ALSO BY THOMAS L. WEBBER

*Deep Like the Rivers: Education in the Slave Quarter
Community, 1831–1865*

Flying over 96th Street

Memoir of an East Harlem White Boy

Thomas L. Webber

SCRIBNER

NEW YORK LONDON TORONTO SYDNEY

SCRIBNER
1230 Avenue of the Americas
New York, NY 10020

Some of the names in *Flying over 96th Street* have been changed.

SCRIBNER and design are trademarks of
Macmillan Library Reference USA, Inc., used under license
by Simon & Schuster, the publisher of this work.

For information about special discounts for bulk purchases,
please contact Simon & Schuster Special Sales:
1-800-456-6798 or business@simonandschuster.com

Designed by Kyoko Watanabe
Text set in Stempel Garamond

Manufactured in the United States of America

1   3   5   7   9   10   8   6   4   2

Library of Congress Cataloging-in-Publication Data

Webber, Thomas L.
Flying over 96th Street : memoir of an East Harlem white boy / Thomas L. Webber.
p. cm.
1. Webber, Thomas L.—Childhood and youth. 2. Whites—New York (State)—
New York—Biography. 3. Boys—New York (State)—New York—Biography.
4. East Harlem (New York, N.Y.)—Biography. 5. New York (N.Y.)—Biography.
6. City and town life—New York (State)—New York—History—20th century.
7. East Harlem (New York, N.Y.)—Race relations. 8. New York (N.Y.)—Race
relations. 9. East Harlem (New York, N.Y.)—Social conditions—20th century.
10. New York (N.Y.)—Social conditions—20th century.
I. Title: Flying over 96th Street. II. Title.

F128.68.H3W43 2004
974.7'043'092—dc22
[B]
2004042998

ISBN 0-7432-4750-7

For
Mom and Dad,
my brothers and sisters,
and Danny

Flying over
96th Street

PROLOGUE

AT 96TH STREET and Park Avenue, train tracks emerge from the underground belly of Manhattan and climb into the sunlight. To the south, Park Avenue is a proud boulevard lined with tall, elegant buildings. The roadway is six lanes wide, separated by long, narrow rectangles of neatly planted trees, shrubs, flowers, and a short half-moon midway where the gray-haired ladies of the Avenue, too slow to make it across on a single light, rest and admire nature's color and man's symmetry while waiting for the light to change. Brassily buttoned doormen whistle down cabs, assist with packages, and stand alert under canopies that stretch to the curb so that no one gets wet in the rain; like castle sentinels, these doormen never sleep. There is no trash here. Garbage is stored in basements, carted away silently in the night, unseen and unsmelled. Life is clean, orderly, hushed. No trucks or buses disturb Park Avenue's serenity, and despite the frequency of my visits, I never see a fire engine invade this hallowed ground. Ambulances I do see: the private ambulances of private hospitals.

North of 96th Street, six-story tenements on either side of the avenue confront the massive stone abutment that serves as the foundation for the elevated railway tracks. Now the six lanes are reduced to one narrow lane to the east of the tracks, one to the west. Cars must proceed in single file, taking care not to scrape against the trestle's jagged stonework. During the long days of summer, beer-drinking men playing dominoes and teenagers talking heatedly above the loud rhythms of transistor radios keep watch in front of their buildings. But in the dark of night or the cold of winter, the youngsters and domino players disappear and no one tarries at the unlit doorways.

Here few pedestrians take two lights to cross the avenue. Even the slow-moving elderly prefer to peer out from the cross-street openings in the stone wall buttress and scurry against the traffic light rather than be stuck in the El's underpass. These tunnels under the tracks are vaulted, dark, and damp. Water rains perpetually from the ceiling, and one must dodge the drops to keep from getting wet. As a young boy, I wonder why the tunnels drip even on dry, sunny days, and I suspect that the trains passing overhead empty their toilets onto the tracks and the contents seep down into the passageways. My theory is supported by the fact that the tunnels smell of urine. I make it a habit to cross on a run.

The streets above 96th Street have their own smell: a combination of sickly sweet, rotting garbage, the musty decay of vacant tenements, and the thick aroma of generously garlicked cooking escaping from open windows of ground-level kitchens, *cuchifrito* stands, and curbside food carts. They also have their own noise: the laughter and shrieks of children dancing in and out of water sprayed by their friends from open fire hydrants; the rhythmic counts of young girls jumping double Dutch or hopscotch on the sidewalks; the calls of "hack" and "double dribble" from basketball players on the many courts; the hubbub of stickball games in the side streets and touch football on the cement school yards; the voices of teenagers and their slightly older mentors engaged in sounding matches or doo-wop concerts on the stoops; the exhortations of Sunday afternoon evangelists from one of the *Aleluya* churches," magnified by portable loudspeaker systems, calling the backsliders, the unrepentant, and the unsaved to come to Jesus; and on the Fourth of July, the whiz and bang of firecrackers from early evening until late into the night. On Park Avenue below 96th Street, I never hear a firecracker. Nor do I ever see a food cart, a storefront restaurant, a stickball game, an open fire hydrant, or hopscotch marks on the sidewalk. They're not allowed.

The human din above 96th Street is accompanied by the sounds of vehicles. The Mister Softee truck, the Pied Piper of creamies, its monotonous jingle luring all kids to its side, rolls methodically from block to block. Fire engines with bells clanging, horns blaring, roar from the station house on 104th Street. Giant garbage trucks devour refuse in the early hours of the morning, the grinding and belching of their motorized stomachs bouncing from building to building. Police cars, sirens sounding, lights twirling, rush from trouble spot to trouble spot. Wailing city ambulances race the sick to Metropolitan Hospital.

The area south of 96th Street is called the Upper East Side or, sometimes, more fashionably, Carnegie Hill. The area north is called East Harlem, Spanish Harlem, El Barrio, or even "the Upper, Upper East Side," this last said mostly in jest. The inhabitants of the Upper East Side are rich, well schooled, and powerful. They rule New York and much of the world. They are white. East Harlem residents are poor, have little formal education, and are, for the most part, politically powerless. They are black and Puerto Rican. Yet, in the midst of its poverty and powerlessness, East Harlem is also a community of dreams and visions; of rhythm, song, and color; of faith, fear, hope, and love. It is a world with its share of saints and sinners, heroes and hustlers, but mostly it is a neighborhood of common people working hard to make ends meet and struggling every day to raise their children the best way they know. It is a world of folks who pray to God and praise Him and who, in 1957 at least, still believed in the American Dream. It is a world that became my world, and this is my story.

CHAPTER 1

THE FIRST TIME God called, my father was standing on the bow of a destroyer escort somewhere in the South Pacific near the end of World War II. God ordered him to become a minister. Dad did. Mom says that, before they married, Dad told her he planned to become a lawyer. Then he went off to war and came back with plans to make her a minister's wife. I guess that's the chance you take when you marry a man who receives direct calls from God.

The second time God called, my father and his friend and fellow Seminary student Don Benedict were walking down the most heavily populated block in East Harlem. Around them swarmed the four thousand plus souls who lived crowded together on 100th Street between First and Second Avenues. They had singled out 100th Street because an article in *The New York Times* had labeled it "the worst block in New York City." Noting the filth, poverty, and absence of even one "mainline" Protestant church, they heard God summon them to found a new kind of inner-city ministry on that very spot. Thus was born the East Harlem Protestant Parish.

The third time God called, Dad convened a family council.

I am eight, in third grade. The family gathers in our living room. My brother Johnny, three years my senior, sits next to me on the couch. Whereas I am stick skinny, Johnny weighs in like a freight train. He's older, bigger, and thinks he knows everything, which he almost does. It's Johnny who has wised me up to the fact that our family councils aren't like a congregation debating the call of a new minister, the way Dad pretends. A Webber family council is more like a call to arms. My five-year-old sister, Peggy, sits on the floor, rocking back and forth against the front of Mom's easy chair. Peggy never sits still, stands still, or does anything still; she even rocks in her sleep. Baby Andy, just turned one, nestles snugly on Mom's lap, attempting to pat the moving target of Peggy's head. Dad sits next to Mom on a dining room chair pulled into the living room for the council. He looms over the rest of us like a minister looking down from the high preaching pulpit of Riverside Church. Outside it's winter. Snow blankets Claremont Avenue and the ivy-covered buildings of Columbia University's Union Theological Seminary, where my father is Dean of Students.

Without warm-up, Dad announces that he and Mom have decided it's time for us to move to East Harlem. He explains how important it is for him to live there and become a more active member of the parish he helped found eight years ago. Working in the Parish on a part-time basis is no longer good enough. He needs to live among the poor, the hungry, and the sick, to share in the lives of the neighborhood people, as do all the other ministers and their families who have joined the Parish over the years. Should anybody need him, he wants to be available even in the wee hours of the night; most human problems, he says, pop up after 5:00 P.M. He has received a call from God, and when God calls, my father always answers, "Here I am, Lord!" He never tries to weasel out with a "Why me, Lord?" or a "Please, Lord, let this cup pass from my lips." Dad never lets any of God's calls pass from his lips.

I'm in shock. My heart is pounding, and I'm fast becoming sick to my stomach. Far from feeling summoned by God like Noah before the flood or Moses in front of the burning bush, I suddenly know how the people of Jericho must have felt after Joshua blew his ram horn and the walls of their safe little city came tumbling down. Johnny's not happy either. One look at him tells me it's only a matter of time before he bursts.

When Dad pauses to let Mom add her support, Johnny shouts, "It's not fair! Just because you want to move we all have to. It's not fair!"

Dad looks surprised and a little hurt, like he hadn't thought in advance about how we might react to his announcement. He's trying to head us off at the pass by acting like it's no big deal, but striking out like pioneers into some unknown land is a big deal. It's a great, big, huge deal.

Glancing over at Mom, Dad continues: "Johnny, sometimes in life you have to do what you think is right, what's in your heart."

"You mean what's in your heart, in *your* heart. *My* heart says stay here," Johnny thunders, tears watering up his eyes.

Peggy chimes in from her swaying seat on the floor: "My heart says stay here too."

At the sound of Peggy's voice, Baby Andy reaches out and claps the top of her head as if he's a cymbal player clashing down the end of Beethoven's Ninth. For a moment I think he's going to speak, which would be a real sign from God, but all that comes out of his mouth is a volley of *ga-ga*s and a long string of drool.

My own heart is stuck in my throat. The thought of moving

chokes me. I love the Seminary, the only home I've ever known. With my two best friends, I roam the halls, classrooms, offices, dormitories, and underground tunnels in search of adventure. We are the Lone Ranger, Roy Rogers, and Hopalong Cassidy. We relieve damsels in distress from their fellow student kidnappers. We ambush unsuspecting outlaw professors. We are princes, and the Seminary is our kingdom.

Because we're the sons of faculty members, the Seminary students, who are all college graduates and only a little younger than Mom and Dad, treat us with careful friendliness. They play along with our pranks, allow us to join in on their athletic contests, and invite us into their dorm rooms, where for the price of a Coke, we gladly spill forth faculty-family secrets. We enjoy the turns of each season: a costumed faculty children's pageant at Christmas; the student drama production of *Billy Budd* in the spring; student-faculty picnics and retreats in the summer; the World Series on the Student Lounge television each fall. Our sidewalk games of running bases are even watched over by a young neighborhood cop named Richie, who reminds us to be respectful of passersby and teaches us how to throw a real curveball.

East Harlem, on the other hand, is a place where I could never be happy. It's an ugly place, full of garbage and strange smells. I know so from visits there with Dad. Worse, it's dangerous. Once when the Parish ministers had a meeting in our apartment, I overheard them talking about how much crime there is in the neighborhood, about how many of the teenagers join gangs and carry switchblade knives and homemade weapons called zip guns.

Stuck in my head is the memory of walking with Dad down 100th Street late one summer afternoon. The block is hot, humid, without a tree or a breeze. Five- and six-story buildings stand wall to wall, so tightly squeezed together that barely any late day sunlight reaches the street. People are everywhere, sitting on stoops, leaning from rooftops, lounging on fire escapes, shouting at each other in a language I don't understand. Small children playing tag run in and out between cars parked in the street, ricocheting off adults jabbering on the sidewalk. Young men play stickball in the street, coolly stepping aside for each passing car, as if the car had better be careful. Many of the people have dark skin, some skin so dark that white teeth explode from their mouths when they smile. Mom says Negroes are the same as other people, only with brown skin instead of white. I'm not so sure. They don't act like the people I know.

In the middle of the block, behind a large sign with two hands, one black, one white, clasped in front of a cross, stands the 100th Street Church of the East Harlem Protestant Parish. Inside the storefront, the space is a sad excuse for a church, just a large, open room with a plain wooden cross on the back wall. It's way too small to be a real church; a thousand churches this size could fit into Riverside Church. All the chairs and tables are pushed to the side, and a fat-cheeked lady with a swirling skirt and a high-pitched laugh is mopping the floor. Soapsuds are everywhere. When Dad introduces her as Mrs. Cruz, she seems amused that I step forward and shake her hand. Five little kids are running back and forth, slipping and sliding on the soapy floor. One girl, about three or four years old, holds on to Mrs. Cruz's skirt and stares at me with wide, curious eyes. Her mother slaps her gently on top of the head and apologizes to my father like I'm not there, explaining that her daughter has never seen a boy with such blond hair and such blue eyes. Your son sure *es muy lindo*, Reverend Webber. You better be careful! Just wait till all the womens get their hands on him!

Dad laughs and put his hands on my shoulders nervously, as if he's worried all the womens Mrs. Cruz is talking about might try to get their hands on him. I know Dad is handsome, and I'm used to women making eyes at him, telling him silly jokes, flirting. But I don't like it. He belongs to Mom.

After Dad arranges the altar table for the next day's Sunday service, we say good-bye to Mrs. Cruz and her children and walk hand in hand back down the street. At the far end of the block, a huge, wide-open warehouse on the ground floor of the corner building extends a third of the way down the street. Peering through the dim light, I see rows and rows of yellow and green bananas hanging from the ceiling. What in the world would anyone want with so many bananas? As I stare, the bananas change themselves into the curved and pointed tusks of crazed, hungry walruses lying in wait to snatch me away from my father and gobble me up.

Thinking about how much I love the Seminary, and how uneasy just visiting East Harlem makes me feel, all I can squeak out is a weak "Do we have to?"

"That makes three," cries Johnny. "Three votes to two. Andy's too little, he can't vote."

And then Mom begins to speak. As I listen to the sound of her calm, soothing voice, my heart sinks from my throat down into my stomach. This isn't about voting. This is about us as a family. About our willingness to sacrifice our own wants and comforts for the needs of others. Moving will be hard, but we'll be together. Every summer we'll still go to Maine as we always do. And, Johnny, next September before we move, you and Tommy will start going to Collegiate.

"Collegiate?" I'm suddenly alert. I've always been a little jealous of my friend Johnny Bachman, who goes there. A private boys' school, Collegiate has athletic teams and lets out early for the summer, three weeks before my public school.

Johnny glares at me and rises from the couch. Dad stands too and tries to make a deal with Johnny. If any of you is truly unhappy after one year, we'll have another family council and talk about returning to the Seminary.

"It's not fair," shouts Johnny. Then he quickly dodges around Dad and stomps off down the hall, slamming our bedroom door behind him. For a big guy, my brother has great moves.

Later that afternoon, when we're alone in our bedroom, I dog Johnny about the odds of our actually moving. I can't believe Dad will go through with it.

Johnny, however, says we're doomed. Dad's gonna make us move. It doesn't matter how unhappy we are or anything else, his mind's made up. He's made a deal with Mom and gotten her to go along; he's even thrown in a call from God to make it final. There's nothing we can do. We're dead.

Not able to bear the finality of Johnny's forecast, I make him enter into a sacred pact, swear a blood oath, like Apache warriors, never to like East Harlem and never, ever, to say anything good about the move. I also pray every night that the move never comes to pass. If God has called Dad, maybe God can be persuaded to call him off. Let Dad be available in the wee hours of the night to the Seminary students, to us.

My mother grew up in a quiet, tree-lined suburb of Cleveland, Ohio. Her father, Granddaddy Barton, a man who loved music, literature, and sports, was an advertising copywriter. I remember once working with him on a list of over fifty ways to say "hit" a home run: blasted, boomed, bashed, creamed, cracked. Both he and Grandma Barton were quiet, gentle people who spoke to their children about the evils of prejudice and racism, but whose actions against injustice were limited to voting for the right political candidates. The last thing they would have wished for their darling daughter, nicknamed Dibby, was for her to marry a minister and move to East Harlem. They wanted her life to be filled with beauty, music, art, literature, and an occasional trip to Yankee Stadium.

Dad spent his childhood in Des Moines, Iowa, a typically segregated midwestern city with only one black student in his white high school. The rest of the black population of Des Moines attended school on the other side of town. When he was a young boy, Dad's sole relationship with a black person was with the family maid. His father, the head of the local Young Men's Christian Association, was charged with putting the *C* back in YMCA, which Grumpa tried his hardest to do. He was an energetic, enthusiastic man willing to challenge local customs and habits, up to a point. When the Tuskegee Gospel Singers came to Des Moines during the Depression, for example, he had them sing at the Y and then invited them over to the house for tea. He was unable, however, to break the long-standing ban against Negroes attending Y camp except for two weeks at the end of the summer, after the white campers had all gone home. Dad's mother, Granmousy, was active in local civic and church organizations, once even helping to organize a local protest when Marian Anderson, the renowned Negro contralto, was denied the right to sing at Constitution Hall in Washington, D.C.

From the stories Dad tells of his childhood, it's clear that the active spiritual life of the Y and church sowed the seeds for his becoming a minister. He speaks of being enthralled by stories of courageous Christian missionaries in foreign lands. Working as a missionary was for Dad the highest possible form of Christian service. Missionary work was selfless, Christ-like, heroic. It appealed to Dad's vision of himself.

Mom and Dad met in the fall of their senior year in college at a Harvard football game, where Mom says Dad made a play for her despite the fact that she was there with one of his best friends. Dad recalls only that he was trying to be friendly. Whatever the case, they started going out together soon thereafter. Mom pictures her Radcliffe years as a magical time in her life. Whenever she talks of those days, her eyes mist over as she recalls friends, professors, and the smell of lilacs in the Cambridge spring. I imagine she's thinking of the spring of 1942, when she and Dad were falling in love, before the war separated them, before they got married, before Dad got his first call from God.

CHAPTER 2

With my mother by my side, I carefully step across wooden planks placed over the mud between the sidewalk and the entrance to our apartment in the newly built Washington Houses. It's the day of our move. I am nine. The pathway leading to the front door is still not finished, even though the opening of our building on 102nd Street between Second and Third Avenues was postponed from January to May. Next to the wooden planks, long chains, looped between low steel poles, keep us off the area where new grass is struggling to push through the mud.

Inside, the elevator rattles up to the tenth floor, and we step into a long, narrow hallway. All the apartments, eight to each floor, are enclosed behind green metal doors with tiny, round windows about two-thirds of the way up. I've never before seen peepholes like this on doors, and assume their purpose is to allow visitors to see if anyone's home.

The apartment is much smaller than our Seminary housing, with three bedrooms, not four, a kitchen too cramped for a dinner table, and no separate alcove for our upright piano, which now takes over the living room like it doesn't belong there. The floors are linoleum, not wood, and the air smells of paint and chemicals. What's more, the apartment's three bedrooms are all huddled together off the same short hallway. At the Seminary, the bedroom Johnny and I shared was at the opposite end of our apartment, far away from the other bedrooms. We could roughhouse, yell, make all the noise we wanted without Mom and Dad hearing. And we had our own bathroom. Here, with only one bathroom for a family of six, who knows how long I'll have to wait.

In the back Johnny shows me with disgust how small our bedroom is and how only the bottom third of each window opens out and down and then sits there right in front of you like a lunchroom tray. When I ask Mom why the windows open so strangely, she says they were built like that so small children can't fall out. When I ask if they weren't concerned about small children at the Seminary, she replies that the Seminary buildings were probably built with a greater concern for beauty than for safety. The way she says this I know Mom thinks these new windows are ugly too.

From our bedroom I look out across the mud and wooden planks to another building exactly like ours. "Projects," Dad calls them, building after building all the same; twelve altogether make up Washington Houses. All fourteen stories high. All built by the city to replace the old, run-down tenements no longer able to house the growing population of Negroes from the South and families flowing in from the island of Puerto Rico. All built so that poor people can live somewhere safe with sunlight, hot water, and heat. Although we aren't really poor, we qualify for the projects

15

because Dad's Parish salary is low and our family is big. Of course, the city doesn't know about the Parish health plan, our private school scholarships, and Dad's housing allowance. Dad says the rules specify salary, and rules are rules and a salary is a salary.

That night I make Johnny renew our sacred pact to let Mom and Dad know at every twist and turn how much we hate it here. In bed I listen to the sounds coming in through the window from the street below: the constant rumble of traffic down Second Avenue; the whining sirens of police cars and ambulances starting in the distance and then getting closer and closer, louder and louder; the snatches of conversation bouncing off the building walls. How can anyone fall asleep with such a racket? At its noontime noisiest, Claremont Avenue is ten times quieter than this neighborhood at night; with our bedroom in the back looking out across a small courtyard to the wall of Riverside Church, I rarely heard a peep.

My great consolation is Johnny in the bunk above me. He will protect me the way he does when we go to Yankee Stadium for Sunday afternoon doubleheaders, sitting far up in the last row of the Upper Mezzanine, surveying the great green ball field spread out majestically below us. Johnny's very smell comforts me.

I fall asleep crying, thinking about my Seminary friends and missing my quiet Seminary bedroom with its familiar shadows on the walls.

It's barely light outside when I am wakened by the crow of a rooster. At first I think I must be dreaming, and I lie in bed listening, not knowing where I am. Then I remember. But what is a rooster doing in East Harlem? I climb out of bed and go to the window. In the distance, a large bridge arcs across the sky like a giant steel rainbow. Closer to earth, I can see the rooftops of the small buildings on the other side of Second Avenue. On one of the roofs a man waves a whiskerless broomstick at the sky. A flock of pigeons flies over his head. When he moves the pole in a big round sweep, the birds follow it, forming a huge circle. When he scarcely moves the pole at all, the birds close in until they look like a huge sky dog chasing its own tail. I watch as the man directs the pigeons down onto the roof, where they huddle around him, bobbing their heads like hungry chickens clucking in a crowded barnyard.

Next to a school on the other side of 102nd Street, I spy two empty basketball courts. On a clear, warm Sunday morning, I can't believe it. Even if some older guys appear later, I could scoot down quickly and get in some practice. At the Seminary my friends and I used to hike over to Riverside Park early in the morning so we could get in some playing time before the older boys arrived and kicked us off. Over the door in my Seminary bedroom I had hung a coat hanger twisted into the shape of a hoop and took shots with a small beach ball. I can never fix up this new bedroom like that: the ceiling is too low, the open space for dribbling too small.

At breakfast Mom lets us choose our own single-serving-sized cereal boxes, a special treat usually reserved for holidays and birthdays. While eating my Sugar Pops, I wrestle over asking if I can go down to the empty courts. Maybe you have to sign up, like for the tennis courts in Central Park. Maybe you can't play on Sunday mornings. Maybe children my age aren't allowed without an adult. I decide to wait. Mom needs more time.

By ten o'clock I have unpacked my clothes and folded them into the dresser, arranged my books by size, put away my games in the drawer under the bookcase, and stored my shoes and athletic gear on the floor in the clothes closet. Four guys are now playing a half-court game on the playground below. A fifth boy is taking shots by himself at the far basket of the second court. Two half courts remain empty. You can play on Sunday mornings.

I find Mom in the kitchen and ask where she's put the high-powered binoculars we take with us every summer for our month in Maine. Mom hands them over with a warning not to invade our neighbors' privacy by looking in their windows. Through the binoculars, I get a close-up of the guys playing on the courts below. They're Johnny's age, maybe older. Most are Negroes. The guy shooting baskets by himself is tall but younger than the others and lighter skinned, almost as light as me. He wears a funny black hat with the front brim pinned back. As I watch him miss shots, I can see he's definitely beatable.

At ten-thirty we leave for church. On our first day, Mom wants us to arrive with time to spare. Dad has already gone over to prepare for the service and put the final touches on his sermon. He's the assistant pastor of Ascension Church, one of the four churches in the East Harlem Protestant Parish and the only one not a storefront. He preaches there once a month, though now that he's working full-time in the neighborhood his main job is to be the chief Parish administrator. In addition to paying the bills and raising money, Dad's supposed to make sure the Parish operates smoothly. When I ask him if he's the head of the Parish like President Van Dusen is the head of the Seminary, he says no, he's simply in charge of carrying out the decisions made by the members of the Group Ministry, who are all equal.

In the nine years since its beginning in 1948, the Parish has grown so rapidly that, in addition to the four churches, it runs a health clinic, a narcotics committee, a credit union, and a youth program that works with gangs. Like drugs, poverty, and no heat, gangs are a big problem in East Harlem, especially when they get into all-out fights called "rumbles" and kids are killed. I wonder if the guys playing basketball are part of a gang and whether they all have switchblades in their pockets and zip guns under their belts. I also wonder if members of different gangs play each other or if they play only against guys in their own gang. And what about boys who aren't in a gang? Who do they play with?

In the elevator, Mom talks with an elderly Negro lady wearing a gigantic hat shaped like a red bowling ball. They chat back and forth about the weather, about the best neighborhood grocery store, about the names and locations of their churches. At the Seminary, Mom had never been such a talker. The lady says she attends something called the Holiness Tabernacle Temple. I wonder if she can possibly be Jewish.

Out on the street, the entire neighborhood is on the move. Large families, small families, people by themselves, people in small groups, everyone dressed up. I'm amazed at how many carry Bibles and figure their churches can't afford enough Bibles to keep one on hand for everyone. Our route carries us past the courts I spotted from my bedroom window. The guy in the black hat is still alone practicing layups. As we walk by, he looks up but doesn't smile. I catch his eye but don't smile either. It's his court, his neighborhood; he should be the one to smile first.

In no time at all, we arrive at Ascension, a four-story brick building near the corner of First Avenue and 106th Street. Inside, there are no windows, just pictures of former ministers and memorial plaques lining the walls. In the front, two small pulpits look down from either side. Mom, Johnny, Peggy, Andy, and I sit bunched together in the second pew. Except for two young men and a young woman who look like Seminary students, we are the only white people present. I've never before been in a room filled with so many Negroes. It feels like we don't belong here. Plus it smells different, sort of musty, like hot dust and sweat. I'm not sure whether it's the Negroes I smell or the church.

Dressed in long black robes, Dad and Libby Newton, Ascension's chief minister, enter from a side door and take their seats on two chairs placed in front of the altar table. As the service begins, I'm horrified to discover that everything is done once in English and then all over again in Spanish. Everything! The welcome, the prayers, the concerns of the church, even the sermon, which Dad delivers first and then a man named Mr. Santiago repeats in Spanish. Not only will the service be twice as long, but it will be three times as boring, with me forced to sit still and listen to words I don't understand. The only Spanish words I recognize are the *Aleluya*s Mr. Santiago shouts at the end of every sentence. I can't tell whether he's truthfully repeating what Dad says or whether he's adding in words and ideas of his own. He definitely slips in his own *Aleluya*s.

I try to concentrate on Dad's sermon about the need for new wineskins, but when Mr. Santiago launches into his Spanish, I can't help looking around the church for boys my own age. I wish we weren't sitting so far up front: even a slight turn of the head draws attention, and I don't want that. It already feels like everyone's looking at us.

Fortunately, the hymns and choir anthems aren't done twice. Instead, one hymn is sung in Spanish.

> *Santo! Santo! Santo! Señor omnipotente . . .*
> *Dios en tres personas, Bendita Trinidad.*

I follow along, sounding out each syllable as I do when I hit a big English word I don't know. My newly created Spanish sounds funny, and I start to giggle, hoping to get Johnny going. One look at my older brother, however, tells me to stuff it.

Toward the end of the service, during the singing of the Fellowship Hymn, the members of the congregation shake hands. Though most of the people stay put in their pews and greet their neighbors in the seats around them, Dad comes down and marches us around the entire church. Everyone smiles and says how glad they are to meet us, how glad they are that we'll be with them every Sunday from now on. I'm tempted to ask a couple of the guys my age if they know about the basketball courts next to the school on 102nd Street, but everything is too quick, and besides, we're supposed to be singing.

After the service, we troop downstairs for coffee hour and I discover that the basement stinks worse than the main church. It's stale and dank despite the smell of the coffee and cookies set out on the table next to the kitchen. Standing next to the wall with Johnny, I survey the crowd. None of the boys my age have come down except for one guy with Mr. Santiago and the rest of his family. Maybe if the boy was alone I'd approach him and start a conversation, but I don't want to deal with his parents.

Dad already seems to know the entire congregation. As everyone lines up to shake his hand and welcome him all over again, he has a smile and some friendly chat for each of them. I can tell he's enjoying himself, like the Prodigal Son at his father's feast, home at long last. I don't recognize anyone except Libby. I had hoped to see some of the other Parish ministers, but they're probably busy running the services of the other churches. Before the move, I had comforted myself with the knowledge that we would be joining a group of people already at home in East Harlem. The members of the Group Ministry are my father's and mother's closest friends; they babysit us, play with us at Parish Acres, an old farm owned by the Parish about fifty miles north of the city and used for retreats. They go to each other's houses for dinners, meetings, and parties, see each other every morning at daily worship, speak constantly to each other on the phone. They are friendly, familiar adults, almost like part of our family. Unfortunately, none of them has any children my age. The closest is a girl four years younger, much too young to play with, except in extreme circumstances.

At Sunday dinner, Dad asks how we liked our new church. Peggy replies that it smells. I say that it's hard dealing with all that Spanish. Johnny is silent. Mom's in the middle of saying how much she liked Dad's sermon, especially the part about the lessons he learned at Y-camp, when Johnny cuts her off in midsentence and asks if he can be excused. Mom and Dad exchange a look before Mom says there's ice cream for dessert. Johnny mumbles something about having lots of homework and leaves the table without waiting for Mom and Dad's okay.

During the first few weeks after the move, what I see of East Harlem, other than church, is limited to what I can see looking out my window and what I take in each day hiking the two long blocks between our building and the bus stop on Lexington Avenue where we catch the city bus downtown. Mom insists that Johnny accompany me to and from school each day. Without her exactly saying so, I can tell she's worried about my safety.

In the morning, most of the grown-ups hurry on their way to work. At the early hour of 7:30, when Johnny and I leave our building in order to make the forty-five-minute, two-bus-ride journey to Collegiate on West 77th Street, few kids are out. On the way home, however, it's a different story. Everybody's on the street enjoying the late May sunshine: men play cards or dominoes around wobbly tables; women gossip and coo at each other's babies; young men on the stoops call out to girls; girls walk in packs, slowing down in front of the boys but never stopping; boys my age careen down the steep 102nd Street hill in soapbox derby specials hammered together with what look like milk crates, old boards, and roller skate wheels. Clotheslines heavy with laundry are strung between tenement windows. Competing flocks of circling pigeons fly overhead. Many of the people shout at each other in Spanish. What amazes me most is how many people there are. At the Seminary, it was rare to see someone walking a dog or pushing a baby carriage on Claremont Avenue. Here people seem to live on the streets.

Occasionally I catch the eye of a man standing around a card table or of a boy carrying his soapbox back up the hill, but nobody says anything as we pass. I figure that everybody, besides us, is either Negro or Puerto Rican, although sometimes I can't tell which until the person starts speaking. I have quickly discovered that some Puerto Ricans are as dark skinned as the darkest Negroes.

Mom was smart to start us at Collegiate last fall, a full eight months before the move. By now I'm used to wearing a tie and jacket every day, eating whatever is served for lunch, and sitting at my desk in the proper manner like a proper gentleman. At first it was difficult to make my way among a group of boys who had been together since first grade, to catch up with their knowledge of multiple fractions, sentence structure, and French; to learn new rules like standing up when your teacher enters the room, never slouching in your chair, and always being on time, strictly on time, better ten minutes early than a minute late. As my first year is ending, however, I feel pretty comfortable at Collegiate except for one thing. My Collegiate classmates always have money in their pockets. They make a beeline every day after school to buy candy, soda, and baseball cards at the "Gyp Joint" or French fries smothered in ketchup from Gitlitz's Restaurant and Delicatessen. They bring so much food onto the 79th Street crosstown bus that from time to time the grown-up passengers complain to our Headmaster and he lectures us on the impropriety of eating on a public conveyance. Birthday parties are especially uncomfortable, as I know that my present will be a good deal less expensive than those of the other guests. My Collegiate friends share their candy and thank me for my gift, but I can't help feeling like the scholarship kid I am, poor in a land of plenty.

When they learn that I've moved to East Harlem, my classmates can't believe it. To them, no one in his right mind would live north of 96th Street, no one, at least, able to live anywhere else. One of my friends asks me seriously if I'm not afraid of the thousands of muggers that walk every street in East Harlem. He's heard they roam around in groups just waiting for private school guys like us. I listen anxiously to what he says. At the same time, I don't believe he knows that much about what things are really like above 96th Street. He's never been there.

Each afternoon on the way home from Collegiate, I try to get Johnny to pass by the school playground on 102nd Street; each day he insists on going straight upstairs. Looking out our bedroom window, I see that both courts are always packed and always with older guys. Through my binoculars, I watch them play; they're good, smooth and confident, talking back and forth during their games. Although they are clearly better than I am, and I know they will never want me on their teams, I like watching them, checking out their moves. I wish I had a magic listening device so I could eavesdrop on what they're saying. From my window perch, I haven't a clue what they're talking about. It's like watching a silent movie.

One night in bed I hear what sound like gunshots. I turn to look at my bedstand clock, wanting to be ready to give reliable testimony if Sergeant Friday knocks on our door and asks if anyone heard shots and, if so, at precisely what time. The next morning when I ask Dad about the gunshots, he replies that they were most likely just firecrackers, people getting ready for the Fourth of July. I half-accept, half-doubt this answer. How can he be so sure? Fourth of July firecrackers in May?

No matter what day of the week it is, the basketball courts are always empty before 8:00 A.M., and on this Saturday after breakfast, it's almost 9:00 and still not a soul stirs in the school yard below. I'm staring out the window, dreaming of playing on my own free court, when Dad comes into the room and stands beside me.

"Seems like a waste, doesn't it? Two empty courts with no one on them. Maybe this afternoon, if I finish up early at the office, you and I can go down together and get in some practice."

Dad played ball in both high school and college and is still pretty good, even though he does shoot old-fashioned two-handed set shots and underhand foul shots. On my desk is a picture of him in his Harvard uniform.

I tell Dad I think the courts will probably be full after lunch. Although at the Seminary I would have jumped at his offer, going down to the courts with my father doesn't seem like the thing to do here. None of the people down there look anything like they could be one of the guys' fathers. I'm almost ten, and I don't want to be taken for a sissy who needs a parent around. And if Dad wears his collar, as he usually does so that people will recognize him as a minister, I will really feel out of place, like we're there to get them to come to church rather than to play basketball. Odds are Dad won't make it anyway. While he's at the office someone will come in frantic over a teenager who's been arrested or a grandmother who's been rushed to the hospital, and he'll get home too late. It's not that Dad loves us less, Mom explains each time he disappoints us, it's just that they need him more.

I change the subject by asking if I have to attend adult service every Sunday. I explain that adult service is too long, that I get restless. Dad says he knows what I mean. When he was my age he wanted to be anywhere but in church Sunday mornings. Only later was he glad he had had to attend. He learned a lot of important things in church, so many things that he gave me the middle name Lane in honor of his minister back home in Des Moines. He never would have become a minister if it hadn't been for Reverend Lane.

Thinking that one day I might follow in Dad's profession, I ask if he's glad he became a minister. Very glad, he replies. He can wear a fancy white collar, little old ladies give him their seats on the bus, and he gets into Yankees games free.

I laugh even though I wish Dad wouldn't make jokes out of my serious questions. I want to know if he ever wishes he did something more fun than being a Parish minister, if he ever gets tired of working all the time, even in the evenings and on weekends, if he ever regrets not having more free time to spend with Mom, with us kids.

On our fifth Sunday in East Harlem, I wake early despite the fact that I spent half the night listening to the pop of what Dad continues to insist are firecrackers and, at one point, got out of bed to watch a shouting match on the corner of Second Avenue grow so loud and out of control that several men started swinging at each other. In the middle of the fight, two police cars arrived, and after much yelling and hand waving, three of the men were handcuffed and taken away in squad cars. I was spellbound watching grown men hitting each other in the face, knocking each other to the ground, kicking and punching.

The clock on my nightstand reads 7:15. I have plenty of time before church. Recalling the events of last night, I try to convince myself there's nothing to worry about. Other than cars and an occasional bus rolling down Second Avenue, the streets are pretty quiet. The men arrested last night are probably still in jail. The muggers and gang members, if there are any, probably sleep late. I've been observing the courts for over a month now and have yet to see anything bad happen.

I dress quickly, walk out to the kitchen, and pour myself some Cheerios, the breakfast of the Lone Ranger. Sitting by myself, I feel like the Lone Ranger, with no Tonto. The apartment is silent, the rest of the family still asleep. I don't dare leave without telling somebody where I'm going, but I also don't dare wake Mom and Dad for no good reason, not on Sunday morning.

I walk across the hall to Andy and Peggy's bedroom, quietly push open the door, approach Andy's crib, lean over the rail, and gently push his chest. He tosses his head from side to side, opens his eyes, lets out a squeal, and breaks into a big, toothy smile. He then turns over, gets up on his hands and knees, grabs hold of the side of the crib, and pulls himself into a standing position. Up, Tommy. Up, Tommy, he calls. Instead of picking him up, however, I quickly back out of the room, waving, smiling, and carefully closing the door to the exact half-opened position it had been in when I entered. Right on cue, Andy starts to cry. I feel bad for him, but not too bad. Mom will be there in a minute. Once she's up, I can tell her my plans.

Back in my room, I hurry to the window. A single figure now occupies the courts. He isn't shooting, just sitting against the fence under the basket. Through the binoculars I can see it's the boy in the black hat, the same boy I saw our first Sunday in East Harlem. As I watch, Johnny startles me by asking what's up, demanding to know why I'm dressed. I tell him I'm thinking of going down and shooting some baskets and ask if he wants to come. Not a chance, he says, in the voice he uses to warn me not to push it. For reasons I don't understand, Johnny isn't into basketball. He's a great catcher on the seventh- and eighth-grade baseball team, and because of his size and speed, he's an outstanding football player. But he never plays basketball.

I can hear Mom in the next room talking to Andy, telling him he needs to sleep later on Sunday mornings. After waiting a few minutes, I go in and let her know I'm going down to play basketball. When I show her how she can check on me by looking out

27

our bedroom window, she has no choice but to set me free. She does say I have to be back by 9:30 to get washed, dressed, and ready for church. Johnny doesn't look my way as I grab my basketball and hurry out.

Downstairs, I realize I'm both nervous and excited about being alone for the first time on the streets of East Harlem. The lack of people walking by gives me confidence: early on Sunday morning, 102nd Street seems almost like Claremont Avenue.

On the courts, two teenagers are now playing one-on-one, and the guy in the black hat is taking halfhearted shots by himself on the next court. He's taller and clearly older than me, with two of the biggest ears I've ever laid eyes on, ears so big I bet the other kids call him Dumbo behind his back. I can feel him looking me over as I start shooting hoops at the far end of his court. The backboard is metal and rattles each time I hit a bank shot. The hoop has no net. But this half of the court is mine, all mine.

I begin my drill with a few easy layups to warm up and get the feel of the ball, then I practice free throws. Dad won his high school foul-shooting contest by sinking seventeen straight. My best ever is nine in a row; my goal is twenty. After I can hit ten in a row most times I try, one day I'll show Dad how good I've gotten.

While I'm taking foul shots, Dumbo walks over to my basket, watches me silently for a moment, then asks if I want to play 5-2. Sure, I reply, glad I know the rules: first you take a long shot from the foul line worth five points, then a short shot for two points from wherever you retrieve your first shot. If you hit both shots, you keep going until you miss. If you miss the long shot, you still get to take the short one, but then your turn is over. I ask him how much wins. He says thirty-one and toes up to the line to take the first shot. Even though I know we're supposed to shoot to see who goes first, I don't say anything.

He makes his first shot and the following layup but misses his second long shot. No one has taught him to bend his knees or to roll the ball off his fingers so that, if he misses, his shot will land nice and gentle and still have a chance of rolling into the hoop. I make my first two sets of foul shots and following layups, and soon reach twenty-eight while he's stuck at eighteen. As I go to the line for what I hope will be my final shot, he announces that the last long shot is from the top of the key. This is something new. The top of the key is too far for me to shoot from easily. In order to reach the hoop, I have to heave the ball with one hand like a huge baseball. I miss the long shot but make the short one. On my next turn I do the same, winning the game 32–20.

With the game now over, the kid asks if I live around here. I point to my building and tell him, Right over there. Before I can decide if I'm supposed to offer a rematch, he says that he saw me going to church and asks why I've never been down before. He seems to accept my reply that we just moved in and tells me his name is Raul but that everybody calls him Rabbit. I say that I'm Thomas and cough, trying to hide my astonishment at his nickname. How can he even think of letting people call him Rabbit? I add that everybody calls me Tommy. He doesn't offer to shake hands so I don't either. Along with his bigger than big ears, Rabbit has a sad look in his eyes, like he's about to cry.

Pronouncing my name Toe-mee, he asks if I want to play some one-on-one and suggests that we use his ball; it's better for outside because it bounces more good on concrete.

In our one-on-one game, Rabbit puts everything he has into winning and just barely beats me. He's taller and can jump higher, which is a great advantage because in this neighborhood, as I quickly learn, the rule is you can go right back up following a missed shot, even your opponent's, without having to clear it out behind the line.

After our game, Rabbit, who is sweating like mad, takes off his shirt and wipes his face with it. His bare back is covered with mean-looking red welts, like a serious rash or something. When he sits under the basket, he's careful how he leans slowly back against the fence.

"You play pretty good," he says as I sit down next to him.

"Thanks," I reply.

"How come you live in the projects?"

"My father works around here."

"No kidding. He a teacher or something?"

"No, a minister."

"What's a minister?"

I can't believe a kid as old as Rabbit doesn't know what a minister is. "You know, like a priest only they're Protestant."

"Priests can't have children," he pronounces firmly.

I assure him that they can if they're Protestant. While he's chewing on this information, I ask if there are roosters somewhere nearby, crowing roosters. He says there are plenty of them in the chicken market over on First, where people buy live chickens and same-day eggs and where they have plenty of cocks to keep the hens happy. He adds that sometimes old guys from the Island hold cockfights and the cocks peck each other to death, going first for each other's eyes. When he says "the Island," I think he means Puerto Rico. Mom has explained to me that most of the Spanish-speaking people in East Harlem are from Puerto Rico. They come to this neighborhood because many of their friends and relatives already live here and because there are not enough jobs on their island. In New York they have to deal with the cold and snow, but at least they have a chance to support their families.

As Rabbit explains about chickens and fighting cocks, I try to imagine why anybody would want to buy a live chicken. Why keep live chickens when you can go to the store and buy one all cleaned and ready to cook? And cockfighting seems cruel, almost as bad as bullfighting, which I thought was a sport in all Spanish-speaking countries until Mom informed me it isn't practiced in Puerto Rico. She says Puerto Rico is an island with customs and traditions of its own, different from those of Spain and Mexico. I wonder if Mom knows that one of Puerto Rico's customs and traditions is cockfighting.

Before Rabbit and I finish our rest, seven or eight older guys arrive together and take possession of our court. On the other court, two half-court games take up both baskets. The two teams in front of us soon race up and down the full court faster than any guys I've ever seen. Their dribbling, passing, and jumping are astounding, but they often miss easy shots, shots I could have made.

Seeing that our court is now permanently taken, Rabbit asks if I want to walk down to P.S. 109, which has four full courts with one always empty. I reply that I have to go home to get ready for church; it's part of the deal when your dad's a minister. As I'm leaving, Rabbit explains where the 109 courts are and says that when I want to go I should come and get him, we'll go together.

I wonder if this sad kid with the big ears and the funny black hat is going to become my first East Harlem friend. I hope so. He seems like he can use a friend and I certainly can, especially an older friend who knows where things are, probably speaks Spanish, and might know how to handle muggers and gang members. An older friend from the neighborhood would be even better than Johnny.

On 102nd Street, I spot a short man with a round stomach and a bushy mustache standing behind a small wooden cart holding a solid block of ice like the ones we used in the old-fashioned icebox in our Maine summer cabin before we got electricity. A thin, white dishcloth covers the ice block. Arranged in square compartments around the ice are tall glass bottles, each filled with its own brightly colored liquid. Big letters painted on the front of the cart announce "5c." The man wears a wide-reaching straw hat and a white undershirt, the kind without sleeves, just thin straps over the shoulders so you can see the hair sprouting from under his arms.

A young woman approaches the cart and speaks to the man in rapid-fire Spanish. In response he produces a metal tool from the side of the cart, whips off the towel, grabs a cone-shaped paper cup from a stack next to the ice, shaves the top of the ice block like my shop teacher planing a plank of wood, and fills the cup with ice shavings. He then lifts one of the bottles and pours red syrup over the ice that reaches up beyond the top of the cup like a miniature red iceberg. The woman takes a bite. As her lips turn bright purple, I can feel the cold ice traveling down her throat.

I am hot, thirsty, and dying to try my own ice cup. I figure they cost a nickel, the sum total of money in my pocket. The problem is I'm not sure how to ask for one. What if the man doesn't speak English? What if they come in different sizes and he hands me a ten-cent large by mistake and I can't pay? With my thirst helping to overcome my jitters, I slowly approach the cart and say, One please. The man grins and spills forth a stream of Spanish. I look back at him blankly, then raise the pointer finger of my right hand and repeat more loudly this time, One please.

The man laughs and asks, "What kind do you wish, my young man?"

"This one please," I say, relieved that he speaks English. I point to the same red bottle from which I just saw him pour. Entranced by the entire process, I stand there dumbly when he hands over my cup.

The iceman says, *"Cinco centavos, por favor,"* raises his right hand, and wiggles all five fingers in my face. *"Cinco,"* he repeats, smiling.

I reach into my pocket and hand over my nickel. *"Cinco,"* I declare, pleased with myself. I have done it: I have gone down by myself, played some basketball, made a new friend, ordered myself an ice cup, and nothing bad has happened. When I take a bite of ice, a cold, sweet cherry taste blasts up through the top of my mouth into my nose. Deeeelicious!

"Se llaman piraguas."

"Excuse me?"

"They're called *piraguas,"* he repeats, chuckling to himself.

"Piraguas," I say carefully. "Thanks."

"Por nada," he says, still smiling.

As I turn away from the cart, I look across the street to our building. By counting up ten stories and across three windows from the stairwell, I find our bedroom. For a moment, I think I see Johnny standing in the shadows looking down at me, and I wave. Before I can be sure, however, the figure in the window disappears. I tell myself I'll save Johnny the last few slurps of my tasty *piragua,* but by the time I get upstairs it has all disappeared.

CHAPTER 3

I'M IN CHURCH the first Sunday in September when a boy about my age sitting two rows behind us across the aisle catches my eye. Squeezed in beside his mother and a woman who seems like either a relative or a close friend, he is constantly fidgeting, with his eyes darting everywhere but forward during the long, hot service. Right in the middle of the Spanish sermon, he lets out a yawn so loud it bounces off the church walls like an award-winning yodel echoing through the Swiss Alps. Much to Mom's dismay, I catch a fit of giggles. Nothing can rein in my laughing, not my mother's dirty looks, not biting my lip or pinching my arm, not even thinking about Jesus hanging from the cross with nails through his hands and feet.

After the service I persuade Mom to let me walk home alone

while the rest of the family attends coffee hour in the church basement. She's relieved not to have to deal with me in front of the disapproving church elders.

The five blocks to and from church and home are familiar now,
and despite the dire warning of my Collegiate classmate, I have yet
to meet up with a mugger. Midway down 106th Street, I feel a
hand on my shoulder, and the boy from church falls into step
beside me.

"Hey, my name's Danny, Danny Strayhorn." He flashes a smile
that spreads across his mouth and lights up his entire face. His two
front teeth are missing, and the jagged, curved edges of the teeth
on either side reach toward each other like two quarter-moons
trying to touch across the gaping crater in the top of his mouth.
Although he's shorter than I am, Danny has long legs and even
longer arms. His skin is a dark leather brown.

"I'm Tommy."

"I know. You're Reverend Webber's son. Don't you hate the
Spanish sermon? Booooring!" His whole mouth moves into
action around the word boring.

"It is a little long."

"A little long? Man, when Aleluya Santiago starts preaching
that Puerto Rican mambo-jambo, it's booooring from the first
blip-diddily out his mouth to his last *Aleluya*. You liked my yawn,
huh?" Danny looks at me with eager, dancing eyes.

"You got me in trouble with my mother. I had to bite my
tongue to stop laughing."

"Better Mr. Santiago bite his tongue."

We are now outside the Italian Bakery on the corner of Second
and 106th, and I hesitate, unsure whether to stop and go in or to
keep walking. All I have on me is the single dime I held back from
the offering plate. Throughout the long service, I'd been dreaming
of a large, ten-cent icie, not a small five-center.

"You want an icie?" I offer, hoping he's either allergic or on strict orders not to eat anything before lunch.

"Sure. Why not?"

Danny pushes open the bakery door and strides boldly up to the counter like he's John Wayne entering a saloon. Behind the display cases, a woman with red hair and painted fingernails is arranging the cream puffs. Danny orders two large icies and slaps a quarter onto the counter.

"What kind you having?" he asks me.

"Chocolate please."

"Make mines lemon."

After the lady scoops two large icies into their white paper cups, hands them over, and picks up Danny's coin, he tells her to keep the change.

Back out on the street, I ask if he always leaves a tip, and he says he does most times because he doesn't want them Italians thinking they're the only ones with money. I say that she seemed friendly enough.

"She's friendly enough when you buying," says Danny. "Otherwise scram."

At my building Danny doesn't wait to be invited in, he just follows me right up. Looking around our living room, he can't believe the number of books that fill shelves covering an entire wall. Enough books for a library, he concludes. He admires our piano, sitting down to pound out "Chopsticks," but is disappointed by the small size of our eleven-inch television set; he says his is a fifteen-incher, and he's pushing his mom to lay away for one of them big twenty-one-inchers. I ask him what his mother has to lay away, and he explains how some stores allow you to buy a big-ticket item like a television and then pay for it a little bit each week.

In our bedroom, I show him the view from our window. He

points out the roof of his building on 101st Street, saying it's the one with the double-decker pigeon cage. "I climb up to the roof sometimes, to get away."

"To get away from what?" I pick up the binoculars for a better look.

"From everything." He grabs the binoculars. "Man, I got to get me one of these. You can see everything."

"Mom says I shouldn't look into anybody's apartment."

Danny takes dead aim on somebody's apartment.

When the rest of the family returns from church, Mom is quick to invite Danny for dinner, which on Sundays we always eat in the early afternoon. The first thing after grace, Peggy asks Danny how he got the hole in his teeth. I try to kick her under the table. Danny looks at Peggy, mushes up his mouth, and scratches the side of his face. Roller skating, he says finally. Peggy is about to ask something stupid like Did it hurt? when Danny cuts her off.

"I'll bet you can't do this." He puts two fingers deep inside his mouth, curls up his tongue, and lets loose with the loudest human whistle in the history of the known world.

At the sound of Danny's blast, even Johnny, who has been secretly scanning the Sunday sports section hidden on his lap under the tablecloth despite Mom's rule against reading at the table, sits up and takes notice. "Wow! Let me hear that again."

"Once is quite enough," cautions my father.

"Yes, sir," says Danny.

There is silence at the table until Dad asks what we all thought about the Prayer Pilgrimage held a few months ago in Washington, D.C. When none of us responds, he tells how thirty thousand Negroes, led by a young minister named Martin Luther King, gathered at the Lincoln Memorial, petitioning the government for the right to vote. Dad explains that Martin Luther King, who I never heard of before, is the same man who led a boycott in Montgomery, Alabama, so that Negroes wouldn't have to stand in the back of the bus even when there were plenty of empty seats up front. In most southern states, Dad says, Negroes are threatened if they try to go to the polls. And those that do make it to the voting place have to recite the Constitution backwards or they can't vote.

"Who knows the Constitution backwards?" I ask.

"Nobody," says Dad. "That's just the point. It's only Negroes they make recite the Constitution backwards. If you're white, you just go right on in and vote."

"That's not fair," says Peggy.

"No, it's not," Dad agrees.

Although I like to hear my father's opinions on things, I sometimes wish he'd be more careful what he talks about. Dad's main topics of conversation are religion and the condition of poor people, which for him are pretty much the same things: to Dad, religion is nothing if not serving the poor. He does sometimes discuss sports, but usually only after Johnny or I start in on the Yankees or the Knicks. At the moment, I wish he'd stop talking about the condition of Negroes. It's like we're talking about Danny ignoring the fact that he's sitting right there. I imagine how it might feel to be sitting with a family of Negroes I'm meeting for the first time and all of a sudden they start talking about white people. I'd want to crawl under the table.

After we finish eating, I ask Danny if he'd like to go down and play some basketball. I'm hoping we can go to the 109 playground, the one Rabbit told me about.

Once she makes sure Danny will stick with me, Mom okays my plan. Danny likes the idea of being my bodyguard and assures Mom that he'll watch out for me good. Before we leave, he asks me to walk him by his apartment so he can change out of his church clothes. I get the feeling he's not too thrilled by the idea of shooting hoops, but I take along my basketball just in case.

Out in the hallway, Danny heads for the stairs, saying that the elevator's too slow, plus it has piss on the floor. I agree with him that the smell of those dog puddles is hard to take. That's not dog piss, that's people piss, he says. Dogs know better, they're trained. Then he suggests that I ride the elevator while he races down the stairs. Before I can agree or disagree, Danny's off like a flash. By the time the elevator comes, stops twice for passengers, and makes it down ten flights, he's waiting for me by the mailboxes, not even breathing hard.

"What took you so long?" He grins. "I been here for days."

When we arrive at his tenement, between First and Second Avenues about two-thirds of the way down 101st Street, Danny tells me to wait on the street while he goes up to change. Although I'm not too keen on waiting by myself, Danny gives me no choice. I figure maybe his room is a mess or his mother has guests over.

The early Sunday morning quiet has given way to an afternoon frenzy of noise and people. Standing all alone, I feel out of place, an easy target for anyone who might want to bother me. It's one thing to be headed toward a clear destination on a known path—to be walking to church, the bus stop, or the basketball court—quite another to be standing all alone on an unfamiliar street. What will I say if someone asks what I'm doing here? What will I do if some kid tries to pick a fight?

As I wait, I watch a bunch of teenagers smack a Spalding off the stairs in front of a building. Three other boys take turns shooting a basketball through the space between the bottom two rungs of a ladder hanging down from a fire escape. On the curbs and in the gutters, kids spin tops, play jacks, shoot marbles, and ping bottle caps around a game board chalked onto the cement. Girls jump hopscotch and skip rope like I've never seen, two or three at a time on the same rope. In the middle of the block, a pack of kids run and squeal in the water streaming from an opened fire hydrant.

39

Whenever a car comes down the street, one of the older boys gets behind the hydrant and reaches around it with an empty beer can, directing the spray up into the air and onto the passing vehicle.

I feel like I'm melting. No breeze cools the air. The warmth of the pavement rises through my sneakers, travels up my legs, across my stomach into my chest and neck, and comes to rest full force in my flushed face. The top of my head feels ready to pop off.

Dressed in a T-shirt, blue jeans, and sneakers, Danny finally returns and catches me in a trance, staring at the water flying from the hydrant, imagining how much fun it must be to direct the spray.

"You ever tried it?" he asks.

I say I haven't, and he asks if I want to. Worried that I might mess up and make a fool of myself, I suggest we play some basketball instead. Danny says it's too hot, grabs my arm, and pulls me into line behind the opened hydrant.

"Next up!" he declares, loud enough to be heard over the swoosh of the rushing water.

The shirtless teenager controlling the spray turns and sizes us up with a quick glance, then offers Danny the empty Rheingold can caved in at the middle. Danny springs into action. Squatting like Yogi Berra behind the plate, he reaches over the top of the hydrant with both hands and calmly lowers the can into the gushing water. The water immediately spurts up into the sky, like a soaring, gravity-free stream.

"You got to hold it real tight and bring it down real slow," he explains, darting the water to the left and right. A pack of half-naked boys scream in delight as the spray rains over them. After several minutes of showing off behind the hydrant, Danny stands up. "Now you."

Exchanging my basketball for his beer can, I try to copy each move I just saw him make. I crouch behind the hydrant and slowly lower the can over the top. As soon as the can touches the water, the force of the current pulls me forward, my chest smacks into the helmet of the hydrant, and I drop the can, which flies out into the street.

"That always happens till you get the hang of it," Danny says as he quickly retrieves the Rheingold can. "This time press up against the back of the hydrant before you lower the can. Then hold on like Godzilla."

I ease my chest against the hydrant and begin to lower my hands inch by inch. This time when the can hits the water, spray ricochets backwards into my face, forcing me to close my eyes. In the darkness, I hear shouts behind me: "Make it. Quick! Here he comes. *Corre! Corre!*"

I feel Danny tugging on my shoulder and hear his voice above the din urging, "Tommy! Come on. *Come on!*"

Nothing, however, can make me relax my death grip on the can. I continue to lower my hands and suddenly, instead of spraying backwards into my face, the water changes direction, shooting up into the air. Opening my eyes, I watch with satisfaction as my own mighty stream arcs into the heavens.

Too late I realize that no one is prancing under my spray. The street in front of me is deserted. Without warning, a huge hand on my shoulder yanks me off the hydrant with such force that I drop the can and fall backwards onto my butt. Standing over me is a pink-faced Goliath of a policeman swinging a giant wrench. Behind him Danny huddles against the wall of the nearest tenement, clutching my basketball like it's a stuffed animal.

"What have we here?" asks the cop, lifting me off the ground by my belt buckle.

Before I can respond, Danny takes a baby step forward and announces in a shout, "That's Reverend Webber's son!"

"And who the hell is Reverend Webber?" bellows the cop, not letting me go.

"Reverend Webber, who runs the East Harlem Protestant Parish and is the pastor of Ascension Church!"

"You don't say. And who the hell are you?"

"I'm . . . I'm . . . his friend."

"Yeah? Well beat it."

Danny retreats a step or two, then holds his ground. The cop glares at Danny, hesitating a second before turning his attention back to me. He sets me on my feet, lets go of my belt, leans his flushed, fat face down toward me, and speaks right into my ear. "Son, I got a piece of advice for you. Don't hang out with these niggers and spics. They'll only get you in trouble." Then he swats the back of my head and proceeds to close down the hydrant with a few twists of his mighty wrench.

I take three steps over to where Danny is standing, and we head down the street, walking double time.

"Wow that was a close one," says Danny, when we have put a full block between us and the cop. "What'd he tell you?"

"Not to let him catch me at the hydrant again or else." I am afraid to repeat what Goliath really said. How could a policeman say such a thing? At home, *nigger* is an absolute no-no, worse than the worst curses imaginable. Dad says calling a Negro "nigger" is the biggest insult you can hit him with, worse than calling him a pig or an asshole even. Just the sound of the word *nigger* sends chills down my spine. And *spic,* I know instinctively what that means: that one's for Puerto Ricans and means they're dirty, ignorant, despicable. I decide not to tell anybody, not even Johnny, what the cop said.

My butt hurts, my chest hurts, my shirt and pants are soaked. I've had enough excitement for one day and decide to head home. We walk in silence to my building, where not wanting Danny to come up, I turn and say good-bye.

Danny asks if he'll see me next Sunday and I say yeah. Then he asks if I'm gonna tell, about the cop and everything. I say not a chance, and he breaks into a big smile of relief.

"And thanks for not leaving me there alone."

"No problem," says Danny. "Just, next time, run when I say so."

Danny doesn't wait until Sunday to reappear. The next Saturday, on my way home from the 102nd Street courts, I find him waiting for me on the bench in front of our building. He greets me with his gap-in-the-teeth grin. I ask him if he wants to go find the 109 courts together. Danny says he's not too big on basketball, so I ask him about baseball. It turns out he's not too big on sports period. Mostly he likes hit songs, TV shows, and movies; at home he's got a stack of forty-fives a mile long.

Together we head inside. Waiting for the elevator is the elderly woman Mom chatted with on the way to church our first Sunday in East Harlem. In place of her red bowling ball hat sits a fruit bowl sprouting bananas, apples, and oranges. Parked in front of her is a shopping cart filled with groceries, and next to her stands an enormous lady. I'm so amazed at the fat lady's size that my mouth drops open; I can't believe anyone so overweight can still walk.

She takes one look at my gaping mouth and in a voice that rattles half of East Harlem shouts at me, "What the hell are you looking at?"

I feel my face get hot, stammer "Sorry," and turn away from her.

"I'm sure Tommy didn't mean to be rude," says the hat lady, surprising me with my name. "His mother and father are fine people. They live on ten."

"Well someone should teach him not to stare."

"I'm sure you just did. By the by, my name's Mrs. Johnson, and this is Mrs. Nicholson."

"This is my friend Danny," I reply, still not daring to look at Mrs. Nicholson.

Danny says, Pleased to meet you, ma'am, twice, first when shaking hands with Mrs. Johnson, and again when greeting Mrs. Nicholson. He proceeds to help Mrs. Johnson maneuver her cart into the elevator and then out again at her stop on four.

After the door closes behind them, Danny lets out a big breath and breaks into hoots of laughter. "Man, did she give it to you. Whoa cat! Next time you got to have a line ready. Like when she blasted you, you coulda said, 'I was just admiring your superior hairdo.' That woulda shut her trap."

Inside our apartment, Danny politely greets my mother, and we head back to my bedroom, where Johnny is reading in his upper bunk.

"You remember Danny, don't you, Johnny?"

"Yeah, sure. The kid with the window-rattling whistle."

"You aint heard nothing yet," says Danny, placing two fingers deep inside his mouth and letting loose with a three-note blast, two low and the last high, like the call of a gigantic bird. This time his whistle really does rattle our windows.

After lunch, when Johnny goes grocery shopping with Mom, we have my bedroom to ourselves. Danny leaps to the radio and tunes into the station playing the top thirty countdown. He knows every song by heart.

"You got any movie mags?"

"No. Only *Sports Illustrated*."

"Never mind. Anybody ever tell you you look like Troy Donahue?"

"Nope."

"Tab Hunter?"

"Nope. Mostly people say I look like my father only with blond hair."

Danny looks me over hard for a moment. "No way," he says. "More like Troy Donahue."

As we listen to the top thirty, we play Parcheesi. Every time Danny rolls a good number, he shouts out "Got dog," careful not to call the Lord's name, or "Gimme some skin," and holds out his palm. He shows me how to slide my hand across his palm real slow, to move my fingers even slower off his, and then to end the exchange with a thumb-and-finger snap. Danny clues me in to the fact that giving skin right is the deal, that you've got to give up some skin whenever something cool happens, like when someone cracks a good one or says something that's right on time. Giving skin right shows you're hip, cool.

When it comes time for Danny to go home, Mom says I can walk him halfway, then come right back. Out on the sidewalk, Danny points to the school across the street, where I play basketball. That's my school, he announces, P.S. 121. Been going there since first grade. I ask if he knows a tall, skinny kid with gigantic ears called Rabbit. Danny laughs and says he doesn't but that if his ears are really that big they should have named him Dumbo. I say I thought the same thing when I first saw him, gimme some skin. Danny reaches out and we skin palms, ease off the fingers, and snap. He seems glad his pupil is catching on so quickly. Then he asks where the school I go to is. I explain that it's over on the West Side and takes two buses to get there: down Lexington and across 79th. Danny is surprised that I walk to Lexington. He avoids Lexington; too many Spanish kids hang out there itching to give someone an ass kicking. He says Spanish gangs got the other side of Third Avenue. Italian gangs got First and Second above 104th. Colored guys got the projects. If he has to go to the subway on 103rd and Lex, Danny starts running when he hits Third, a block before.

"Don't nobody bother you when you making tracks," he says.

I ask what happens if he walks down the wrong block. Danny

says he gets his butt beat. When I ask if he fights back, Danny replies that he has no choice, that if he didn't fight back they'd call him a sissy. Mess with him all the time. Take his money. Rank out his moms in front of everybody. Pretty soon he couldn't walk nowhere.

Danny points to the movie theater on the other side of Third Avenue and says it's the Eagle but everybody calls it the Bird. On Saturday afternoon the Italians, Spanish, and coloreds all jam in there together, and they have some hellified food fights, near like riots. Sandwiches and shit flying all over the place. Sometimes so bad they have to call the police. He says his brother, James, used to take him before he went into the army. Now Danny mostly walks down to the RKO or Loewie's on 86th.

"I like them movie houses better. They're cleaner, more quieter. Nobody bothers you. If I aint got money for a movie, sometimes I just walk and walk. I dig Park Avenue the best. Clean and pretty with flowers and bushes and trees right in the middle. I check out them rich people's buildings with the suited-up doormen. Inside some got gold on the walls. Can you believe that? Gold. Right on the walls! Below 96th people look at me funny, but I don't mind. At least I know they aint gonna mess with me."

"For me it's the opposite. It's in East Harlem people stare. Like I'm out of place. Like I must be lost or something."

"That's cause they aint used to seeing someone who looks like you north of 96th. Even the Italian boys aint got hair like you."

When we lived at the Seminary, before our move to East Harlem, Johnny and I went to Sunday school at Riverside Church. Mom and Dad made us attend adult service only on special holy days like Easter Sunday. Since our move, though, we've been doing the opposite: going to adult service but not Sunday school. Now, with a new school year about to begin, Mom thinks it's time for us to start attending both Sunday school and adult service. But this morning, as we are supposed to be getting ready, Johnny announces he's not going. He's thirteen, and Sunday school is for little kids. After a heated discussion, Mom and Dad back down and agree that Johnny no longer has to go to Sunday school. As part of the deal, however, he has to attend confirmation class for ten weeks after Christmas. Listening to their argument, I know there's no way I'll get out of Sunday school until I, too, am thirteen. But I don't mind, not really. I hope there'll be some guys my own age at Sunday school. And besides, I like it when we dress up and go to Sunday school and church just like other East Harlem families; it feels like we're almost part of the neighborhood.

Fourth- through sixth-grade Sunday school is held at the home of a church elder named Leonard Answick, a dark-skinned, lanky, white-haired man dressed in a navy blue three-piece suit despite the stuffy heat of his tenement apartment. Bent over like a long fishing pole dipping with the weight of a heavy sinker, Mr. Answick looks like someone who's been through hard times.

After Dad drops me off on his way to church, I'm left alone with Mr. Answick, who seats me in the kitchen and asks questions about how I'm doing at school. For a moment I panic, thinking maybe I'm the whole Sunday school class. Soon, however, there's a knock on the door, and Angel and his pretty sister, Evelyn, the children of Aleluya Santiago, come in. Five or ten minutes later, another kid about my age named Alfred arrives, and nearly a half hour late, in walks a girl who smiles boldly at me and says her name is Janice. Just as on the basketball court, I'm the only white kid present. It's a situation I'm quickly growing used to.

Mr. Answick starts off with a slow, boring telling of an Old Testament story. At first I don't quite understand what he's saying. He sort of mumbles, so it's hard to understand him, plus my attention is stuck on a gigantic roach making its way down the side of the kitchen cabinet.

When his story is over, Mr. Answick tries to get us talking by asking us questions. No one is saying anything. On my first day in class I certainly don't want to do all the talking and have the other kids think I'm the know-it-all son of the new minister. Finally giving up, Mr. Answick excuses himself to use the bathroom, and Janice, who is sitting next to me, leans over and whispers in my ear that my blue eyes make her melt. What am I supposed to say to that? I look straight ahead and don't say anything. Janice is nice looking, with a slim body and long legs, but her dark skin makes me uneasy, like her boldness. Besides, it's Evelyn I'm interested in. Quiet and soft, she seems more like the girls I knew at the Seminary. Evelyn sits across the table from me next to her brother, listening to everything with her deep brown eyes. Her dark hair is tied behind her neck with a red ribbon. When I catch her eye, she smiles shyly, then looks down at the table.

Upon his return, Mr. Answick announces that today is Communion Sunday. Right after the offering, we are to walk up and stand around the communion table but not to take any of the bread or wine, just pass it along. We aren't allowed to partake of communion until we're old enough to join the church and have been properly confirmed.

"Who can tell me the meaning of communion?"

"The bread is the body of Christ," says Evelyn, her soft voice hitting straight into my heart. "The wine is his blood."

Pleased with this answer, Mr. Answick adds that when we take communion we are remembering that Jesus died so that those of us who believe in him shall not die but shall pass over to the other side, where we will join together with friends and family and live life everlasting in company with Christ and the angels.

"We're already keeping company with Angel," says Alfred,

trying to make a joke and impress Janice. Clearly he isn't disturbed by her boldness.

At the end of class, Mr. Answick walks us to church, where I go immediately in search of Danny. When I find him, I demand to know why he wasn't in Sunday school. He explains that Sunday school is too early, that he can't be getting up at eight o'clock, not on no Sunday morning. I remind him that Sunday school's not until 9:30, and he replies, "It takes time to get ready, don't it?"

Danny is always neatly dressed and combed, with white baby powder under his arms and around his neck when it's hot. He also smells like some kind of strange lotion. Everything in East Harlem looks and smells so different that I assume this is just one more thing Negroes do different from white people.

During the service, when it comes time to celebrate the Lord's Supper, Danny and I stand around the communion table while the adults and those teenagers who have been confirmed break pieces from a common loaf of Italian bakery bread and drink La Lupe's Liquor Store wine from a common chalice. We all sing "Let Us Break Bread/Drink Wine Together on Our Knees." Noting that no adult is denied a chunk of bread or a gulp of wine, I wonder how we can be sure that they've all been properly confirmed. Couldn't one of them be Catholic or even Jewish? When I ask Dad about this later, he laughs and says God won't mind as long as they make a contribution when the collection plate is passed. Danny says if the Parish keeps it up, half the winos in East Harlem will come piling in on Communion Sundays and they won't be making no contribution. Dad says God won't mind that either, anything to get them into church. In my family, God doesn't mind a lot of things. Not even that at lunch Mom and Dad drink what's left of the communion wine and we all finish up the communion bread, both now miraculously returned to their normal states after a brief life as the blood and body of Jesus.

CHAPTER 4

EVERY NIGHT AFTER supper, right at seven o'clock, Mom and Dad, when he's home, watch the evening news with Walter Cronkite. If it isn't my turn for the dishes, I sit with them. To my parents, watching the news is an acceptable excuse for postponing homework. It's important for us to learn about what's happening in the world.

For several weeks running, Walter Cronkite's main story is the court-ordered integration of Central High School in Little Rock, Arkansas. We watch as crowds of cursing white demonstrators try to prevent nine Negro students from attending all-white Central High. In order "to protect and preserve the peace," Governor Orval Faubus stands in the school doorway blocking the entrance of the Negro teenagers.

Dad wonders out loud who is protecting and preserving the Constitutional rights of the nine Negro students, where the white people of conscience are. He says he'd like to see just one elected official, one teacher, one white minister stand up and proclaim for all to hear that segregation is wrong, that racism is wrong, that justice knows no color line. Dad makes being a minister sound heroic. Mom says that hate's not something you can talk people out of, that hate has to be taught and now it has to be untaught. Her tone suggests she's worried Dad might suddenly receive a call from you-know-who ordering him to become that one standing up white person he's looking for.

A few days later, President Eisenhower finally sends in federal troops, and we cheer as armed soldiers escort the Negro students through the angry crowd into the school building. I'm still hoping to see one white person stand up and declare that segregation is wrong. The only whites I see doing anything to help the Negro students are wearing helmets and carrying rifles.

I ask what's going to happen to them inside, and Mom assures me they'll be all right once they're away from the crowds and the cameras; inside they'll make friends with many of the white children. I hope she's right, but I'm not so sure. Making friends with kids who hate you because of the color of your skin couldn't be that easy.

At Collegiate the integration of Central High doesn't cause half the stir it generates in my house. The big news at Collegiate this fall is the launching of *Sputnik*. Our teachers say it's terrible that the Russians have gotten so far ahead of us in space, that it's a shame we've let our postwar military superiority slip away. They encourage us to do better in math and science so that America will stand a fighting chance against the Russians and all of us won't have to live someday behind the Iron Curtain.

When I talk with Danny about what's happening in Little

Rock, he seems almost as uninterested as my Collegiate friends. He wants to know what the big deal is: his school doesn't have any white kids. I argue that that's different because no white people live in East Harlem, whereas lots of Negroes live in Little Rock, and there they've got two high schools, a good one for whites and a bad one for Negroes.

"Italians live in East Harlem," says Danny. "*You* live in East Harlem."

I repeat to Mom what Danny said, and she admits that he makes a good point, that we need to improve and integrate the schools in East Harlem as well as those in the South. I suggest that maybe I should go to Danny's school, even though I know I don't really want to. I'd like to be brave and heroic like the nine Little Rock students, but I have no desire to leave Collegiate, where I've grown comfortable, made friends, and like my teachers.

Mom says that she and Dad want us kids to go to the best school possible.

"What about Danny?" I ask. "Shouldn't he go to the best school possible?"

"Yes, he should."

"But he doesn't."

"No, he doesn't. Perhaps you can grow up to be a leader who will change things, who will know how to make all schools good schools."

"You want me to become a leader? Like Daddy?"

"Sort of like Daddy," Mom replies.

Mom wants us kids to become what she calls "movers and shakers." She's only partly joking when she says she wants one famous author, one celebrated statesman, one well-known artist or musician. She dreams of us becoming people who influence not just the lives of individuals but the course of human history. I sometimes wonder if she's imagining the kind of person she hoped

Dad might become before he got his first call from God and threw his law books overboard into the ocean.

Immediately after Thanksgiving, all of East Harlem prepares for *Navidad*. Green and red reflecting paper and brightly lit stars crisscross Third Avenue from streetlamp to streetlamp. Christmas carols in English and Spanish sound from every store entrance. Christmas toys, gifts, and candy beckon from every store window. The tall buildings of the projects, their apartments twinkling with multicolored lights, shine into the night like giant rectangular Christmas trees. At Ascension, candles and wreaths adorn the nave, and a large crèche is placed beside the altar. Outside the Catholic churches, larger than life Nativity scenes light the sidewalks. No one dares think of stealing away with Baby Jesus or taking a ride on the dutiful brown donkey.

Seeing East Harlem's preparations for Christmas, my brain aches with memories of Seminary Christmases past. As far back as I can remember, we've attended the Christmas Eve party at President Van Dusen's gigantic apartment, where gray-haired Mrs. Porter would sit at the piano and play all the Christmas carols without any sheet music and Derek, the youngest of the three Van Dusen boys, just home from college, would sing so loudly we were sure he was sneaking liquor into his Christmas punch. We could drink as much punch and eat as many Swiss chocolates as we wanted so long as we didn't squeeze first to determine what lay inside. "If you squeeze it, you eat it," that was the rule strictly enforced by my brother Johnny, who appeared from nowhere, like Jiminy Cricket, whenever I approached the chocolate table.

At the end of the evening, all the lights were turned out and President Van Dusen would read the King James Version of the Christmas story in his deep, rich bass, like the voice of God emerging from the darkness, even if his name was Pitney and his friends called him Pit.

> And it came to pass in those days, that there went out a decree from Caesar Augustus that all the world should be taxed. And all went to be taxed, every one into his own city. . . .

In the Christmas darkness, the tree was lit with real candles, like those in Dr. Van Dusen's native Holland. Whenever a candle began to burn dangerously low, it was put out by one of the Van Dusen boys with the long-armed, golden candle extinguisher borrowed from the Seminary chapel. I would watch as each candle burned closer and closer to its branch, threatening a blaze that might set someone's dress on fire, like what happened to poor Mrs. Longfellow, the wife of the famous poet. And then, in the tree-lit darkness, we all sang "Silent Night," and all was calm and bright round yon virgin mother and child and I felt cozy and full of chocolate, snugly surrounded by friends and family. Best of all, the next day was Christmas.

I know that the Van Dusen party will be held this year just as it has been every Christmas Eve of my life. Mrs. Porter will play the Christmas carols without looking. Derek will sing too loudly. Dr. Van Dusen will read the Christmas story in his voice of God bass. And the tree will be lit with real candles that will burn dangerously low if somebody isn't carefully watching. When I ask my mother if we might attend, she says somewhat sadly that we won't be going this year; the Parish has its own Christmas Eve service.

Even without the anticipation of our traditional Seminary Christmas Eve at the Van Dusens', I can't help getting caught up in the Christmas spirit. Each Sunday in church we light a new candle for the next of the seven O's that begin each verse of the

Christmas carol "O Come, O Come, Emmanuel." I love how the O's, like the windows of our Advent calendars, help us count down the weeks until the birthday of Jesus. By the time we light a candle for the sixth O, one week before the long-awaited coming, I am in a high state of Christmas readiness.

> *O Come, thou Dayspring, come and cheer*
> *Our spirits by thine advent here . . .*

At home, my family does its own preparations for Christmas. We get out the Christmas plates, set up our homemade crèche on the living room altar in front of the cross and opened Bible, make a list of the presents we want, and plot how to afford gifts for our family and close friends.

As he does every year, Dad suggests that this year, for once, we do without presents. Christmas, he says, is becoming too much about buying and selling and too little about Jesus. He is mostly joking, but joking, as he often does, to make a point. Fortunately for us, Mom does her best to make sure each of us gets the top item we're hoping for, as long as it's not too expensive. Peggy's yearly request for a dog is denied as usual. Mom repeats her standard line that the city is no place to raise a dog and this year adds that, in any case, dogs are not allowed in the projects. Just as they always do, Mom and Dad say we needn't waste any of our savings on them. Despite her words, I know Mom will be disappointed if I don't at least make her something.

Three Saturdays before Christmas, we set out as a family to buy our Christmas tree. After some exploration around the local streets, Dad has concluded that the only trees to be found in East Harlem are the fake plastic ones sold in Woolworth's. Rather than travel just a few blocks south across 96th Street, where there are rows and rows of real trees, Dad insists on packing us all into the

Carry All and riding up to the Bronx Terminal Market, where he has heard trees can be had for cheap. Once we arrive, Dad tries to head us in the direction of the smaller, misshapen, less expensive trees, but Mom puts her foot down, insisting on a well-shaped, fresh evergreen. She finally settles on a perfectly shaped balsam, tall enough so that the star of Bethlehem, which will soon be shining at its top, will reach just below the ceiling. To Mom, purchasing a proper tree is no waste. She scrimps and saves on clothes, food, and entertainment, but on things like school, music lessons, books, holidays, and birthdays she can be relied upon to overrule Dad's distaste for spending money.

We tie our tree onto the car roof and ride back down into East Harlem, creating a commotion on 102nd Street. All our neighbors smile and joke and comment on how big our tree is, whether or not it will fit into the elevator, how lovely it smells, on how this year they may well have to break down and buy a real tree themselves. I hate each step of the endless journey from our car to the elevator. Once again, we are on display, the subject of notice and comment. Worst of all, Mom tries to get us singing "O Tannenbaum" as we march along carrying—or, in the case of Peggy and Andy, pretending to carry—the Yule tree. When I don't sing, I feel disloyal to Mom, who only minutes earlier stood up for us and bought a great tree. When I do sing, I feel like we're complete idiots, more conspicuous than ever: six crazy white people, singing in German while carrying a live, full-grown, bushy tree through the streets of El Barrio.

Upstairs, I lobby hard for blinking lights, like the ones in all the East Harlem windows, timed to go off and on so that they look like a flowing stream. Mom's answer is a short and final no. Blinking lights are fine to look at from outside, she says, but inside they'd give us all headaches.

When our tree is finally up and fully decorated with the usual colorful but unexciting lights, a fresh fir scent fills the apartment and it truly does feel like Christmas.

On Christmas Eve, we go together to the Candlelight Service at Ascension, where we listen to the Christmas story and sing all of the familiar carols in total darkness, except for the soft light of the altar candles, representing the Seven O's from "O Come, O Come, Emmanuel," and the light reflecting off the crèche. Like the little town of Bethlehem, the world lies still, quiet, expectant. At the end of the service, our head minister, Libby, lights her candle from the candle of the Seventh O, and shares her flame with Dad. Then they both step down into the congregation and pass the light until every person is holding a twinkling candle and the entire church is ablaze.

At the first hint of sunlight on Christmas morning, I hop out of bed and wake Johnny. Together we wake Peggy and Andy, and the four of us rush into the living room. Our bulging stockings are spread out across the floor in front of the Christmas tree, and the plate of cookies and the glass of milk we had helped little Andy put out for Santa and his reindeer the night before are empty. At breakfast Dad asks us questions about the birth of Jesus to make sure we remember to put Christ into Christmas—as if, living with him, we could ever forget to put Christ into anything.

Then we march in size order, hands on the shoulders of the person in front of us, Andy leading the way, into the living room as we sing "Joy to the World." Finally, we can start opening our presents. My best one, the one Mom knew I wanted most of all, is a guitar. I took piano lessons at the Seminary, but they were interrupted by the move. Now I have convinced Mom I will be more likely to practice with a guitar. She has already signed me up to start guitar lessons after New Year's at a program on 104th Street called Union Settlement. I can't wait to start learning "Hound Dog."

We have to hurry in order to make it on time to Christmas service at Ascension, where we will once again put Christ into Christmas. I know Christmas isn't about presents, or parties, or fancily decorated trees. Christmas is what you carry in your heart. It's the Christmas Angel appearing to Mary. The innkeeper turning Joseph and Mary away because there is no room at the inn. The wondering shepherds. The adoring Magi. Herod throwing a fit and ordering the slaughter of all babies under the age of two, and the Three Kings being warned about it in a dream and going home by another route. The miracle that God has sent his only Son into the world to be born in a lowly manger, that through him we might all be saved. And to add to the story, there is the music. To me nothing is sweeter than "Lo How a Rose E'er Blooming," "O Little Town of Bethlehem," "I Wonder as I Wander," sung in Choir Director Ted Ward's full baritone. As I sit in church, I know that no matter where I might be, no matter where I might wander, I will always carry the joy and wonder of Christmas in my heart.

After church, just as we are about to sit down for Christmas dinner, Danny arrives bearing gifts, not just for me but for every member of my family. He gives me a pair of soft leather gloves with real fur inside, by far the nicest gloves I've ever owned. He is pleased when he unwraps the three forty-fives I bought him and doesn't seem to mind that no one else has a present for him. He loves my guitar and eagerly checks out my other presents. When I ask him what else he got, all he says is, Nothing much.

"Like what?"

"Like a pair of underpants from my brother, James," Danny says matter-of-factly, placing one of his new forty-fives on my record player and beginning to dance and pretend he's onstage singing into a mike.

I'm dumbfounded by his brother's present. We never buy each other clothes at Christmas, certainly not underpants; clothes are what your parents have to buy you anyway, not something they'd ever give you as a gift.

"That's nice," I finally say.

"Yeah," says Danny. "He knew I needed them."

On the way to and from school, church, the courts, and my newly begun Saturday afternoon guitar lessons, I often run into one of our neighbors from the building, many of whom seem to be elderly ladies. Since my first encounter with Mrs. Johnson and Mrs. Nicholson, I have learned always to say good morning, or good evening, and, if they are having difficulty with their shopping carts, to help them in and out of the elevator. Saying hello is what everybody does in East Harlem each time they meet; not to is an insult, like you think you're superior or something. Children are expected to answer immediately and politely when spoken to, to carry packages, open doors, and never speak back. Speaking back is a great sin, a sure sign of a bad upbringing. The older the person is, the more respect he or she is given, and all respect is doubled for grandparents and tripled or better for great-grandparents. Around old people, East Harlem kids act like different human beings. If you saw Danny just around old folks, you'd think he was a little saint.

On warm days, I often see Mrs. Johnson or one of the other ladies from my building resting on the bench beside the entrance path. They can be counted on to tell me who in my family just came down or went in, and occasionally, they call me over and ask about my guitar and how my lessons are going; if I'm learning to play any gospel, blues, jazz. Not yet, I always reply, unsure I'll ever make it to rock and roll, let alone jazz. My guitar teacher is a large, sweating, balding man named Blake Hobbs. He lives in a ground-floor apartment next to the settlement house and favors old-fashioned folk songs. The Music Man, as the students sometimes call him because he teaches a long list of instruments from trumpet to drums, has started me off with lonesome cowboy songs like "Down in the Valley" and "Green Grow the Lilacs," not "Hound Dog" or "Wake Up, Little Susie." When he sings, his voice deepens, turns sad, and you can picture him all alone in front of a lonely prairie campfire surrounded by lowing dogies and the howl of coyotes in the distant foothills.

One afternoon as I'm lugging my guitar home from Union Settlement, I discover Mrs. Johnson and a group of our neighbors milling around in front of the mailboxes. Both elevators are out. The two ladies standing next to Mrs. Johnson look determined to camp out in the lobby forever if necessary. I'm eager to get upstairs and see how the Knicks are doing. The older of the two women says they've been here a full half hour and haven't heard a thing. Nothing's moving. I put an ear to the glass window. Not a sound comes from inside the darkness of the elevator shaft. No motor purr, no clanking chains, nothing. A young man with a small child cradled against his chest begins banging the elevator button.

"Do you really think that's going to help?" asks Mrs. Johnson. A brilliant purple doozy of a hat sprouting long, brightly spotted feathers sits on her head today. She looks as if, at any minute, she might soar into flight.

The young man continues to bang the button; it might loosen things up. The young woman beside him comments that all it might loosen up is his finger. After a few more minutes of waiting with no results, I decide to walk up. Although I feel guilty abandoning ship, there's nothing I can do to help by staying put. And besides, the Knicks must be well into the third quarter. As I make the stairway door, Mrs. Johnson asks if I would help her up to her apartment on the fourth floor. She could surely walk up herself, but her cart might be a bit much. I balance my guitar inside her shopping cart on top of the bags, and Mrs. Johnson tops off the load with her gigantic purse. On the stairs, I climb ahead, bumping the cart up behind me one step at a time. At each landing I pause and wait for Mrs. Johnson to catch up. Her feathers arrive several steps before she does.

We finally reach her apartment. By the time she's located her keys from inside her pocketbook, I've managed to free my guitar and have begun my getaway. Before I can make it back to the stairs, however, she asks me to come inside for a moment. There's something she wants to show me. It won't take but a minute.

In her kitchen, I lift her grocery bags onto the counter. Mrs. Johnson motions for me to follow her into the living room, where she points to a faded photograph on top of the television. She explains that it's a picture of the cabin she was born in fifteen miles north of where her mammy and pappy grew up on the biggest slave plantation in Mississippi.

"Your parents grew up on a slave plantation?"

"Sure did. On Mammy and Pappy's plantation they had so many pickaninnies of so many shapes, sizes, and colors nobody knew for sure who their father was. Except of course for those little high yellers who looked just like Massa."

"What's a pickaninny?"

"A slave child too young to work."

"What's a high yeller?"

"Half-breeds. Mulattoes. White fathers, slave mothers. On Pappy's plantation, Massa himself wasn't so bad. But his four sons. Watch out."

Before the move Mom threw out the Aunt Jemima and Uncle Joe salt and pepper shakers we had on our kitchen table, explaining she wouldn't want our new friends and neighbors to be reminded of that time in American history when Negroes were made to plow the fields and pick cotton for no pay and children could be sold away from their parents. Mom's description of slavery made getting rid of our salt and pepper shakers seem a small price to pay for not reminding anybody of those days. Now here's one of those very neighbors telling me all about it. Even worse, she's telling me about slave masters and their sons having children by their own slaves. Wasn't that breaking one of the Ten Commandments? Wasn't it adultery? And what would happen to those half-white slave children after they were born? Would they become slaves too? Even though the master was their father? And if they did, would they sometimes be sold just like other slaves were sold? That I can't believe. Even the most hateful, evil person, even Hitler, wouldn't sell his own son or daughter.

"Slavery was pretty bad, huh?"

"Slavery days was about as terrible as they come. Nothing but beatings and whippings, weeping and wailing. After Freedom wasn't so good neither. But at least you owned your own shack and your own truck patch, if you was lucky, and nobody could snatch away your children. Anybody ever tells you things aren't better now than they were back then, wasn't there. Only it's important we don't forget. White folks should never forget either."

"How can I forget what I never knew?" I ask.

"You know now," says Mrs. Johnson.

CHAPTER 5

Aᴄꜰᴛᴇʀ ᴀ ʟᴏɴɢ ᴡɪɴᴛᴇʀ of no outdoor basketball, I resolve at long last to go in search of the 109 basketball courts. Although I'm getting used to living in East Harlem, it's especially lonely on Saturdays. Except for Danny, who's over at the house a lot, I have no close neighborhood friends. The guys I've met at Sunday school and church, like Alfred and Angel, I see only on Sundays. Weekdays I don't get home from school until right before supper, and Sundays there's Sunday school, church, and homework in the afternoon. It's Saturdays that stretch out long and boring. Occasionally some of my Collegiate classmates invite me to join them on Saturday afternoons; when they don't I'm stuck playing with Peggy or trying to persuade Johnny to do something with me, which he seldom does. Johnny mostly stays in his room reading, doing homework, or scribbling away in one of his notebooks. I fear he's angry at me for not being true to our pact. Each time I grab my basketball on my way out to play, I feel his eyes on me like I'm Benedict Arnold going over to the other side.

Sometimes I see Rabbit hanging around on the courts, but this morning when I look out my window, he's nowhere to be seen. I wish he was there to come with me. Despite my determination to find the 109 courts, I'm worried. Maybe there won't be an empty court like Rabbit predicted. Maybe younger kids or new kids aren't accepted. Maybe gangs rule the 109 courts the way Danny says they rule certain streets and projects. The one thing I figure for sure is, the earlier I get there, the better.

At the breakfast table, I casually mention to Mom that I'll be walking a few blocks downtown to P.S. 109, not to the usual courts she can see from our bedroom window. She is not pleased. Even after I explain how the P.S. 121 courts fill with older guys and how 109 has four courts with one usually open, she says that it's too soon, that I'm still learning my way around the neighborhood. I counter that it's been almost a year and that, besides, there's nothing to learn, the 109 courts are right there, right through the projects. Mom seems about to put her foot down when Dad speaks up and assures her I'll be all right. Dad is big on letting us do things by ourselves if we think we're ready. When I was just starting fourth grade two Septembers ago, he convinced Mom it was okay for me to take the bus alone from the Seminary to Collegiate. And before that, when Johnny was ten and I was seven, he persuaded her to let us travel by ourselves to Yankee Stadium.

I wolf down my last spoonful of cereal and head out with my basketball. While most of East Harlem sleeps, I travel south, hiking in the direction Rabbit pointed out. All is the typical Saturday morning quiet on the concrete path that cuts through the many buildings of Washington Houses. Then, before my journey has barely begun, without crossing a single street, there they are: four beautiful, nearly empty, full-length basketball courts glimmering in the sun before me like a great prize. I have reached the Promised Land.

Inside the playground, I hesitate, considering whether to join the only kid in the huge school yard or to start off on my own. The boy shooting baskets has brown skin like Danny and looks slightly older. As I watch out of the corner of my eye, I can tell he's good, very good. Not especially tall, he is smooth and quick, and most of his shots are falling. He's absorbed in his practice and doesn't seem to notice me. I choose the court next to his and begin my warm-ups. It's a bright, fresh morning that smells like spring with a hint of coming summer. I'm in heaven, basketball heaven.

When I stop for a breather, I notice that the boy on the next court is practicing foul shots. I count in amazement as he sinks five in a row from the line, then moves to the top of the key and sinks four of five from there. I find myself hoping that he will turn and call me over to play with him. I shoot by myself awhile longer then, determined to take a chance, walk toward him.

"How you doing?" I ask, unsure of what to say. "You wanna play some one-on-one or something?"

He looks at me for a moment, his huge hands nearly encircling his basketball. I don't know whether he's sizing up how good I might be or is about to say, Get lost.

"If you'd rather play five-two or H-O-R-S-E or something else, that's all right too," I add. "Anything's okay."

"Go ahead," he says, motioning me to the top of the key. He places his own ball against the fence under the basket, then walks toward me. "Ready?"

"Ready."

As I start to dribble toward the basket, he takes two slow steps in my direction. Then, with a lightning-flash move, he knocks the ball out of my hand, scoops it up, jumps high into the air, and buries a beautiful one-handed jump shot.

"Nice shot." I hurry to retrieve the ball and throw it back to him.

"Two," he says, catching the ball and retreating beyond the top of the key. "Ready?"

"Ready."

He slowly dribbles toward me, looking me dead in the eyes. At my first step forward, he swerves past me and in three long, smooth strides sinks an easy layup.

"Four."

This time, when I back off as he comes toward me, he simply stops and sinks a floating set shot.

"Six."

This kid is, without a doubt, the best ballplayer I've ever played against. Dad says you learn more by playing with guys better than you. If that's true, just being near this guy will improve my game. The final score is 32–4. I make my only buckets on rebounds from two long bombs he barely misses.

"You sure can play," I say after he hits his final shot, a soft running layup that he sinks effortlessly with his left hand as I try to block his right.

"You're not bad, yourself." I think he's pulling my leg, but he continues. "You just need to learn to dribble with both hands, without looking at the ball."

He throws me the ball and says to try and dribble past him. As I start to dribble, he moves his body into my path, effectively blocking me without raising a hand.

"See? I know where you're going before you go there. You always dribble to your right, never to your left. You're scared of your left hand. Plus you don't see me coming. Instead of watching me, you're watching the ball."

This guy knows what he's talking about, and I like that he's willing to teach me.

"Thanks, my name's Tommy." I hold out my hand.

"William," he answers and reaches out to shake.

We are about to start a second game when two guys, neither of them carrying a basketball, walk onto our court. One is brown like William and looks as old as Johnny. The other is lighter skinned and closer to my age. Whether he's a Puerto Rican or a Negro, I'm not sure.

"Hey, William. What's up, my man?" asks the older guy, looking me over as he advances in our direction. He reaches out and slides his right hand over William's, giving skin just like Danny taught me, only without the finger roll or snap.

"You baby," answers William.

"Hey, William. What's good?" the other guy asks with a slight accent. He steps toward me and introduces himself as Junie but doesn't offer to shake hands or skin them. "And this here's Charles," he says indicating his companion.

"Tommy," I reply.

Without greeting me, Charles says, "Let's go two-on-two. Me and William against Junie and the white boy."

Because of my blond hair, I've been called Whitey several times by fans at Yankee Stadium. But that felt friendly, like being nicknamed Whitey Ford or Whitey Lockman. Charles's "white boy" doesn't sound so friendly and I know he's not talking about the color of my hair. The tone of his voice is threatening. It occurs to me he might be a gang member, a rumbling kind of gang member.

"No way," objects Junie. "Yous twos against us twos? No way José!"

"I'll team with Tommy," announces William, shutting down further discussion.

This game is closer than my one-on-one with William had

been, but not by much. Whenever I'm thrown the ball, all I have to do is get it back to my teammate and we have a sure two points. William and I win easily.

We're resting and shooting lazy hoops before the next game when Junie turns to me and asks, "So, Tommy, what are you anyway?"

I have no idea what he's talking about.

"You know, like Jewish or Italian or what?"

Now I understand what he means, but I'm still clueless how to answer. Although I've lived in East Harlem less than a year, I can already sense the importance of making clear what group you belong to. What group, however, do I belong to? At home, we've never talked about being anything except Protestant. We aren't Catholics because we don't believe in the Pope, and we're not Jews because we do believe in Jesus. I know that Protestant isn't the right answer, however. Junie's not asking about my religion.

Finally I blurt out, "American," figuring that has to be all right. If I'm anything, I'm surely American.

"We're all Americans." Junie glares at me. "We're all here Americans."

"Yeah, we're all Americans," cuts in Charles. "Only some folks are more American than others. Take William and me, we're two niggers. It's you Spanish guys think you're something special."

"Spanish are Americans. We're born citizens, just like you," says Junie.

"Yeah," Charles snorts. "Americans with an accent."

Later that morning, as soon as I enter the apartment, I find Mom and ask her what we are. At first she doesn't understand what I'm asking her about, just as I hadn't when Junie asked me. I explain that I want to know what we are like some people are Spanish, Negro, or Italian. She says that her mother, Grandma Barton, is Irish. That makes me one-quarter Irish. Granddaddy

Barton is English, so that makes me a quarter English. Grumpa Webber is Dutch and she thinks a little German. Granmousy is English and Swedish making me one-eighth Swedish, at least one-eighth Dutch, a little German, and more English than anything else.

"Webber with two b's is Dutch," she says, "if that's helpful."

At Mom's laundry list of our family's ancestry, my heart sinks. This isn't the answer I was looking for. Quarters and eighths will never fly on the basketball courts of East Harlem. I need something clean and simple, something the guys on the court will accept immediately. Dutch doesn't seem right; all I can picture is a rosy-cheeked blond boy wearing wooden shoes and sitting under a windmill like in *Hans Brinker.* I decide to try out "English" the next time someone asks. If that doesn't go over too well, maybe I'll add, "And a little Irish." I decide to let the Dutch, Swedish, and German parts rest in peace.

As for the guys on the court calling themselves niggers, I know better than to ask Mom about that one. Questions about niggers and white boys will only worry her, and that's the last thing I want. Instead, I turn to Johnny. Even though he seldom leaves the apartment except for school, I know he understands things that I don't. At Collegiate, he's always first or second in his class. And he reads constantly, anything and everything. He knows about history and science and rivers and deserts in faraway places I've never heard of. I'm not sure he knows about niggers and spics, but there is no one else I can ask, not even Danny. Not yet.

"Johnny," I begin that night as we lie in our bunk beds in the dark. "This morning a guy on the courts called himself and one of the other kids 'niggers.' Just like that. I thought you weren't supposed to call people niggers."

"You're not. Don't ever call anyone a nigger."

"I know. I won't. But what should I call them?"

"Negroes, call them Negroes. And make sure they hear you right."

"I don't think they like being called Negroes. I never hear them say Negro. Mostly they say colored. Danny says colored."

"That's strange."

"Yeah. Like somebody colored them."

"Can't you just call them by their names? They have names, don't they?"

"That's a good idea," I say, pleased with this simple solution. "I'll stick to their names."

I pause for a moment, then dare a second question: "And, Johnny? There was this other guy they called Spanish. You don't think he's really Spanish, do you? Spanish like from Spain?"

"Most likely he's Puerto Rican."

"Then how come he calls himself Spanish?"

"Probably because he speaks Spanish. Like they call East Harlem 'Spanish Harlem' sometimes."

"You mean sorta like calling yourself English because you speak English and at least one and maybe two of your grandparents came from England?"

"Yeah," says Johnny, "like that."

The first Monday morning of my summer vacation the 109 playground is bursting with little kids. Since finding these courts, I've been playing here a lot, two or three days a week after school and just about every Saturday morning. In the afternoons and on weekends, with the younger kids gone home, guys my age and older take over the playground. But I had forgotten that the public schools finish three weeks later than private schools like Collegiate, and little boys are running, yelling, pushing, and zigzagging from one activity to the next. Girls in groups of four and five talk excitedly at each other; one group jumps rope, another slaps their hands, chests, and legs in some kind of rhythmic body-patting game. Four of the older boys are trying to play basketball in a free space hardly big enough to shoot layups.

At Collegiate, we're allowed to enter the building at whatever time we arrive. We can go up to our homerooms and hang out with our friends, finish our homework, talk to one of our teachers. This doesn't seem to be the case at P.S. 109. I wonder what happens on rainy days, or cold days: are the kids allowed in early then, or do they have to stand outside? And what's the school like inside? Is there as much pushing and shouting inside as there is outside?

Suddenly, a buzzer blares across the playground. In no time the kids arrange themselves, from the smallest to the biggest, into a series of double-file lines. At the sound of a second buzzer, the boys and girls march into the school building. Within minutes, the playground is empty.

I choose a basket next to the huge, flat school wall that blocks the blinding rays of the sun and begin my warm-ups. After several minutes practicing dribbling to my left, I look up to find a dark-skinned teenager standing at the top of the key. He is tall and strong looking and, despite the warmth of the June sun, is wearing a black leather jacket sparkling with brightly sewn stars and moons. The words MIGHTY GENTS are written in silver capital letters across the chest. I haven't heard of the Mighty Gents, but I have a good idea that, whoever they are, this guy is one of them, there are others, and when they get together they form a gang.

Without saying hello, introducing himself, or smiling, he orders me to give him a shot. I throw him the ball, suddenly aware of how quiet the school yard is. This guy's sour attitude reminds me of Charles, only worse. He acts like I'm insulting him just by being here.

Mighty Gent takes a long set shot, and the ball bounces high off the rim toward the sideline. He walks slowly over to retrieve it, calmly dribbles to the basket on the next court, takes a layup, and continues taking shots, ignoring the fact that I'm standing behind him waiting to get my ball back.

"Want to play five-two?" I ask. In truth, I have no desire to play 5-2 or anything else with this kid. All I want is my ball back.

Instead of responding, he turns and dribbles to the third basket. One more court and he'll be out onto Third Avenue. On his next shot, I try to jump in front of him for the rebound, but he blocks me out with his body and catches the ball. Turning to face me, he says, "Beat it."

"Give me my ball."

"What did you say, punk?" He pushes me backwards.

"It's my ball."

"It was your ball," he snaps, then punches me hard with a right fist to the chest that causes me to bend over in pain. The blow is a surprise. I start to cry.

"Give me my ball," I shout between tears, desperate not to have my ball stolen. I'd rather get punched again, punched a thousand times, than lose my ball.

I'm about to give up hope when a tall Negro man carrying a wire bristle broom emerges from inside the children's playground at the south end of the school yard. He's wearing the army green uniform of the New York City Parks Department. Mighty Gent sees him coming and takes off toward the street with my basketball. Mr. Parks Department immediately drops his broom and lights out in hot pursuit, running in long, awkward strides.

Sensing he's losing ground, Mighty Gent turns and throws my basketball hard at his pursuer. In one easy motion the man catches the ball and shouts after the retreating teenager to stay out of his park. Breathing heavily and now limping, my savior heads toward me. I try to wipe away my tears quickly.

"Here," he says, handing me my basketball. "Those kids better not try their mess on my playground. You okay? He didn't hurt you, did he?"

"No. It's nothing." My chest is sore, but I'm relieved to have my ball back and grateful he doesn't mention my tears.

"Some reason folks not in school today?" He stoops to pick up his broom.

"My school's out for the summer," I explain, looking up at him. He's super tall, with sharp, broad shoulders that jut out from his body.

"You don't say. What school's that?"

"Collegiate," I reply, leaving out the "School for Boys" part.

"Collegiate? Aint that a high school?"

"Sort of. It goes from first grade through twelfth."

"Catholic?"

"Private."

"Bet it costs plenty. Now listen here. I don't allow no hooky players on my playground. No hooky, no nooky. On school days the playground's closed till three o'clock."

"But it's not a school day for me."

"So you say. But if I find out you have lied, from these courts you'll be denied. You can stay till first recess, ten-thirty. The other rules are simple. No litter. No fights. No beer. No wine. No liquor allowed of any kind. And no gangs neither. You got that?"

"Yes, sir."

"Okay then. You're a good kid. I been watching you."

"You have?"

"Yeah. This here's my playground. I know everything that goes on here. Everything. I've seen you with William. He's a good little ballplayer, but I've still got my old-man tricks."

"Like what?"

"Like giving him a sharp poke just before he shoots. He's too proud to call hack unless I directly hit his shooting arm. A sharp little poke in the ribs throws him off. It's the only way I still beat him."

"You beat William?"

"At the moment. Not to be uncouth, but no one beat me in my youth. See here."

He indicates for me to throw him my ball, and he sinks a long set shot.

"I'm getting a little rusty. Don't play as much as I used to. It's the knees. If that guy shows again, just call, I'll be keeping an eye out. See you, Tommy."

"You know my name?"

"Like I said, I know everything."

"What's your name?"

"Aaron Levy," he replies, slapping his heart where the letters A. LEVY are sewn into his uniform. "Mr. Levy to you," he adds, then returns to the children's playground.

After Mr. Levy has left, I realize that I'm trembling, like I'm having some kind of delayed reaction and am more scared now than I was while under attack. I want to go home before Mighty Gent gets it into his head to return for a second shot at me and my ball, even if Mr. Levy is keeping an eye out. But I can't leave yet, I've only been out a short while. If I return too early, Mom will be suspicious. I'm certainly not going to tell her what happened, not after her efforts to keep me from the 109 courts in the first place. And I want Mr. Levy to think that I really am all right, that a small thing like a punch in the chest isn't going to run me off the courts like a scaredy-cat. I'm ashamed that he saw me crying, but glad I stood my ground, even if I didn't punch back. I can't imagine actually trading punches with someone a lot bigger than I am. Living with a ten-ton older brother taught me a long time ago there's little to gain and much to lose by hitting a kid twice your size.

Despite the growing soreness in my chest, I can move my right arm and take easy shots without too much pain. I kill time around the basket until 10:30 sharp, when just as Mr. Levy predicted, the school doors fly open and children gush out onto the playground. Taking this recess as my cue to leave, I hurry home, where I head straight for the bathroom, take off my shirt, and examine the purple punch mark spreading below my collarbone. Just when everything was starting to go so well, just when I was beginning to feel safe and confident, this had to happen. I wasn't doing anything to bother that guy, nothing. I wonder if Mighty Gent picked on me because he wanted my basketball or because I'm white. If it was because I'm white, what am I supposed to do about that? Sitting on the edge of the tub, I feel like crying again.

For several weeks, I can't bring myself to return to the courts. From a distance every Negro teenager I see on the street looks like Mighty Gent. Although I try to convince myself that it's not his skin color that made Mighty Gent so scary, I know I wouldn't have been half so frightened if he were white. Fighting with an older white guy would seem more like fighting with Johnny. Even if I got hurt, I wouldn't be frightened. Negroes seem more dangerous, more likely to do something really bad, like pull out a knife. My fear traps me inside our apartment. When Mom asks why I'm not going outside anymore, I make an excuse about how it's not fun playing by myself while everybody else is still in school.

On Saturday, Danny phones and suggests that we go have us some fun. I ask like what and he replies like lots of things, as if he has a secret adventure tucked up his sleeve. Before signing off, he tells me not to go nowhere, that he'll be right over. Two hours later, Danny arrives, hot to take off. I demand to know where he's been and angrily remind him that he said he'd be right over. He says he had to eat and dress, didn't he?

"Right over means right over."

"Well here I am."

I'm quickly learning you can't stay angry at Danny.

In my bedroom, he lays out his plans. We have two choices, he says. It's either Coney Island or the Staten Island Ferry, depending upon how much money we've got. Coney Island isn't much fun unless you've got mucho money for the rides and everything. He empties his pockets onto my bedroom floor, counts out one dollar and thirty-five cents, and asks how much money I have. All I have is the weekly fifty cents allowance Dad gave me this morning. Danny thinks I'm holding out on him, but I assure him it really is all I have.

Not wanting to quit on Coney Island too easily, I say that maybe I can get Mom to give us some more. Danny suggests I tell her we need ten dollars. I'm shocked that he thinks I can ask my mother for that much money. Even though our clothes and sneakers are cheap, from Alexander's or Thom McAn, and I don't own expensive toys or equipment like fancy record players or radios, Danny, like most of the kids in East Harlem, still thinks we have lots of money. He thinks that being white equals being rich.

I tell him Mom might give us fifty cents each for the movies, if we're lucky.

Danny moans that it's not enough, that we have to have four or five dollars each, minimum; the Cyclone alone costs fifty cents. As I picture Danny dragging me onto Coney Island's gigantic roller coaster, Staten Island suddenly becomes more appealing and we settle on the ferry.

Danny still encourages me to get what extra change I can from Mom. "Tell her we need some money for the movies. The double feature at Loewie's don't get out till late. We'll have more than enough time. Tell her we're both dying to see *Gunfight at the O.K. Corral*."

I'm not in the habit of lying to my mother, but taking the ferry alone with Danny is too tempting. When I ask her for some movie money, Mom hands over a dollar easily, and I think we're home free until she asks if we'll take Peggy with us. I panic. Fortunately, Danny, always ready with a quick comeback, up and says we'd been sort of hoping to go alone, just us two, close friends like. Mom thinks for a moment, then gives in, saying maybe Peggy is too young for a gunfight movie.

With $2.85 between us, we start out. On the way to the subway, Danny informs me that he plans to jump the turnstile, thereby saving the fifteen-cent fare. "You should do it too, Tommy. That'd be a second fifteen cents saved. Even if the token man sees you, he aint gonna do nothing. No way he's coming out that booth."

"I'll watch you. See how it's done. Then maybe on the way back."

"Watch me good."

At Third Avenue, we break into a slow run. Although it's early in the day for gangs to be on the prowl, Danny says you can't be too careful. Don't nobody bother you when you making tracks. Inside the subway station, we wait on line and I buy a token. There are several grown-ups in front of us, but thankfully no cops. I try to walk slow and casual. As I put my token in the slot, I turn to watch Danny. The smooth quickness with which he hops over the turnstile is a minor miracle. If I hadn't known to watch in advance, I wouldn't have noticed anything more unusual than the quick lift of his upper body.

Downstairs, next to the train tracks, Danny leads me to the head of the platform so that when the train comes we can stand at the front car window. Danny says he likes the first car better than the last because he wants to see what's coming toward him, not what has already passed him by. When the uptown express roars through the station without stopping, he opens his mouth wide like he's silently screaming. After the train has whizzed by, he asks if I heard anything. When I reply no, he seems disappointed. He was singing a high note. Someday he's sure that, while the train is roaring past, I'll be able to hear. He wants to be able to say he sings louder than a locomotive.

Standing at the front window, Danny gets me singing doo-wop songs with him. In response to our rendition of "Get a Job" a male passenger throws us a dime, and Danny gets the idea that singing in the subway might be a quick way of earning the money needed for Coney Island.

"We could be a duo," he suggests. "Strayhorn and Webber. All we need is a hat for the money."

At 42nd Street, we switch to an express train across the tracks. Whereas Danny obviously knows his way around the confusing subway system, it's the first time I've ever ridden a subway without one of my parents, except when going to Yankee Stadium with Johnny. I ask Danny if he's done this before, and he says lots of times. Some days when he feels like playing hooky and it's cold outside, he just rides the trains. He's seen some amazing stuff on subways. Once he saw a woman give birth. No fooling. She was on her way to the hospital and didn't make it. By the time the train got to the next station, her baby was already screaming. Another time, he saw a wino piss into an empty Coke bottle. The old man kept going right up to the top, then stopped, didn't leak a single drop.

I'm not sure whether all of Danny's stories are true, and usually I just listen and let them slide by. This one, however, about the lady giving birth, interests me too much. If she actually gave birth in the subway car, she must have been naked, at least below the waist, right there in front of everybody. Hoping that Danny will supply

78

more details, I ask if she delivered her own baby. Danny says she didn't. There was this older lady on the train who seemed to know what to do. She shooed everyone away, laid the woman giving birth down over the subway seat, and talked to her real calm, telling her everything was gonna be all right and stuff. Then when the baby came, she caught it and held it until emergency medical arrived.

I suggest it was one pretty exciting subway ride. Danny replies that it was so exciting he nearly threw up when he got off the train.

At the stop for the ferry, we get off the train, walk upstairs, and cross the street to the terminal. Danny pays his fare along with everybody else, proclaiming loudly that at a nickel it's still the best bargain in New York. Onboard, he again wants to ride in front, this time so we can watch the ferry bang into the wooden barriers as it docks. That's the best part, he says. On windy days, when the captain can't control the boat too good, it slams into them piles like a mofo. Crack! It's outa sight. I say it reminds me of the Macy's Thanksgiving Day Parade when the wind pushes one of the big balloons and it crashes into the side of a building.

"I aint never been to no Macy's Parade," says Danny.

As the ferry plows its way toward Staten Island, he shouts above the wind, pointing out everything like he's a tour guide and I'm a tourist: the Statue of Liberty, Ellis Island, Jersey, the *Queen Mary* resting in her port up the Hudson River waiting to take a new load of rich passengers across the ocean to England. When the ferry arrives at Staten Island, it eases into the platform, barely nudging the wooden barriers, with more of a thud than a crack.

"Damn," complains Danny. "I've heard better when the wind aint blowing."

We walk off the boat with the other passengers, then turn around and walk back on with the incoming crowd. Danny explains that there's nothing to see on Staten Island. He walked around once and I should trust him, there aint nothing to see. On the return trip, we again position ourselves on the side deck near the front and watch how the skyscrapers of Manhattan look like cliffs coming right down to the water's edge. When I point this out to Danny, he thinks for a moment and says they're more like a mirage in the desert, that as we get closer they keep moving further away. Before I can ask him where he ever saw a mirage, he starts leaning way over the rail trying for a better view of the waves and the spray.

I tell him to be careful. He asks if I'm scared and sits on the railing. The next moment he rises to his feet on the railing and starts walking toward the stern of the boat, stretching his arms out like he's a tightrope walker high above the circus crowd. I'm frozen to my spot on the deck, terrified he'll lose his balance and topple into the water. Danny, get down, I plead. I'm serious. Get down! He takes two or three additional steps, then casually jumps onto the deck. My fear quickly turns to anger. Don't ever do that again, I shout, marching into the ferry's enclosed area. I want to get him as far away from the railing as possible. To my relief, he follows me. I'm beginning to wonder if hanging out with Danny is such a great idea after all. What if something really bad were to happen? What if we got arrested, or suppose Danny fell overboard? What if he drowned?

I tell him that if he wants to go places with me, he's got to promise not to do anything crazy like that again. Danny looks at me like I'm the crazy. Finally he says that he won't but that he wasn't in no danger, he's walked the rail lots of times.

For the rest of the ferry ride, we sit in silence. Trying to sing louder than a locomotive is one thing, risking your life for a cheap thrill is something else. It's stupid.

On the subway home, we count out our money: $1.75 remains between us. Danny asks what we should do with our cash, and I suggest that we save it up so that we can go to Coney Island one day. Danny's eyes brighten. He likes my idea and is happy that I'm still okay on going places with him. He tells me to hold the money and hands me the entire pile.

"If I keep it, I'll spend it," he says. "Every week I'll give you more, like a Christmas savings account. Soon as we get ten dollars, we'll make it to Coney Island."

"I'm going to camp for July. Then to Maine in August," I say, suddenly realizing that a country house in Maine, even a small log cabin without running water, is probably something no other kid in East Harlem has. Certainly something Danny doesn't have.

Danny frowns and says he had plans for us to go to Orchard Beach, the Bronx Zoo, the Circle Line, the Statue of Liberty, walk the George Washington Bridge.

I offer to give back his ninety cents, suggesting he might need it.

"Nah. You keep it for me. We still got to save up for Coney Island, aint we? We'll go first thing you get back. When you get back?"

"Labor Day."

"Bet," says Danny. "We'll make it to Coney Island first thing you get back."

When Mom asks how I liked the movies, I say that they were both great, but that she was right: Peggy wouldn't have liked *O.K. Corral*, too many people getting shot.

A few days later, I boost up my courage and return to the 109 playground. I want to play there at least once more before I leave for the summer. Otherwise, I'm afraid I might never go back. When I arrive, William and Charles are engaged in a half-court game with Junie and a guy named Samuel, who I've seen before but haven't talked with much. All I've noticed about him is that he seems almost as careful around Charles as I am.

As I approach, Charles calls out, "Well, lookie who's here. Mr. America hisself. What's happening, white boy?"

"You baby," I reply, trying to act like Charles doesn't scare me, which he does.

The playground rules are that the winning team stays on the court and the first kid waiting to play chooses the new challenging team. When it comes time, I pick Junie over Samuel both because he's better and because I want him to forget that I called myself an American. Once that happens he might begin to like me, and once he begins to like me, he might persuade Charles to lighten up on the constant heckling. I tell Junie I'll guard William. He looks at me as if I'm deranged, then goes to stand in front of Charles, who's holding the ball, ready to begin.

During the game, I test Mr. Levy's trick. Whenever I'm close enough, I give William a slight push with my lead guarding hand just before he shoots. It works, especially on jump shots. Junie and I still lose, but between William's unusual missed shots and Charles's hotdogging, the game is closer than it should have been. They only double our score, 32–16. William says that he can tell I've been talking with Mr. Levy. I play dumb and ask who Mr. Levy is.

"That old lame nigger with the Jew name who thinks he runs everything," says Charles.

Junie says he does run everything. Charles declares that Mr. Levy doesn't run his everything, that no man name of Levy is gonna boss-man him. Not on no public court. William says Mr. Levy is okay, that he's a good ballplayer and must have been great when he could move. Now he can hardly walk without his broom. Samuel adds in that he knows a colored guy name of Solomon. Charles says that Solomon don't count because it's a first name. I ask what's up with his rhymes, remembering too late that I'm not supposed to know Mr. Levy. Fortunately, William lets me slide and explains that it's one of Mr. Levy's old-time things that comes in handy when he's playing the nines.

"I just wish he'd cut out the pushing," says William.

"What's that?" asks Charles.

"Nothing," says William. "Let's play ball."

CHAPTER 6

JOHNNY AND I SPEND July at the New York City Mission Society's Camp Sharparoon and then go to Maine with the entire family in August. In addition to coming from East Harlem, the boys and girls of Sharparoon are from other poor parts of New York City, places like Harlem, the South Bronx, the Lower East Side. Mom has the idea that the camp will help ease our way into East Harlem, that maybe we'll make friends with guys from the neighborhood. For most of my fellow campers, it's clear that this is their first experience away from the city. They are both fascinated and scared by deep, dark forests and quiet, spooky nights with no people shouting and no sirens screaming.

Unlike camp, which feels like East Harlem transported to upstate New York, the quiet village of Sorrento, Maine, feels like a different planet. When I was two, Mom and Dad used just about all their savings to buy a small log cabin without heat, electricity, or running water, on the shore of Frenchman Bay across from Bar Harbor, and we've been going there in August ever since. In the morning I lie in bed listening to the call of gulls, the cawing of crows, and the putt-putt of lobster boats motoring out into the bay. Still under the covers, I can sense the fine, sprinkled dampness of the fog before the sun burns it off the water. At night I am lulled to sleep by the lapping of the waves on the rocky beach below our cabin, especially if it's high tide and there's a wind over the water. No place could be more different from East Harlem; even China couldn't be more different. Only the roosters crowing each morning at the chicken farm next to the golf course remind me of 102nd Street.

The best thing about Maine is the daily presence of my father. Although he sets aside the better part of each morning to work on his Ph.D. dissertation, which he hopes to turn into a book, Dad emerges from his study just before lunch and spends the rest of the day being with us. Fishing for flounder in Frenchman Bay. Swimming in Flanders Pond. Throwing a baseball. Playing badminton, croquet, or golf on the miniature nine-hole golf course we have created around the outside of the house. And on Sunday he doesn't work at all. Before we head off for church, Dad makes us pancakes in the shapes of animals, sometimes filled with the blueberries we picked the day before. As we eat, he tells us Bible stories. He can make the adventures of Joseph, King David, and even Saint Paul sound more exciting than pirates and hidden treasure.

We drive back to the city the day before Labor Day, and as soon as we get home, I call Danny. The next morning he arrives at the house around ten. We mess around for an hour or so in my bedroom, then he invites me over to his house for lunch. He's dying to show me his movie mags and play me his new forty-fives.

It's the first time Danny's invited me over, and I'm curious to see what his apartment is like. With Danny's assurances that he's gotten his mother's okay, Mom agrees I can go.

Inside Danny's building we are met by a short man holding a broom. Behind him, the door to the ground-floor back apartment is open. The sharp, garlicky scent of Puerto Rican cooking hits me full in the face; the Negro food of the projects smells more like Mom's cooking, only thicker.

"Buenos días, Señor Comacho!" calls out Danny, bounding up the stairs.

"Buenas," Señor Comacho replies, barely moving his lips.

"I didn't know you spoke Spanish," I say, trying to follow as close behind Danny as I can.

"I don't really. Only out here, you got to *habla* a little *español*. That's our super, Mr. Comacho. I call him Mr. Caramba behind his back cause he aint too friendly. Always bugged out about something. That's how come I *buenos días* him to death."

Danny lives three flights up. Although the stairs are well swept, graffiti covers the walls, and the halls are so dimly lit it feels as if we're descending into a dark cellar, not climbing upward.

To enter his apartment, Danny has to open three locks. The last one releases a skinny iron pole reaching from his door to a bolt in the floor. Loud music blasts from inside the apartment. Noting my look of surprise, Danny explains that you can't be too careful, that they keep the radio on when they're out to fool robbers into thinking someone's home and not break in. I wonder out loud if maybe my family had better start leaving the radio on. Danny assures me I have nothing to worry about, that no one's going to get through one of those solid steel project doors unless I let them in. Though Danny's words make me feel better, it occurs to me that if thieves rob your apartment when they don't hear any noise coming from inside, they might also break in when you're reading quietly in your bedroom or asleep at night. And suppose they knock on your solid steel door first, saying they're selling something or pretending they're maintenance: What if you open the door and let them in by accident?

I'm surprised to find Danny's living room furniture covered with plastic sheets. It looks like they're preparing to be away for a long time, either that or getting ready to paint. On the coffee table in front of the couch stands a large, framed picture of a young man in an army uniform; Danny says it's his brother, James. I ask if he has other family and learn that he has two sisters older than James who don't live with them anymore, and his moms, of course.

Danny leads me to his bedroom and proudly shows me his collection of forty-fives stacked neatly inside a row of old milk crates and arranged in alphabetical order by singer. After popping a disk onto his record player, he swings his arms and shoulders to the rhythm of the music and rummages through the many magazines strewn on the floor beside his bed. He soon finds what he's searching for. Look here, he says, and points to a picture of a tall, blond man. See what I'm telling you? You look just like Troy Donahue. Checking out the picture, I can't see it. Except for the fact that we both have blue eyes and blond hair, I don't look a bit like Troy Donahue. Only thing is, Danny continues, you put grease on your hair like the Italian boys. Troy goes in for the dry, natural look. Danny is right, I do comb my hair wet, parting it in a neat line at one side and using Vaseline or Vitalis to hold it in place. On bitter cold days, my hair freezes.

Danny tells me I should wear my hair dry like Troy, that nobody wears their hair wet anymore. He goes to the bathroom and returns with a towel and a strange looking black comb shaped like a small pitchfork. Motioning me to sit on the edge of his bed, he uses the towel to rub up as much of the Vaseline as he can, then sets to work combing and recombing my hair. Not until he's perfectly satisfied will he allow me a look in the mirror. When I do look, I like what I see. I imagine myself a teen idol emerging from the stage door of the Ed Sullivan Theater to the wild screams of adoring female fans. With my hair dry, parted to the side, and patted into a casual sweep over my forehead, I feel different, older.

Danny's mother doesn't sit with us during lunch as she serves boiled hot dogs, potato chips, and Cokes. A small, dark woman with glasses, Mrs. Gomez smiles frequently but doesn't say much. I figure that if her name is Gomez, and Danny's name is Strayhorn, she must have married again after Danny's father died or they got divorced. I assume Mr. Gomez is probably Puerto Rican, but I'm not sure because he isn't around either, not now or any Sunday in church. Danny's mother doesn't say anything about Mr. Strayhorn or Mr. Gomez or about whether Negroes often marry Puerto Ricans, and I don't ask. Instead, Danny does most of the talking, going on nonstop about movie stars, TV shows, the Coasters, the Rays, the Del Vikings, and about how he's going to form his own group someday. It's not like he's boasting—more like he's letting me in on a piece of the future.

After lunch, we climb up to his roof at the top of the stairs past the fifth-floor landing. When Danny pushes open the heavy door, I see two large, double-decker pigeon coops containing a flock of at least twenty-five birds. Thinking we're going to feed them, they begin to coo and call. I move closer for a better look.

"These pigeons belong to Jesus," Danny explains.

"Give me a break," I say, sure he's pulling my leg.

"No, for real. The guy who owns and trains these pigeons is named Jesus. He lives downstairs."

"Who'd be crazy enough to name their son Jesus? That'd be like naming him God. Can you imagine? God Strayhorn. God Webber."

"Well, that's his name. When they have contests, Jesus has his homers trained good. They usually capture a lot of the other guy's birds. Any pigeons what fly home with yours are yours to keep. Only thing is, I don't like how he keeps them all crammed up on top of each other, hopping on each other's crap, no freedom like birds should have. Sometimes I feel like breaking that lock and letting them all fly free."

"Birds probably don't care too much about freedom," I suggest, worried that Danny might actually do what he's thinking about.

"Bull jive! Birds got to fly free. Any bird what can't fly free aint hardly a bird."

"Maybe they don't care as long as Jesus gets here on time with their next meal."

"How you know? You aint never been no bird."

With that, Danny heads past the coops and shows me how his building is attached directly to the two buildings on either side so that you can jump from one roof to the next. It comes in handy when you running from the cops, he mentions matter-of-factly. You can run up the staircase of one building and down the staircase of another.

I look down at the people walking in the street below and gaze out over the rooftops of East Harlem. Danny says that he likes it up here all quiet and peaceful. He gets in some good thinking alone with the pigeons. Pointing downtown at the tall buildings in the distance, he names the Empire State and the Chrysler Building. I ask if he's ever been up the Empire State, and he replies that he hasn't. When he learns I've never been either, he suggests that we go check it out, right now. I say I can't; Mom has told me to be home early to get ready for the guests we're having over for dinner. Danny wants to know what's to get ready and agrees when I say that moms are always worrying about something. He falls silent for a moment, then starts up again pointing out the East River and the Triboro Bridge.

I admire the bridge and the river running under it and begin to understand why Danny likes his roof. Up here it feels like you own the things you're looking at, like it's your bridge and your river and your Empire State, even if you've never been to the top. I turn and look west and north. In the distance I spot the unmistakable high tower of Riverside Church. I point out the church to Danny and tell him that I used to live right next to it, so close it was all I could see from my bedroom window. I tell him that sometimes they took our Sunday school class up into the bell tower. From there you can see the George Washington Bridge, the Statue of Liberty, and if it's a clear day halfway across the ocean to Europe.

"That tower has tons of bells, some as big as elephants. If you're up there when the bells start ringing, you can get blasted right into the Hudson River."

Danny studies the distant church. "You had colored friends over there?"

"Nope."

"How about at your school?"

"Nope. There are no colored boys at my school."

"But you got lots in the neighborhood."

"Not so many. The guys I know I mostly just play ball with."

"How about Maine? They got colored folks there?"

"No way. Not a single one. In Sorrento, Maine, they don't even have any Jews."

"That's impossible." Danny grins. "They got Jews everywhere." He turns away and stares silently at the faraway church tower. "You miss being over there?"

"Sometimes. Sometimes I miss the Seminary and my old friends so bad I try not to think about it. We're never moving back there, you know. Dad's decided our life is here now. Someday on one of our trips I'm gonna show you around my old neighborhood. We'll go up into the tower when they're playing 'Our God, Our Help in Ages Past.' You won't believe the bells."

"Bet," he replies with his wide grin.

We climb over to the roof of the next building, and Danny leads the way down its stairs. When we reach the ground floor, he puts a finger to his lips and motions for me to follow him around behind the stairway, where a door opens to the basement. Halfway down the stairs he stops and sits. In the faint light coming in through the small windows just above the sidewalk, I can dimly make out two young men asleep on the floor, propped against the side of the basement wall. One of them, apparently hearing us, grunts and turns his head in our direction. Struggling to wake, he raises his eyebrows and opens his eyes partway. As he tries to push himself to his feet, his legs buckle and he falls back to the floor. *Vete al carajo!* he shouts, startling awake his sleeping companion.

Danny and I dart back up the stairs and out the doorway onto the street. He explains that the junkies won't chase us; they're so doped up they can't walk straight. Danny wobbles down the street with his knees half bent, his shoulders hunched over, his chin jerking up and down, and his eyelids at half-mast.

Although I've never heard the word *junkie* before, I have heard about drug addicts. But I pictured them as old men wasting away in opium dens like in the Sherlock Holmes mysteries, not young men sleeping in the basements of old tenements or walking with weak knees down 101st Street. I ask Danny if there are lots of junkies in the neighborhood, and he says there are tons.

"East Harlem aint got nothing but junkies, junkies and winos. Winos are okay, they only bother you for some change to buy T-bird. But junkies? Watch out! A junkie what needs a fix will rob his own mother."

"Are they worse than gangs?" The very word *junkie* sounds frightening, like a dog with rabies or a zombie or something.

"Worser. Gangs just help guys feel big and bad, junkies are desperate."

When we reach the corner of Second Avenue, I turn to Danny. "Thanks for lunch. You don't need to walk me home. I'm fine by myself."

He looks at me for a moment, then keeps walking beside me. "That's okay. I'm your protection."

That night in my bedroom, I gaze out my window over at Danny's building with its Spanish-speaking super, Mr. Caramba, its pigeons, and its pigeon trainer named Jesus. Yesterday morning I ate breakfast in Maine looking out our living room window at the fog resting on the water in front of our house, fog so thick I could see only the tops of the pine trees leaning off the shore of Preble Island. For nine years, I sat upon the wide sill of the window in my bedroom at the Seminary looking out onto the quiet courtyard separating McGiffert Hall from Riverside Church. Now I'm staring out a window ten stories up, looking down on the noisy streets of East Harlem. Each of my windows makes the world seem different. Yet it isn't really. The trees on Preble Island are still there, shining now in the late afternoon sun even though I can't see them. The Seminary courtyard is still there, the same as it has always been; only now another boy is sitting on my sill looking out across at the massive wall of Riverside Church.

Collegiate starts later in September than the public schools, so for two weeks I have the 109 courts to myself until first recess. Each day, I follow a set schedule. In the morning, I practice on the courts for the two hours between 8:30 and 10:30, always going first into the children's playground to say good morning to Mr. Levy. Then I return for another two or three hours in the afternoon between 3:00 and 6:00. Although I keep an eye out for Mighty Gent, I see no sign of him. The pain of getting punched has now faded to a dim memory, and unknown Negro teenagers have long since begun to look like themselves.

Each morning Mr. Levy limps over on his broom and shoots hoops with me. While giving me pointers on my game, he tells stories about the way it used to be in East Harlem during the old days before World War II.

"Back then things were different. There weren't drugs and gangs and all this fighting. It was safer, better. People watched out for each other and each other's children like they was their own. In them days, weren't many Spanish. Not like today. Around here was more like Little Italy. They even had an elevated train on Third Avenue. Of East Harlem I've heard tell, to get there you just take the El."

I tell him I like his rhymes. He smiles and explains how he and his buddies made up rhymes to keep themselves amused, sometimes even holding rhyming contests.

"Playing the nines?" I ask.

"You got it," he says.

Although the kids I play with on the courts change from day to day, I'm getting to know a few of the regulars. William appears almost every day right at 3:00. I study how he handles himself, how he seldom calls hack unless it's a clear foul in the middle of shooting, how he sets himself to block out his opponent when going up for a rebound, how during warm-ups he always throws the ball back when you make your shot. Basketball is serious business to William, and I can tell he likes having me for a teammate. We both play basketball as a team sport, not as a showcase for fancy moves, although William's normal dribble or pass is the best of fancy moves.

I'm also getting to know the serious kid named Samuel. When we're around the older guys he's quiet, but when we're alone he asks tons of questions about places I've been and things I've learned about in school, like the Amazon rain forest and why leaves turn colors in the fall. He comes down early on Saturday morning, and we talk before the courts get crowded. What I like most about him is how he always seems just himself. He never tries to show off or say something just to impress the others. In fact, once the other kids arrive, he hardly talks except when he comes out with a strange fact or observation, like did we all know that when a gorilla is scared he beats his chest.

Junie is also starting to like me and has taken it upon himself to teach me short Spanish sentences like *"¿Qué pasa?, nena"* and *"Aquí viene la policía."* He also teaches me curse words. Along with *"Buenos días,"* and *"Me llamo Tomás,"* I can say "go to hell," "faggot," and "eat shit" in perfect Puerto Rican–accented Spanish. Shouting out a Spanish curse when missing a basket or dropping a pass is a surefire way to get Junie laughing. When I curse in Spanish, it doesn't really feel like cursing. It's nothing like saying one of the four-letter English words that would raise the roof at home.

William and Charles both occasionally call Junie "Junie Fingers" because of his two missing fingers, but he doesn't seem to mind. Junie gets along with everyone, seldom takes offense, unless someone puts down being Spanish, and is constantly telling funny stories and cracking jokes. Before drinking from a new bottle of soda, he always pours out a sip as a sign of respect for his dead ancestors. I get a kick out of this custom and, much to his delight, begin doing it too. It makes me feel cool, like one of the boys.

Charles, I notice, is as unhappy as Junie is happy. He puts down everything and has what Mom would call a large-size chip on his shoulder. His constant digs and sour attitude make him no fun to play with. He seldom passes the ball, hogs most of the shots for himself, and when we start losing, as we always do with William on the other team, says I don't help him guard his man, that I miss easy shots, that I don't jump high enough or quick enough to catch his wild passes. Everything is my fault.

Charles's hostility is so hard to take that I often play one-on-one with Samuel on our own court rather than join in where Charles is playing. When I do play with him, I try every trick I know to make him like me. I smile. I say I'm sorry when I drop a pass or miss a shot. I praise his nice moves and shots. When nothing works, I only try harder. I'm convinced that if I can get Charles to like me, I can get everyone to like me and then my tryout will be over. I'll be accepted on the courts. I keep hoping Junie or William or even Samuel will tell Charles to quit riding me, but they never do.

Going to school at Collegiate was no big deal when we lived at the Seminary. Although most of my classmates are from families a lot wealthier than mine, and many are Jewish, the atmosphere inside the school isn't so different from the Seminary. The entire school sings Christian hymns at Monday morning chapel services, recites the Lord's Prayer in French, sings "We Gather Together" in the original Dutch, and takes Bible class with Boss Hoffman.

Now that we live in East Harlem, however, the contrast between my school and my home neighborhood smacks me in the face every day. I wake up in the morning in a project building lived in by Negroes and Puerto Ricans poor enough to qualify for public housing. I pass through halls covered with graffiti, ride an elevator that stinks, and walk streets filled with litter, garbage-strewn vacant lots, and crumbling tenements. Less than an hour later, I enter the Collegiate School for Boys, the oldest, most elite private school in America, founded by the Dutch in 1628. My schoolmates are the sons of the men who rule American business, government, and even entertainment, like Arthur Rubenstein, Robert Ryan, and Don Budge. Most live on the Upper East Side in large, palacelike apartments with fourteen rooms and original Picassos on their living room walls. All are going to college, the only question being which of them will get into Harvard, Yale, and Princeton.

At first, I attempt to lessen the divide between my two worlds by carrying pieces of East Harlem into Collegiate. One day I'm caught teaching my fifth-grade classmates how to pitch pennies the way grown men do against the walls of the East Harlem tenements. Another time I'm apprehended entertaining my friends in the locker room with a song I overheard on the streets: "You get a lot when you smoke pot." In each case I'm threatened with a Saturday Detention and told never again to gamble or sing about illegal substances in school.

Most East Harlem customs are not appreciated in school, just as many Collegiate practices don't play well in East Harlem. The kids on the streets, for instance, wear T-shirts, jeans, and sneakers, whereas at Collegiate we have to wear a jacket and tie. In El Barrio my school clothes make me stand out, make me feel like a private school rich kid. The Catholic school boys do dress in formal slacks, white shirts, and ties, but even the church school nuns let up on the jacket. My solution to this problem is to remove my tie as soon as I enter the elevator and to fling my jacket casually over my shoulder as if it's an unneeded sweater. As the weather gets colder, I pull the knot of my tie down out of sight and bunch up the bottom of my formal jacket so that it can't be seen under my winter parka. On really cold days, I fasten my hood tight around my face so that only my eyes and nose poke out into the winter's air. That's the best; when I'm all bundled up in the cold of winter, no one can see that I'm white.

I've begun to think about 96th Street as an invisible wall separating the two halves of my city. East Harlem kids rarely venture south and then only with varying amounts of anxiety. Danny is the exception that proves this rule; he's bold enough to walk anywhere. Collegiate boys venture north never, no exceptions. Some Saturdays, rather than walk the few blocks north to P.S. 109, my Collegiate friends and I traipse for miles searching in vain for a free basketball court below 96th Street. On several occasions I've invited classmates over to our apartment, but they always make excuses, so I've stopped inviting. Their parents will not let them visit. I'll bet they've heard stories and read articles about muggings, drugs, and gang violence. Whatever their reasons, I conclude that it's a given, a universal rule among white, rich people: You just don't go north of 96th Street.

In East Harlem, I try to act and talk like the guys I'm with. Although we know not to "talk fresh" in front of church ladies, cops, or parents and grandparents, when we're alone together we all talk slang. Whereas Collegiate gentlemen are admonished never to stoop to the use of slang, East Harlem boys speak street lingo with pride. Breaking out with the latest slang expression before the others have heard it makes you hip. Using fancy, ten-dollar words, as Junie calls them, makes you suspect, trying to act superior.

In school, I'm even reprimanded for singing on the stairways. Gentlemen, my French teacher informs me, do not sing in public. In East Harlem, singing in public is common. Groups harmonize doo-wop hits on every street corner. Puerto Rican bands with at least one tall drum and a guitar play Spanish songs in front of every grocery store. Music blasts from open apartment windows, storefront churches, bars, and handheld transistors. In El Barrio it's never surprising to pass someone singing to himself on the street and to hear someone else encourage him with a "swing, my man, swing" or a *vaya,* baby."

At Collegiate all the East Harlem skills I'm learning—how to diddy-bop, talk slang, give skin, curse in Spanish—are strictly forbidden. All except one. My emerging basketball ability, hardly noticed in East Harlem, is greatly respected.

Sometimes I think about how the rules of Collegiate and East Harlem are so opposite and how they got that way, but most of the time I just try to get along the best I can. If I act differently at Collegiate than I do in East Harlem, I also act differently in Sorrento, Maine, at home, at church, or at my grandmother's house. Each place requires its own set of manners; I just need to remember which way to act in which place.

As I make my way between Collegiate and East Harlem, I do sometimes feel as if I'm acquiring secret information about both worlds, information that only family members should know. I witness family fights and petty quarrels. I learn where Mr. Weiss, a business executive, hides his girlie magazines. I listen to the cries of the two children next door as their mother beats them. I notice Mrs. Mitchell's lip tremble as Dr. Mitchell, a famous surgeon, informs her over the phone that, once again, he'll not be home for dinner. I come to understand that both rich and poor have problems, fears, sadness.

Now that I'm eleven and in sixth grade, Mom agrees that I can travel home from Collegiate by myself. This change is necessary because Johnny's in ninth grade and stays late every day to play on the varsity football team. On the way home, I remove my tie and jacket while waiting for the bus at the corner of 79th and Lexington. As it rumbles uptown, the bus gradually discharges its white passengers. By 96th Street I'm always the last white person still riding. After 96th Street, people stare. Someone, usually an older woman, asks if I'm lost. Trying to avoid these predictable offers of assistance, I read a book or stare out the window. I'm embarrassed by people trying to come to my rescue, like I'm a helpless little boy. Don't they see that I'm confident, mature, that I know where I'm going?

* * *

From my bedroom window I spot a familiar figure sitting under the basket, his funny black hat pulled down over his eyes. When I arrive on the 121 playground I find Rabbit sound asleep. Because the court is still empty, I decide to practice here and let him wake up on his own time.

My warm-ups have progressed to working on my foul shots when Rabbit opens his eyes and looks at me.

"Hey, Rabbit."

Rabbit stands up, rubbing his eyes with both hands like a baby. "Toe-mee, where you been?"

I throw him the ball, and he takes a sloppy shot, barely hitting the rim. "Didn't get much sleep last night, huh?" I ask.

"The roof's hard," he mumbles.

"You slept on the roof?"

"Yeah. Fridays my father gets paid."

I have no idea what his father getting paid on Fridays has to do with his sleeping on the roof, but I hesitate to ask him for fear of prying into his personal business. "Want to come with me over to the 109 courts?" I ask.

"Okay," says Rabbit, like it doesn't matter to him what we do.

At 109, we find William practicing by himself on his usual sun-free court next to the school wall. I introduce him to Rabbit, and they say hello without shaking hands. Rabbit seems shy, almost withdrawn. I can tell he's surprised I know someone on these courts. While William and I are talking, Rabbit retires to a seat under the basket and looks like he might fall asleep again. When I suggest a three-way game of H-O-R-S-E, however, he stands up.

Once Rabbit realizes that William is not going to miss anything easy, he attempts crazy shots, not coming close on any of them. Each time Rabbit misses, he mutters an excuse about usually making that one. It's clear to William and me, however, that no player alive usually makes the shots Rabbit is missing. He acquires his "E" and is out of the game while I'm still at "H-O" and William hasn't gained a single letter. Complaining that he isn't used to my basketball, Rabbit again sits under the basket.

William seems to have improved each time I play with him, shooting with more ease, more accuracy. He misses only one of my shots, a miraculous hook shot I somehow sink from the corner.

After the game is over, I'm about to suggest that William take on the two of us in a regular game when Junie arrives, chowing down on what looks like a long, thin piece of brown, crispy pancake held between the folds of a greasy paper napkin. When I introduce him to Rabbit, Junie says something in Spanish.

Rabbit frowns and responds in English, "No thanks, I don't eat that food."

"How about you, Tommy?" Junie asks. "You wanna bite?"

It's a rule in East Harlem always to pass around whatever food or drink you have when others have none. If you're too hungry or too poor to share, you're supposed to find a place to eat in private.

"What is it?"

"*Bacalaíto*, man. Aint you never tasted no *bacalao*?

"Nope. What's in it?"

"It's *bacalao*, man. Puerto Rican food. Try some. It's good. Real good." He tears off a piece and hands it to me. On closer inspection, it looks more like some kind of thinly sliced fried chicken. I hesitantly raise the greasy morsel to my lips and take a bite. Junie's right: it is good. It tastes like a deep-fried, mushed-up French fry, only sweeter and crunchier.

"Hey, William," I call out, offering him my remaining piece. "Try some of this. You'll like it."

"No way. I don't eat pig for breakfast."

"It's not pig," protests Junie.

William scowls. "It looks like pig to me. All that *cuchifrito,* Puerto Rican food is pig."

"I tell you it's not pig," insists Junie.

I say that it doesn't taste like pig, and Junie repeats that it's not pig, that it's *bacalao.* I ask Rabbit what *bacalao* is, figuring that, since he's Spanish, he can set us straight.

"How should I know?" Rabbit replies in a voice that makes clear he wants nothing to do with Junie's food, Junie's Spanish, and perhaps even Junie himself. I'm not sure whether he's just tired and grumpy or whether there's something about Junie he doesn't like.

"It's some kind of fish," responds Junie. "Like eel or something."

"Eel?" I stammer, gagging.

"Yeah. Good, huh?"

I pretend to take a final bite, then spit my entire mouthful into the napkin while wiping my mouth and casually backhand it into the rear pocket of my blue jeans.

"I still say it's pig," pronounces William, banking a long jump shot.

After Junie finishes his breakfast, he proposes that we play two-on-two; himself and William against me and Rabbit.

I say that William and I would be fairer, that Junie and Rabbit beat me and William beats Junie so that's the fairest. Pleased I told the others he beats me, Rabbit okays my pairings and Junie is stuck.

During our contest, Rabbit and his game are both missing, and I blow past him with ease. And, of course, Junie is no match for William.

When I make a shot, Junie tells me to shout out *"¡Gracias a Dios!"*

Rabbit warns I shouldn't do that, and Junie asks him why not. It's not right, says Rabbit. You shouldn't make fun of God. Junie says that he's not making fun of God that he's thanking Him. Plus, Toe-mee's not Spanish, adds Rabbit.

"You never know." Junie grins. "His mother might be a Gonzalez."

Junie's comment makes me laugh. It also makes me wonder if I could ever be mistaken for a Puerto Rican. After all, Puerto Rico is an island, not a race, and anyone can move there to raise a family, in which case the children, if not the parents, will become Puerto Rican. If I learn to speak Spanish and declare that my name is Tomás Gonzalez, who can swear I'm not Puerto Rican? Anything would be better than being the white son of a white minister who decided to move to East Harlem. To the kids on the courts, no one in his right mind would ever choose to move to East Harlem. Most of them are dreaming of the day when they'll have enough money to move out of East Harlem.

The game is nearing its end when Charles diddy-bops onto the playground. After making clear he has winners, he starts in with a series of puzzling comments: "Hey, homeboy, how was them grits this morning? What do you say, country? When does the rain start? Dig it, Junie, check out them serious high waters. We better get us on home, must be a serious flood coming."

At first I have no idea what Charles is talking about; I think maybe he's ragging Rabbit about his dirty clothes. Soon I realize, however, that he's making fun of my blue jeans, which happen to end several inches above the tops of my sneakers. The two general rules of the East Harlem dress code are not to look poor and not to look country, which amount to about the same thing. Never dress raggedy, dirty, or like you're down to your only pair of pants, and never look like you've just gotten off the boat from San Juan or the Greyhound from Alabama. I try to ignore Charles, but instead of letting up, he quickens his jabs, determined to get a rise out of me.

"God damn, he said he was American, but I didn't know he was from Alabamie. Must be some heavy water conditions down on that white boy farm."

Although I know better than to let Charles think he's getting to me, I feel like hitting him and wonder if maybe I should. I'm worried that if I don't show I'm willing to fight, he'll continue to make fun of me and all the guys will think I'm a sissy. Then the word will get around and everyone will mess with me, take my money, rank out my Mom in front of the entire neighborhood. Trying to keep my voice calm, I announce that I like my pants this way, their lightness gives me speed.

"Speed-jumping from puddle to puddle," cracks Charles.

For the next game, Charles chooses Junie as his teammate, and Rabbit sits. Charles elects to guard me and puts Junie on William. During the contest, he continues his digs, calling me "whitey," "white boy," "Mr. America," and shouting, "Don't let no white boy dribble past you, Junie," or "Even Mr. America aint allowed to hack." Whenever I pass the ball he says, "What's the matter, whitey? Scared to take a shot yourself?"

Toward the end of the game, Charles makes a nice jump shot over my outstretched hand and mocks me with "In your face, white boy. In your face."

This last taunt pushes me over the edge. I'm not sure what I'll do if Charles hits me, but I know I can't let him keep bullying me. I can feel William and Junie waiting for me to do something, waiting for me to stand up for myself.

I retrieve the ball and walk straight up to where Charles waits at the top of the key.

"Tommy," I say loudly. "My name's Tommy." I don't throw him the ball as he expects. I just stand there, waiting for him to do or say something. I'm glad the others are here watching, but rather than involve them, I keep my eyes glued on Charles. He looks surprised and doesn't say anything, so I continue. "I call you by your name. You call me by mine. Tommy. That's my name. Tommy."

"I don't like it when you call me Charles. I like nigger. You should call me nigger."

"I don't think so," I say slowly but clearly, aware that Charles is trying to trick me into saying something that will turn the others against me. "I'll call you what your other friends call you."

"You aint my friend."

"Just call me Tommy. Okay?" I hold the ball, determined to have an answer. "Deal?"

He looks me in the eyes. I hold his gaze. Finally, with the faintest hint of a smile, he says, "I don't make deals. Now throw me the ball, Tommy."

CHAPTER 7

W<small>E'VE NOW LIVED</small> in East Harlem for a year and a half, and I'm slowly beginning to discover how my new neighborhood is organized. My knowledge comes from Danny, from the guys on the courts, from listening to people talk in the elevator, in church, in the bus, and while waiting on line at the grocery store. It also comes from what I see as I walk through the streets. Much of East Harlem is divided into racially separate mini-neighborhoods. Each set of projects, and there are many, is like its own village and seems to be filled mostly with Negroes. Puerto Ricans occupy the tenements between First and Second Avenues from 97th to 103rd and up the entire length of Lexington Avenue. Each block is its own self-sufficient world, with its own bodega, *cuchifritos* stand, beauty salon, Laundromat, bar, and church. Italians live between

First and Second Avenue from 104th up to 120th and all around the Pleasant Avenue area, where the majestic Benjamin Franklin High School dominates the landscape like a large fort guarding the East River. Although I see a few colored people living on the Puerto Rican blocks, and a few Puerto Ricans living in the projects, I never see a Negro or a Puerto Rican hang out on an Italian block or the other way around.

Italians attend one of the local Catholic churches and send their children to Parochial schools. Puerto Ricans also go to one of the Catholic churches or to one of the many Evangelical, *Aleluya* churches that I see on every block. Some Puerto Rican families, perhaps those that can afford it, send their kids to Parochial school; the rest go to public schools. Colored people attend a variety of Protestant churches in the neighborhood, both large, established churches and smaller storefronts founded by self-appointed pastors. Colored kids all seem to attend public schools.

Because no Italians live in the projects or play ball on the public playgrounds and they all attend Catholic church, I do not know a single Italian boy my age. The only Italians I've become friendly with are the adults who own and operate the stores we go to: Pat the shoemaker, Sonny the pizza man, the Puglisi brothers who run Puglisi's meat market, Regina the kindly pastry shop lady on the corner of 106th, who welcomes me with a big smile and scoops my Italian icie especially high after church each Sunday.

Kids in the neighborhood refer to each other according to where they live. Your block or your project is part of your identity. It's your turf, where you're from. When guys introduce themselves it's first name, short pause, block number or project name, as in I'm Freddie . . . Freddie from 105th, or I'm Ray Ray . . . Ray Ray from Carver Houses, or You know Moody . . . Moody from 100th Street. In East Harlem your block or your housing project is what tells you apart from all the other Freddies and Ray Rays and Moodys in the neighborhood.

In addition to identifying who you are, where you live also affords status, or lack of it. The bottom rung of East Harlem's social ladder is occupied by the homeless, especially if they're junkies, as most of the people I see sleeping in vacant houses, or huddled in empty lots, appear to be. Homeless junkies are both feared and pitied; even their own families have turned them out. Then come the people who live in the tenements, which except for the many projects, make up just about all the buildings in East Harlem. Tenement dwellers are respected if they settle in, help to maintain their building, and fix up their apartments. Far too often, however, tenements become run-down, lack heat or hot water, and have rats and roaches. Often families are forced to move in search of better conditions or to escape paying their back rent. Tenements are also more likely to have thefts or fires, the two great worries of life in East Harlem.

Several rungs up the social ladder, looking down upon the tenement dwellers, are the people lucky enough to have gotten into the projects. Dad says more Negroes live in the projects than Puerto Ricans because Negroes have been in New York longer and have more political pull. Whatever the reason, project dwellers have heat, hot water, elevators, few if any rats, and a maintenance department that comes and fixes backed up toilets and leaking pipes, if you're willing to wait. Projects are made of bricks and cement and don't burn and have impenetrable steel doors that prevent break-ins. Among project residents themselves there is an internal hierarchy based upon how well your buildings are maintained, who has the best outside gardens, whose lobbies are cleanest and sport the best decorations at Christmastime, whose tenant associations are most sought after by the local politicians. The guys on the courts have their own distinctions. Jefferson has the toughest kids, second only to Wagner further uptown. East River shelters the most kids whacked out on drugs. Carver has the baddest gangs. Washington has the best basketball players. We have William.

Even higher on the East Harlem social ladder than the project residents are those favored few who have saved enough money to move out of El Barrio altogether and are now living in honest to God one-family houses on Long Island or in Jersey. At the very top of the ladder, floating in the clouds of local lore, reside those legendary heroes who have retired to their beloved Puerto Rico or moved back to their childhood homes in the South.

"Have you guys ever seen the Egyptian tomb at the Metropolitan Museum?" I ask.

Samuel, Junie, and I are standing under the overhang of the Parks Department building in the kiddie playground south of the courts, waiting for the rain to stop. Junie has just entertained us with scenes from *The Ten Commandments*, currently playing at the Bird. After he closes with a dramatic description of the Red Sea closing down over Pharaoh's army, I tell them about the Egyptian tomb at the Metropolitan Museum, how they brought every stone over from the Egyptian desert and you walk into a long, dark tunnel like it's actually inside a pyramid. Samuel and Junie seem intrigued by this information, and Samuel asks where the museum is. I say it's at Fifth Avenue around 82nd and ask if they want to go. I'm unsure how much of the city either Samuel or Junie has seen, whether they've ever been to a Broadway show, the Central Park Zoo, or any museum. It seems as if they, unlike Danny, have never been anywhere, not even to Staten Island on the ferry.

Junie says to count him out. He doesn't travel south of the DMZ unless he has to. I ask what the DMZ is, and he explains that it stands for demilitarized zone, 96th Street. Rich folks to the south, Spanish Harlem to the north, the 96th Street DMZ between. Just like North and South Korea.

Silently I thank Junie for merely saying rich folks to the south. He could have said rich white folks or even just white folks period.

I turn to Samuel and ask what about it. He agrees to go, and I make a final attempt to get Junie to come with us. Junie repeats to count him out. I can't tell whether he's nervous about traveling below 96th or simply not interested. Junie doesn't seem like the scared or cautious type, but south of 96th may be a world he stays away from.

Samuel and I reach the museum just as the doors are opening. Samuel stares in wonder at the high, domed ceiling and at the wide stairway leading to the second floor. In addition to seeing his mouth falling open like mine did when I first caught sight of the fat lady at the elevator, I can feel him tensing up beside me. He has entered unknown territory.

A museum guard steps in front of us and tells us we have to check our basketballs. I ask where, and he points in the direction of the coatroom. After we have handed over our basketballs and our jackets, a young lady at the information desk informs us that the Egyptian tomb is down the hallway to the right. On our way to the tomb, we find ourselves in a room filled with figures from a medieval battlefield. Covered in armor from helmet to boots, life-size figures of knights resembling King Arthur and Sir Lancelot ride equally armored horses. They carry spears, lances, and creepy weapons like metal balls with sharp spikes attached to chains on clubs. I point to the spiked ball and ask Samuel how he thinks they used that one. Like he's in a library or something, Samuel whispers that the spikes could penetrate the armor. More like penetrate the skull, I say.

Finally we reach the Egyptian tomb, and I direct Samuel to the small opening leading under the pyramid. As we walk down the tunnel, Samuel murmurs out of the corner of his mouth that there's a guard watching us, that he's been following us since we came in.

"He watches everybody," I say. "That's his job."

"Not like he watches us," grumbles Samuel.

At the end of the tunnel, a rope halts our further progress. Behind a thick glass partition rests the mummy of some long forgotten Egyptian pharaoh. Around the mummy are gold plates, goblets, knives, spoons, forks. Everything gold. I wonder out loud where they thought his food would come from.

Samuel is silent, reading about the life and death of the Egyptian pharaoh-mummy. Then he says that Egyptians believed cats were gods.

"I know," I say. "Sort of like Indians from India believe cows are gods."

"Hindus don't believe cows are gods. They believe cows contain the souls of the dead. Reincarnation."

"How do you know all this stuff, Samuel?"

"*National Geographic.*"

I don't say so, but I'm impressed that Samuel reads *National Geographic.* I find it boring, except for the pictures of women from the Fiji Islands with their grass skirts and naked breasts.

When we emerge from the tomb, the guard's still there. I hate to think he's following us because Samuel's colored, but I can come up with no other good reason. I wonder what he thinks Samuel is going to do. Mug somebody? Grab King Arthur's spike ball and start swinging? Punch out the window and steal the mummy's golden goblet?

"You wanna see something else?" I ask as we reenter the main entrance hall.

"No. Two things are enough. I like knowing there are more exhibits for another day. That they're here just waiting for me."

Outside, the rain has stopped and the sun is trying to push through the clouds. Looking down the stairs toward the street, Samuel suggests that we walk home. I wonder if maybe he doesn't have money for the return bus ride. I've known Samuel for more than a year, yet he's never been over to my house and I've never been over to his. I don't know if he has brothers or sisters or even a mother and a father. All I know about him is that he's serious and knows more strange pieces of information than an encyclopedia. At the moment, I'm unsure if he has fifteen cents in his pocket for the bus ride home. And Samuel's no exception. I don't know much about the families or private lives of any of my East Harlem friends. In East Harlem, families are private matters, out-of-bounds. Except for my family, of course: my family is open to all comers. That's why we moved to East Harlem in the first place.

We walk up Fifth Avenue and then, at 96th, cut down the street to Third in order to avoid the steep 102nd Street hill. When we reach the 109 playground, Samuel marches straight through the courts and asks if I want to come over for lunch.

Samuel's Washington Houses building is just north of the courts. Inside his apartment, the closed windows, the heat from the radiators, and the steam rising from a pot boiling on the stove make the air feel like the hottest, most humid summer day ever, despite the fall coolness outside. In the living room sits Samuel's grandmother, reading a book of meditations. A huge dictionary spread open on its own stand dominates the room. Samuel's grandmother, a very old lady with a kind smile, says I should call her Mrs. Dilliard and seems pleased that Samuel has brought me home for lunch. She insists that I phone my mother to ask permission, which I promptly do.

While Mrs. Dilliard prepares lunch, Samuel shows me his bedroom. Two large bookcases are stacked neatly with hundreds of *National Geographics* and the many volumes of the Encyclopaedia Britannica. There's not a single other book on any of the shelves. Samuel informs me proudly that they are complete sets going back to nearly when the magazine first started. They were Grandpa's before he died. Now Grandma keeps the subscription going for Samuel.

I see no evidence anywhere of Samuel's father, mother, or any brothers and sisters. But I don't ask. Instead I ask why the apartment's so hot. Samuel says that his grandma has cold in her bones.

At lunch, Mrs. Dilliard bows her head and says grace out loud before serving milk, chicken wings, and a wet green vegetable, something like spinach, out of the steaming pot on the stove. She also serves us each a doughy biscuit called a "hoecake." I'm relieved that the hoecake tastes good and that Mrs. Dilliard doesn't seem to notice that I adjust and readjust my clump of greens without eating any. While Samuel and I chew our food, his grandmother does the talking.

"When I was growing up in Georgia, we endeavored to make our hoecakes right in the middle of the fireplace. We heaped the glowing coals all around. If the coals weren't hot enough, they'd get stuck to the dough. Lord, Lord that was one mess. Saturday afternoons I carried hoecakes to the white family where my mother worked. Mrs. Grice it was who taught me to read. She said our hoecakes were just about the best biscuits she ever tasted. Have you ever been down south, Tommy?"

Mrs. Dilliard makes down south sound like a country all its own, like England or France. I tell her the farthest south I've ever been is Washington, D.C.

"Washington, D.C.," Mrs. Dilliard continues, "is barely the South. The real South gets going about South Carolina and justly arrives in Alabama, Mississippi, and Georgia. That's what I call down south. Where the cotton grows white and full and shines in the glow of the afternoon sun. Where it's always warm and seldom if ever snows or gets cold."

"Yeah," Samuel bursts out. "The glorious old South where they've got the KKK and another lynching every day."

"You just hush now about any KKK." Mrs. Dilliard looks dead straight, and drop dead angry, at Samuel. "And in front of your guest too. They never did bother anybody who was respectful and knew their place. You hear me, Sammy?"

"Yes, Grandma," says Samuel.

After lunch I thank Mrs. Dilliard and explain that I have to get home in time for my guitar lesson. Samuel accompanies me to the elevator, where he asks if I have any more museums up my sleeve. I tell him about the Museum of Natural History, where they've got animal scenes behind glass windows, rooms filled with giant dinosaurs, and a whale as big as Moby Dick. When Samuel asks if I'm serious, I assure him that I am, that they even have his gorilla standing up on his legs and beating his chest.

"He must be scared about something," says Samuel. "Will you take me someday?"

I say sure, no problem, but not to wait for me if he doesn't want to: all he has to do is hop the 79th Street crosstown.

"No, that's all right," says Samuel. "We'll go together. You're my protection."

Danny and I are in the habit of doing our weekend homework in my bedroom on Sunday afternoons after church and dinner. He has few assignments and, while waiting for me to finish up, entertains Peggy and little Andy. I hear him joking with them in the next room. Danny is not much interested in academics, although he gets okay grades. Mom says his problem is that no one ever taught him the basics. When we first started doing homework together, I spent many hours unsuccessfully trying to help him memorize the multiplication tables until one day Mom hit upon the idea of singing them out. After Danny put the numbers to a beat, he learned them in a flash, just like he memorizes the words to every song he hears on the radio after hearing them only once. I know I'm better at school than Danny, but I don't think I'm smarter than he is. I just know more about the kinds of things you learn from books: geography, mathematics, history. Danny knows about show business, the subway system, and how to make sure no one messes with you on the streets. And he thinks more quickly than I do, never at a loss for what to say next.

During one of our homework sessions, I confess to Danny my love for my Sunday school classmate. Evelyn, with her dancing brown eyes, soft, shy voice, and long, dark hair tied back with a red ribbon, is driving me crazy. I think about her constantly. At eleven o'clock service, I try to sit in the pew behind her so I can stare at the back of her thin neck and greet her during the Fellowship Hymn. When we shake hands while singing "Blest Be the Tie That Binds," she keeps her eyes lowered, but I feel sure her warm, soft hand lingers a little longer with me than it does with anyone else. Unfortunately, except for our walks from Sunday school to church in the company of her ever-watchful brother Angel and those thrilling moments during the Fellowship Hymn, I am too shy to approach Evelyn and talk to her. Besides, along with Angel, her father, mother, and younger brothers form a human wall of constant protection around her.

Danny proposes that I write Evelyn and offers his services as official go-between. We labor long and hard over the letter, convinced that the success of our efforts hangs on the power of each word. Danny is determined to discover just the right tone of lovesick longing mixed with clearly honorable intentions. We don't want her to think you're just out to snatch some pussy, he declares. You've got to ask for a date, say you want to take her somewhere nice, not just write how much you like her.

At the last moment, I lose my courage and refuse to let Danny deliver the letter. Suppose she says yes? Where can I take her? And suppose Aleluya Santiago gets wind that I'm sweet-talking his daughter? Suppose he gets upset and complains to Dad? Suppose my love for Evelyn becomes a scandal, or worse, a source of humor, the talk of the church? I feel like I'm beginning to understand the rules that East Harlem boys live by: how to talk, how to carry myself on the courts and on the streets. But dealing with girls is a different matter entirely. When it comes to girls, I'm lost for advice. Johnny is out. He's almost fifteen and hasn't had his first date yet, or if he has, he's keeping it to himself. And Dad is hopeless when it comes to girls and sex. He can't talk about the subject without turning red. I turn to Danny only because there's no one else to turn to. But I don't completely trust him. He's too bold.

Danny takes it on himself to speak with Evelyn on my behalf, without my permission. How he gets past her moving wall of family protection I never learn. He reports back that she isn't allowed to go on dates and that her father would kill her if he found out she had a boyfriend. She thinks I'm cute, but a date is out of the question. Cute! That's the exact word Danny says Evelyn used. Cute like a baby. Cute like a little boy too timid to speak for himself. I destroy the letter, which I kept without telling him, just in case.

Now I feel ashamed whenever I see Evelyn in Sunday school. I no longer try to catch her eye or make her smile. At Sunday service I sit as far away from her as possible, on the other side of the church. I've learned my lesson. I know without anybody having to coach me that if I want a girl to know I like her, I have to screw up my courage and tell her so myself. When Dad first proposed marriage to Mom in a letter, she didn't respond until he called and proposed to her properly. Even with a war on, so that he had no choice other than to ask her over the phone, Mom still wanted to hear how much Dad loved her out of his own mouth.

In March, Danny invites me to his twelfth birthday party. When I enter his apartment I'm embarrassed to find that I'm the first guest to arrive. Danny's mother, one of his older sisters, and two teenage female cousins are cooking, cleaning, and in the early stages of decorating. Danny is taking a bath. When he emerges from the bathroom, he's distressed to see me and asks why I'm so early. I remind him that he told me the party would start at three. He says that three doesn't mean three, that there's not no way three means three.

Guys on the streets joke about what they call CPT (colored people's time) and EHT (East Harlem Time), but until this moment, I wasn't too sure what they meant. In my house, three definitely means three. And at Collegiate, 8:20, when school starts, means more like 8:10 or 8:15.

By five o'clock Danny's apartment is clean, decked with signs and balloons, and ready for the party. Danny and I helped decorate and put out the drinks and food, including a three-layer, bakery-made birthday cake decorated with flowers made of different-colored frosting and the words "Happy Birthday Danny." As if on cue, the guests begin arriving, and the apartment quickly fills with people of all ages. They eat ribs, fried chicken, and potato salad, drink beer and liquor, and shout at each other above the nonstop music from the record player spinning Danny's favorite forty-fives. I sit in the corner smiling at Danny's aunt, who is perched in a large easy chair opposite me like a giant queen bee. Although this is Danny's party, there are no other kids our age present and I feel out of place. I wonder why Danny hasn't invited other kids, if maybe I'm his only friend.

Suddenly, one of the older female cousins stops the music and yells, It's spanking time! Danny starts running toward the door in a halfhearted attempt to escape. If Danny really wanted to escape, he would motor. Cousins and friends grab him by the arms and legs, lay him out, stomach down, on the quickly vacated couch, and take turns smacking Danny's butt. They aren't soft spanks either. The idea is to see who can land the hardest hit and record the loudest smack. Danny doesn't struggle, but as the spanks mount, tears form in his eyes and he grits his teeth the way he does when he's trying to keep from saying something he might regret. They don't stop at twelve but keep right on going, adding one spank for good luck, one for good health, one for a sexy wife, one for a rich wife, on and on until everyone has had a turn. Everyone except me.

Next comes the singing of "Happy Birthday" and the cutting of the cake. I eat my piece topped with a scoop of ice cream, wait a polite few minutes, and then tell Danny I need to be getting home.

"You can't leave yet. I haven't opened the presents."

"Danny, it's late. I told Mom the party started at three."

"At least let me open your present," he says, taking me by the hand and pulling me into his mom's bedroom, where the presents are piled across her coat-strewn bed. I retrieve my gift and hand it to him. In a flurry, Danny rips the wrapping paper off the book filled with pictures of Hollywood stars. He hungrily leafs through the volume and its larger than life portraits of past and present movie greats.

"I hope you like it. It's got pictures and a story about each star."

Engrossed, Danny studies a photograph of Audie Murphy and reads its accompanying bio. For a moment, he forgets my presence. When he finally looks up, he puts his hand on my shoulder. "Thanks. This is the first book I ever owned."

Danny turns away from me, tosses aside coats, and searches

through the other presents lying on the bed. Finding what is obviously a softball, he holds it out to me.

"Here, you might as well have this. I'll sure never use it."

"Thanks. I needed one."

Danny hands me my winter jacket and pulls on his own coat.

"You can't walk me home. You can't leave your own party."

"Nah, that's all right. They won't miss me."

I'm tossing my new ball into the air as we walk down 101st Street when a man leaning against the wall of a small grocery store asks for a throw. He reeks of beer and has a greasy, overgrown mustache. I toss him the ball. He throws it over to a friend, and they begin playing catch. I ask for my ball back, explaining that I have to be getting home. The man ignores me. I ask a second time, adding that if I'm late for supper I'll catch a beating. This line works wonders with the guys on the courts. The man stops throwing, bends down, puts his face right in front of mine, and says in a beer-blowing whisper that I can have my ball back if I give him a kiss. I hesitate, then quickly press my lips to his cheek. It seems a small price to pay for getting my ball back, and after all, pressing isn't the same as kissing. The man, however, fails to honor my distinction. Squealing in delight, he jumps up and down like a crazy, rolls his eyes, and points to his cheek, shouting in Spanish something about *un beso, un beso*.

Danny goes berserk. He grabs the ball from the man's hand, slams him in the chest, and screams that he'd better not mess with me again or he will kill him, kill him, *kill him*. Danny then turns, grabs my arm, and drags me roughly toward Second Avenue, continuing to shout curses back over his shoulder. Danny has a temper and I've seen him hot on several occasions before, but this is the first time he's completely lost control. I can tell he's angry for me but also at me. Until he exploded, I didn't think it was such a big deal. I just wanted my ball back.

When we get to the front door of my building, Danny says that if I ever do something stupid like that again, everyone will make fun of me, kiss at me, call me a faggot.

"If they do, I don't care. I know I'm not one."

"What you are doesn't matter. It's what people think you are that matters."

"I don't care what people think."

"Just don't do it ever again."

"All right. I won't."

Danny turns to go, but I call him back. "Danny?"

"Yeah?" he asks, only half-turning.

"Happy birthday."

"Thanks," he says, sort of quiet, without his usual Danny smile.

Rabbit and I meet occasionally on the 109 courts, and one Saturday morning after playing basketball, I invite him to come up for lunch. He jumps at the idea. Just like Danny, he's astounded by the entire wall of books in our living room and wants to know where they all came from. When I say that Mom and Dad bought some of them in college and that the others are gifts, Rabbit is amazed that people give my parents books. I explain that everybody who knows my mom knows how much she loves to read. Rabbit says quietly that he does too, especially books about far-off countries, princes and kings, real-life adventurers. I lead him back to our bedroom and point out *Robinson Crusoe, Treasure Island,* and our mythology book. He asks what mythology is, and I explain it's about the Greek gods and their adventures: Persephone going down to hell, Athena being born from Zeus's brain when he gets a headache. I remove *Greek Mythology for Children* from our bookshelf and turn to the page showing Cyclops with Odysseus hiding behind the sheep.

This is some great stuff, says Rabbit as he takes the book from my hands and turns to the next page, where Prometheus, bound to a rock, is being eaten by an eagle. He then sits on the floor and is soon lost in the land of Greek mythology.

I pick up my latest Hardy Boys mystery and begin reading on the floor next to him. Looking over at Rabbit, I find it hard not to feel sorry for him. It pops into my head that he's one of those guys Mom would call a lost soul. He seems so sad, so out of it, he makes me feel ashamed of having books and never having to sleep on the roof because my father gets paid on Fridays.

When Mom calls us to lunch, Rabbit carefully replaces the book in the bookshelf, like he's memorizing exactly where it is. We all sit down to the table, and I ask where Dad is. Mom says he's over at the office dealing with an emergency. Apparently this morning one of the ministers discovered twenty-five people living in coal bins in the basement of a building on 100th Street. Seventeen of them are children. Dad's trying to help them find apartments.

"What's a coal bin?" asks Peggy, trying her best not to stare at Rabbit's ears. The first thing I told her after we came in was that she'd better not mention his ears.

"It's where they used to store the coal before the building switched to oil heat," Mom explains.

Later that afternoon, as he's about to leave, I hand Rabbit the mythology book and tell him he can bring it back when he's finished. Rabbit looks at me hopefully and strokes the book like he can't bear to part with it a second time. Then he hands it back, asking me to keep it for him here. He says that if he brings it home his father will say he stole it and give him a beating. I want to know how often he gets beaten and with what and how bad it hurts. I want to say how terrible it is, what a mean father he has, how I wouldn't blame him for sleeping on the roof every night or for running away even. But I don't. I don't want him to think I feel sorry for him.

Once Rabbit is gone, I find Mom in Andy and Peggy's room. She's dressing Andy following his afternoon nap. Peggy, now eight, is sitting on her bed reading a Mrs. Piggle-Wiggle book. When I tell Mom that Rabbit's father beats him, she halts in the middle of pulling Andy's shirt over his head and asks how I know. I tell her what he said about the book. I can see she's upset and unsure what to say. Peggy, who has stopped reading and is listening intently to our conversation, says that Mom and Dad spank us sometimes.

Mom says that her spankings are different, that they're more an idea of a spanking than a real spanking.

"He sure has big ears," says Peggy.

"He slept on the roof last night," I continue, "because he doesn't want to be home on Friday nights when his father gets paid."

Mom is quiet for a moment, pulling on Andy's socks. Then she tells us she's been thinking about starting a reading program, a program where my friends like Rabbit and Danny can go after school and borrow books and be encouraged to read. A quiet, safe place, sort of like a lending library with tutors. Peggy says that starting a reading program won't stop Rabbit from getting beaten, and Mom has to agree. I ask what we can do about that.

Finally, after a long moment of silence, Mom says, "Be a good friend to him."

One morning while looking out my window, I realize we've lived in East Harlem for almost two years. The first anniversary of our move has long since come and gone without comment, with no new family council, no outcry from Peggy, no moans from me, without even a sarcastic comment from Johnny. I try to imagine what this means. One thing for sure, we are here to stay. Another thing for sure, I'm not the same. Two years ago, I didn't know much about anything outside Union Seminary. Now I know about gangs and junkies and why you need to break into a run when you hit Third Avenue. I know about the Bird, *bacalao,* and why roosters crow in East Harlem. I know about calling hack and pouring out a sip of soda before drinking. I know about colored and Spanish, Negro and Puerto Rican. I still have dreams of myself back at the Seminary, but they are dreams of a time and a place far away.

Looking down on the street, I spy the *piraguas* man on the corner of 102nd , the same man who taught me my first word in Spanish. *Cinco.* Now I can curse in Spanish and recite a growing number of Junie's useful Spanish phrases, like Hi there, baby, and Here come the police. The *piraguas* man is serving a woman and her two children. I watch as he scrapes the ice, piles it high, and pours on the sweet syrup. On my way home from guitar class, I'll be sure to buy a cherry-and-grape combination, my new favorite.

That night in bed, I realize I no longer want to return to the Seminary, even if we could. Sometime during the last year, the determination to hate East Harlem has oozed out of me slowly, like the water dripping from my blue jeans on the wooden rack suspended over our bathtub. In fact, I'm growing pretty content with my life except for one thing, my pact with Johnny. I have gone back on our sacred blood oath. The weight of my betrayal is so heavy I can't sleep. With my light off, I lie in bed waiting for Johnny to finish his homework. Finally, I hear him click off his light, sigh, and turn over onto his side.

"Johnny?"

"You still awake?"

"Yeah. I can't sleep. I been thinking. I been thinking about the Seminary. About our friends there and everything . . . About our pact."

He takes a deep breath, and I watch as the weight of his body shapes the mattress on the crisscrossing springs above me. Then his head pokes down around the side of the upper bunk. "What about it?" he asks.

"I've been thinking about how everything's different now. About how we're both older and everything. About how things feel sort of . . . different." I pause, but Johnny doesn't speak. "Would you wanna move back to the Seminary if we could?"

Johnny's face withdraws to the upper bunk. I can hear his breath going in and out. My own breath is hardly moving.

"Look, I know what you're trying to say, and it's okay. I don't think about returning to the Seminary because it's not going to happen. We're here and we're here to stay."

"What about our pact?"

"I never believed in it. I knew once we moved we'd never return."

"You never believed in it?"

"No."

"Then how come you shook on it and went along and . . ."

"For you, you dummy. You were so unhappy. The pact seemed important to you. You wanted to believe in it so bad. East Harlem's not so bad. And Dad and Mom. They're happier. Can't you tell?"

"They seem the same. The same like always."

"Well open your eyes."

At that moment, however, relieved of a great weight, instead of opening my eyes, I shut them and fall fast asleep.

CHAPTER 8

OTHER THAN CHURCH, our apartment, and the basketball courts, Union Settlement is the East Harlem place I spend the most time in. It's been on 104th Street between Second and Third since it was founded in 1895 and is a place where children go for music and drama lessons, sports, Boy Scouting, and after-school tutoring. Burt Lancaster attended his first drama classes there, and many neighborhood hopefuls perform in the annual talent show as a warm-up to their long-hoped-for appearance "Amateur Night at the Apollo." Like sports, show business is seen as a possible path to the fame and fortune dreamed of by neighborhood kids. Mom says few, if any, of them will ever make it and they'd do well to spend more time reading and less time on their routines. I know when she says this she's thinking of Danny.

I've been taking guitar lessons at Union Settlement since our first winter in East Harlem, and Johnny and I both sometimes perform in the annual talent shows. Last year Johnny won second prize for his rendition of "On the Street Where You Live" from *My Fair Lady.* When Johnny sings, you know God has given him a special talent. Mom says he sings with the sweetness of a violin. Since we've moved to East Harlem, however, Johnny won't perform at home. No matter how much Mom begs, like when we have guests over for dinner, he always refuses. I play my guitar and do one of my Elvis routines and everybody laughs. But I know it's Johnny Mom really wants to hear sing.

The first time I appeared in a Union Settlement Talent Show, Danny and I performed as a duo singing "Little Liza Jane" with canes and top hats and doing a soft-shoe number that Danny worked out. We practiced our routine for days, with Danny insisting that I get the steps just right, with my legs all loose like James Cagney in *Yankee Doodle Dandy.* On the night of the performance, everything went well through the first two verses. I was doing great, keeping my arms and legs loose, matching Danny step for step. Then, suddenly, at the beginning of the final verse, Danny jumped out of formation and began executing leaps and turns I had never seen before. As he danced around the stage and around me, the audience went wild. I didn't know what else to do, so I kept dancing the simple steps we had practiced. Right before the end of the song, Danny jumped back in beside me, and we side-stepped together offstage, shaking our straw hats at the audience.

I was furious. "You made a fool out of me," I accused Danny. "Everybody was laughing."

"No one was laughing," said Danny. "They thought it was part of our routine."

"Yeah, well it wasn't. You said you wanted to keep everything together, mirror images of each other. You're a jerk. A total jerk."

"I'm sorry," said Danny, quiet like I'd never seen him. "When we got onstage, something lit into me. I could feel the audience wanting more. It just sprang out. I didn't mean it."

"We were supposed to be a team."

"I'm sorry," Danny repeated.

"Sorry is too late."

"No it's not. Sorry is never too late."

"I never know what you're going to do next."

"That's why you like me." Danny grinned with his big gap-in-the-teeth grin, the liveliness returning to his eyes. "Now take it back. Take back calling me a jerk."

"You are a jerk. A big, complete, one hundred percent jerk."

"Take it back," repeated Danny, waiting.

"I take it back." For the first time I can ever remember, Danny let me have the last word.

In September, Danny and I decide to join the Union Settlement drama class. He has the idea that he needs to become a triple-threat performer, able to act as well as sing and dance. I've loved being onstage ever since I can remember, since the Seminary Christmas pageant, since my family started creating skits out of fairy tales like "The Giant Who Loved Chocolate Cake."

One day the class works on silent, solo scenes we've improvised ourselves. I do a sketch about a young man making a phone call to his pregnant wife, becoming more and more anxious each time he gets a busy signal. I had worked hours on my piece, practicing over and over dialing a seven-digit phone number. The trick is to concentrate so completely on the specifics of the scene that you forget people are watching. I'm so sure I've successfully created my own world onstage that the lack of audience response disappoints me. One wiseass in the class says it looked more like I had to take a piss than it did that I was worried about my old lady.

When it comes Danny's turn, he performs an extended skit about a happy-go-lucky wino out for a country spin in his souped-up Model T Ford with a windup crankshaft in front to start the motor. Driving blissfully along, tipping his hat to people and enjoying the scenery, he periodically takes a long pull from the flask carried in his back pocket. From time to time the car stalls, and the woozy driver climbs out of the front seat to crank the car started again, nearly getting whirled aloft by the shaft each time the motor catches. Finally frustrated and unable to get the car going after the third stall, he has the brilliant idea of adding some of his booze to the gas tank. The motor starts right up. The Model T purrs smoothly. The old wino takes one last pull on the flask, flings the empty bottle into the nearby fields, and drives happily off into the sunset. During the scene there's lots of laughter. At the end, the applause is thunderous. Even our teacher claps loudly.

On the way home, Danny admits that he lifted the entire routine from Sid Caesar's *Your Show of Shows.*

"That's what artists do," he says, always glad for an opportunity to teach me something. "They borrow bits and pieces from other artists."

"Yeah, sure they do. And then everyone goes around saying they're funny but not that funny. Not funny like Sid Caesar."

"Are you jealous?"

"No way. Why should I be jealous when you can't even make up your own skit and had to copy one?"

"You *are* jealous," declares Danny.

On Friday afternoons Collegiate lets out at one o'clock, and when I arrive well before two at the bus stop on 102nd Street and Lexington, I decide to make a one-block detour to the candy store in front of the 103 subway stop. Although straying from my usual, well-beaten route home is a gamble, it's the only store in the neighborhood where I know I'll find the salty, buttered, ten-cent bag of popcorn that I love. I make my purchase, then walk east on 103rd Street, stopping every few steps to set down my book bag so I'll have a hand free to help myself to more popcorn. Halfway down the block, I'm suddenly surrounded by four Spanish teenagers. They're all wearing jackets decorated with the faces of fire-spitting monsters and the word DRAGONS, written in bold letters across both the front and back. My path toward Third Avenue is blocked by three of them. The fourth kid walks around me like I'm a horse he's about to lasso. He's tall and skinny, with a red birthmark covering his left cheek.

"*Mira* what we gots here. A greaser eating supper on our block with no manners. Not even no spaghettis to share." He reaches out and snatches my bag of popcorn. "No guineas this side of Third." He stuffs his face with a fistful of my popcorn, then passes the bag on with a big grin. "Vanny, have some Italian popcorns."

My heart is pounding. Here in the flesh is one of the gangs I've heard so much about, a fighting gang, a rumbling gang, a gang getting ready for a butt beating. I should have been running like Danny advised always to do west of Third Avenue.

Not wanting them to think I'm a kid from outside the neighborhood, I tell them that I'm sorry to be on their block, that I was just on my way home. The leader of the gang stops circling and looks at me like he's never heard the word *sorry* before. In reality, I'm far from sorry. What I really feel like telling him is to bug off.

"Where you live at?"

"Washington Houses." I try to focus my thoughts through my fear and ready myself to duck if he or one of his guys tries to punch me.

"The projects? *Pato,* who you kidding? Aint no Italians live in the projects. More like 104. Hey, Vanny, you know how God made Italians? He took a pile of *mierda* in one hand and another pile of *mierda* in the other hand and smacked them together, *wop*."

"I do live in the projects, and I'm not Italian," I state firmly, with the faint hope that it's Italians he has a problem with, not whites in general. "I'm English and a little Irish."

"Hey, Vanny, *mira*, we got us a mick. The last mick in El Barrio. How much money you got, mick? Gimme your money and maybe I let you go without a stomping."

I feel myself start to tremble. I have fifteen cents in my front right pocket, the change from the quarter I used to buy the popcorn. My left pocket contains a dollar. Slowly I reach into the right pocket and withdraw the dime and nickel. I offer up my two coins and say, "This is all I've got."

"Don't gimme no *mierda*. Paddy boys always got money. Turn out your pockets, mick face."

I'm determined not to cry. After breaking down in front of Mr. Levy, I swore to myself I'd never again cry on the streets. Instead, I stand still, frozen between fear and the injustice of giving up my dollar. Before I can decide what to do, one of the guys who's blocking my advance, the one called Vanny, speaks up. The top of his left ear is missing, like someone took a bite out of it.

"Aint you the minister's son?" he asks.

"Yeah," I say, glad to be talking about something other than giving up my money.

"Don't he run the church over on 104th where Councilman Ríos preaches? Strewbee, you know Reverendo Ríos. The one with the three fine-looking daughters."

Vanny is confusing my father with one of the Parish ministers who works at the church on 104th. Somehow I don't feel like correcting his mistake.

"So what if I do?" demands the head Dragon, whose name I

now take to be Strewbee. "That don't mean Paddy boy gets to walk down our block without paying for the privilege."

"No, Strewbs, he's the minister's son. We can't mug a minister's son. It's bad luck."

"Fuck that, Vanny. Maybe we let him go without a stomping, but first we see what he's got in his pockets."

Strewbee and Vanny are face-to-face, eyeing each other, a standoff. The two others are distracted by the argument between their leader and his lieutenant. Quickly, I duck around them and run for it. I run as fast as I can.

At Third Avenue, I turn the corner, bang into someone, and fall to the sidewalk. Not hurt, I jump to my feet. Before I can resume running, the guy I bumped into throws his arms around me in a bear hug.

"Lemme go!" I shout, struggling to free myself.

"Tommy, it's me, Tito. What's the matter?" There in front of me, like a life buoy thrown to a man overboard, stands Tito, a friend from last summer at Camp Sharparoon, the boy who'd ruled our cabin and taught me to pitch pennies and hustle candy money from the other campers. The somewhat older boy who, once he learned I was from East Harlem like he was, called me his Barrio blood and took me under his wing. I've never been so glad to see anyone in my life.

"Nothing." I look behind me for advancing Dragons. Suddenly I remember my book bag: I took off without it.

"You were jugging pretty fast for nothing," says Tito, slapping my shoulder and grinning.

"I was running from some guys trying to take my money. They stole my popcorn."

He brushes sidewalk pebbles off my coat. "Who were they? Was it the Dragons? One guy with a giant strawberry on his cheek, another guy with half an ear?"

"That's them. You know them?"

"Strewbee, Van Gogh, and their bopping buddies? Let's say they know me. They want me for their war counselor. So far I've stayed out, but not much longer. They own 103rd. Any kid between ten and twenty walks down that street got to pay tax or get his ass beat."

"I left my book bag. When Van Gogh began arguing with Strewbee, I left my book bag and ran. It's got all my school stuff in it."

"Let's go get it."

My book bag is open in the middle of the sidewalk, with three books lying beside it. No sign of the Dragons. I pick up the bag and examine the remaining contents. Tito asks if everything is here and I nod. Books and papers are clearly of no interest to Dragons.

As we make our way back toward Third Avenue, Tito asks if I've ever been hassled before. After I tell him about the guy from the Mighty Gents, he says that I should never carry big money in my pockets, any bills I should put inside my socks. If the same guy keeps bothering me, I should tell him off good. Go for him first. Punch him in the face as hard as I can. Pick up a trash can top, a soda bottle, anything. Go for his head. Scream out Motherfucker, motherfucker and try to kill him. Tito says I might get my ass whipped, but after that he'll let me alone, everybody will let me alone. It'd be better for me to get beat once and prove I have *corazón* than to get turned into a faggot and get offed every time I walk down the street.

Though I've often fought with Johnny, I've never been in a real fight. I don't think I'd know what to do in a real fight. Defend myself maybe. But start a fight? Hit the guy first? Try to kill him? I stood up to Charles without fighting, maybe I could have talked my way out of a fight with the Dragons, maybe I could have explained about my father and the Parish, gotten Strewbee on my side along with Vanny. One thing is certain: I wasn't going to give up my dollar. That would have been worse than giving up my basketball. Paying your way out of trouble is what rich kids do. What downtown white boys do.

We cross Third and walk down 102nd Street. "You wanna come up? Meet my family?" I ask as we near my building.

"Maybe another time, I got something to do. Now I know where you live at, I'll know where to find you. You don't have to worry about Strewbee and Van Gogh or any of the other Dragons, I'll talk to them. Once they find out you're my friend, they'll leave you alone, probably even watch out for you."

When I tell Danny about my run-in with the Dragons, he decides to give me some more lessons on the facts of East Harlem street life. Everyone, he tells me, is a little nervous when walking through the streets. Even adults. Even colored folks. Even himself. I've just got to learn to be careful and do what he says. First off, I'm to never let no one know I'm afraid. People are like dogs, if they sense you're scared they get excited. Danny helps me learn to walk with a diddy-bop in my step so I'll look confident on the street. Diddy-bopping right announces that I'm from the neighborhood, that I know the score, that I'm not worried about a thing; not nobody, not no thing.

Second, I've always got to watch my back. I've got to learn to know, without directly looking, who's in front of me, who's off to the side, and who's behind. I've heard the great Boston Celtic guard Bob Cousy explain how a good basketball player knows at all times where every player on the court is and where both ball and basket are. Cousy is famous for his passing. He can hit the open man without looking at his target. This 360-degree vision I try to perfect on the streets. I soon convince myself that, without turning to look, I can sense when someone is coming up behind me.

Danny's next piece of advice is to stick to streets alive with people. Muggers and gangs don't like crowds. I'm coming to know the streets from 96th to 106th, between Lexington and the East River so well I think I could walk them with my eyes closed. I know which blocks are full in summer, which in winter, which route to take at night, which during the day. Whenever the streets are empty, I break into a run.

Looking a dude who's trying to start something in the eye is also a big no-no. If you do, it's a challenge and he has to fight. I protest this warning because if I don't look him in the eye he'll know I'm afraid and Danny just said never to let anyone know I'm afraid. Danny explains that I should ignore any kid bent on starting trouble, act casual and keep walking. Then, and only then, when there's no other choice, I'm to look him dead in the eye and, if I don't like what I see, run like hell. You've got to study on people, Tommy. Learn to tell what they're gonna do before they do it.

In an attempt to help me sound cool, Danny constantly teaches me the latest slang, words like, *boss, skank,* and *doofus.* He shows me how to change the meaning of words by sounding them from my chest, or rolling my eyes, dragging out the vowels, as in "she's *sooo* fiiine" or "he's baaaad." He also gives nicknames to our friends and even to my own family members. Peggy is Pegasus from my Greek mythology book because it feels so good to say, or sometimes, "Your baby sister Louise," which is part of a taunt as in "Your mother, your father, and your baby sister Louise." Johnny has been dubbed Bluto after Popeye's archenemy because of his size. Mom is christened Bubblegum Butch, but never to her face. Mom is the opposite of a true Bubblegum Butch, and she never chews gum of any kind, let alone bubblegum; the name's very outrageousness is why Danny loves it. Thanks to Danny, our family name for baby Andy is now Blip, short for "He's a real blip." Poor Andy's too young to complain.

Danny also teaches me the fine points of sounding matches. "Sounding" is another way to be hip, especially if you're good at it, know the latest snaps, and can so upset your opponent that he can't continue. The four topics sure to be in any sounding match are your momma, your looks (including how you dress), roaches, and welfare. If you let someone sound on your momma without making him take it back or fighting him, it means that what he said is true. Outside of a sounding match, making fun of someone's mother is always just cause for a fight.

DANNY: Your momma wears combat boots.

TOMMY: Your momma's feet are so big she don't fit her combat boots.

DANNY: You're so ugly when you were born the doctor slapped your momma.

TOMMY: You're so ugly the doctor slapped you and your momma and your fadder and your baby sister Louise.

DANNY: You're so ugly the roaches run in fright.

TOMMY: Your house is so full of roaches you need a baseball bat to fight your way into the kitchen.

DANNY: Your family's so poor even the roaches are on welfare.

TOMMY: They call your family the welfare kings.

Because matches so easily turn into fights, I usually pretend I don't know what's going on, especially with guys I don't know and trust. With another colored kid, Danny can say, "Your hair's so kinky your mother uses your head for a scrub brush." I would be courting disaster to use such a line. When forced into a match, I stick to old, played-out comebacks that have no real snap, such as "Your mama wears combat boots" or "Your sister looks like a Noxzema sandwich." Even these can lead to trouble, though, especially if the kid's sister does look like a Noxzema sandwich from all the cream she uses to cover up her pimples.

One day Danny and I are well into a sounding match that started out with a normal round of roaches and combat boots when he startles me with "Your father buys his clothes at John's Bargain Store." This statement is true and causes both amusement and a touch of embarrassment in our family. Despite Mom's efforts to get Dad to buy trousers that fit, he invariably slips off to John's Bargain Store and buys another pair of "saggy baggies." To Dad, the fit doesn't matter as long as the clothes are indestructible and cheap; even high waters don't faze Dad if they're cheap.

What surprises me is that Danny is bringing fathers into one of our sounding matches; he has never done so before. I counter with "Your father's so weak, cheap, can't afford, he steals his clothes from John's Bargain Store."

"Your father's so cheap he thinks a Carry All is a Cadillac," says Danny, who has the unfair advantage of knowing my father. Not knowing anything about his father, I can only fire wildly, hoping for a lucky hit: "Your father has so many children by so many wives, he thinks he's the Sheik of Monte Sheba."

Danny's face sets stone-cold. "Your father's so full up with God he don't make time for his own children's birthdays."

Dad had, indeed, missed my last birthday party, off as usual on Parish business. That it hurt, I had confided only to Danny.

"Your father's so full up with himself he doesn't have time for his own children period!" I shout, wanting to hurt Danny, to hurt him bad, like for some reason he is trying to hurt me.

Danny shuts his mouth and pulls back his hand to hit me. "You don't know anything about my father," he says, tears filling his eyes. Instead of swinging, he stares at me, grinds his teeth in fury, then grabs his coat and storms out. I have won the match. Instead of feeling a sense of victory, however, I feel shaken, ashamed.

The next Sunday in church neither of us mentions what happened, but all sounding matches between us are ended forever.

When the phone rings about 10:30 on Saturday morning, I assume it's Danny calling to let me know what time he'll be over—we have plans to go Christmas shopping. Instead I hear Samuel's voice asking me to take him to the Museum of Natural History like I said I would. He wants to check out his gorilla. For a moment I hesitate, knowing Danny won't be pleased. For Danny, plans are plans, and he hates changes. But I also want to make good on my promise to Samuel, so I ask if he minds my friend Danny coming along. Samuel says to bring him along, to bring anybody I want.

The minute Danny arrives, I inform him of the change in plans. The first thing he wants to know is what's to do in a museum. I say there's lots of things to do, they've got animals, whales, dinosaurs, a giant squid, all kinds of stuff.

"Dead stuff!" Danny groans.

Danny and Samuel are so different. Danny wants action, lights, cameras, people. He's outgoing, talkative, looking for adventure. Samuel's interested in natural history, science, geography. He's quiet, thoughtful, cautious. I wonder which one I'm more like and think maybe I'm a combination of the two, adventuresome and cautious at the same time.

As it turns out, Samuel and Danny already know each other from their days at P.S. 121. "Aren't you the kid who dances?" Samuel asks when they shake hands. To my surprise, he's dressed for church, in creased slacks, dress shoes, a formal jacket, and even a tie under his winter coat. "You should see this guy dance," Samuel says. "How he jumps and turns is stupendous." Danny smiles, clearly pleased.

The huge, cavernlike entrance hall of the museum has a musty smell like Ascension's basement. Although I've been to the museum four or five times with my parents and on school trips, it's the first time I've come here without an adult, and I'm unsure where things are. An elderly lady at the information desk informs us that Samuel's gorilla is in the African Mammal Hall and that Danny's dinosaurs are on the fourth floor. She circles each location on one of her little floor plans and hands a pamphlet to each of us.

In the middle of the dimly lit African Mammal Hall, six life-size elephants thunder across the plains.

"These are African elephants," explains Samuel. "See the long tusks and the big, fanlike ears? Their ears are larger than those of Indian elephants."

"I wouldn't want to be walking down 101st and see them mambo jambos coming at me," says Danny.

"Actually, they're pretty friendly," says Samuel. "They don't bother people unless you interfere with their food or their young, especially their young."

"I aint interfering with their nothing," cries Danny.

I turn away from the elephants and spot the object of our search. We advance to a large glass window showcasing a life-size gorilla beating his chest. A mother gorilla sits under a tree, a toddler at her side, and another gorilla approaches on all fours through the tall grass. Samuel tells us that the gorilla is beating his chest to get his blood circulating. Danny says that he's also probably warning the other gorilla to stay away. Samuel, happy as a pig in slop, agrees.

Danny and I leave Samuel reading about the scene and move on to the next window, a group of animals and birds gathered around a watering hole. By the time we've circled the hall of maybe fifteen or twenty scenes, Samuel has progressed only to the third window, which features two lynx. At this rate, Danny and I will be able to see the entire museum and eat lunch before Samuel finishes with the African mammals. When Danny suggests we go and check out the dinosaurs, Samuel protests that he's just begun his way around the room. Danny says that we'll go without him and report back when we're finished. Although Samuel agrees to this plan, I'm not sure: Samuel's dressed in a jacket and tie and knows more about gorillas than any boy his age, but I'm supposed to be his protection. Danny is straining at the bit, however, and who knows how he might break out of it.

"Don't leave this room," I tell Samuel on our way out.

By the time Danny and I race up to the fourth floor, check out the dinosaurs, get lost, and finally return to the African Mammal Hall, Samuel is nowhere to be seen. I tell Danny that I knew we shouldn't have left him alone; Samuel could be wandering anywhere.

Suddenly, like an echo in a tunnel, we hear Samuel's voice calling, "Gentlemen." Danny and I look in all directions. No Samuel. "Look upward, gentlemen," we are commanded. At the far end of the hall, Samuel is leaning over a balcony about three tenement stories high. There are more scenes up here, he says, waving and smiling broadly.

"You been here all this time?" asks Danny, when we arrive upstairs.

"Most definitely," says Samuel. "Everything's so real."

When Samuel finally finishes the balcony exhibits, Danny announces he's had enough museum. I ask if he doesn't want to see the giant squid hanging right off the ceiling, but they both agree it's time to go. Samuel, who has been no further than the African Mammal Hall, says he's going to examine one entire exhibit each time he comes; that way he won't finish them all too quickly.

"You're coming back?" asks Danny.

"Absolutely," says Samuel.

Outside, it's still snowing. Drifts are piling up on the museum steps, and a silvery winter light filters through the clouds and illuminates the swirling snowflakes. Danny suggests that we take a cab home; between the three of us he figures it'll cost only a little more than the bus. Not waiting for either Samuel or me to agree, he dashes down the stairs and runs out into Central Park West, waving both arms. Despite Danny's long arms and loud whistle, not a single cab stops, even though several are empty. One slows down for a closer look, then speeds away. Samuel shakes his head and says that no cab's going to stop.

"Why not?" I ask.

"You kidding? You never noticed all the gypsy cabs in East Harlem and so few yellow cabs?"

"How come?" I know why, but I don't want to admit it.

"They're scared," replies Samuel.

"Yeah, because they're yellow," I joke. Samuel doesn't laugh. I know the cabs aren't stopping because Danny's colored. It makes me feel embarrassed to be white. You'd think that at least one cabbie would stop.

As Samuel and I reach the bottom of the steps, Danny is still whistling and flailing away. Finally, he jumps back onto the sidewalk, pushes me out into the street, and tells me to try it. I raise my right arm, wave my hand, and call out "taxi" in my loudest voice. In less that a minute, a cab screeches to a stop in front of me. Danny jumps off the curb, opens the door, and shouts, "All aboard." Samuel, however, doesn't move from the sidewalk. He announces that's he's going to walk. Danny asks if he's crazy—it's cold, snowing, and a long walk home. Samuel replies that he doesn't care and starts off down the street.

Obviously Danny doesn't give a fig whether the cabbie's prejudiced or not. Samuel, however, won't ride in any cab that won't stop for him because he's colored. But how does he know that this cabbie wouldn't have stopped for him or Danny? He doesn't know, not for sure.

Danny angrily slams shut the cab door, and we walk up Central Park West until we can enter Central Park at 81st Street. Kids on sleds are everywhere. The snow piling up on the ground and sticking to the trees fills the world with Christmas spirit.

Danny lets go of his funk and rushes ahead, sliding through the snow like his shoes are skis. As we approach the lake in front of the weather station castle, he turns back to us and shouts, "Hey, check it out, the castle of the Three Kings of Orient Are."

"That's more like King Arthur's castle," I call back through the snow.

"It's our castle now," says Danny.

"Ours?"

"We're looking at it, aint we?" demands Danny.

Slowing down to walk beside me and Samuel, Danny starts singing, "We three kings of Orient are, bearing gifts we traverse afar." I put my arm through his, and we begin walking faster and faster as we pick up the beat. To my amazement, Samuel joins in. With arms linked, we get louder and louder, faster and faster, like Dorothy and her friends skipping down the yellow brick road. When we have burst our lungs and run out of breath, Danny falls to the ground and cracks up, laughing and rolling in the snow.

"Melchior, Caspar, and Balthazar. That's us," he says, getting up and brushing off the snow. "I'm Balthazar. He was the colored one, right?"

I say I think the colored one was Caspar, but Samuel says no, Danny's right, it was Balthazar. I know that if Samuel says it was Balthazar, it probably was. He goes to church every Sunday with his grandmother, and together they read and study the Bible almost as much as the Parish ministers.

"Either way I'm Balthazar, King Balthazar!" declares Danny. "Balthazar is a kick-ass name. Aint no one gonna mess with no dude named Balthazar. You're Melchior, Tommy, and you can be Caspar, Samuel. Caspar the friendly ghost."

"It's all right with me," says Samuel. "Balthazar's the one who gives the myrrh."

"What's myrrh?" asks Danny.

"Like it says in the song. A bitter perfume. They used it on dead people."

"Dead people?"

"Yeah, dead people."

"Then how come Balthazar's giving it to baby Jesus?"

"Because he knows Jesus is going to need it."

"Got dog," exclaims Danny. "How you know all this stuff, Samuel?"

"I learned it studying up on the Egyptians. After Tommy took me to see the pharaoh's mummy, I read about the Egyptians."

"I'm glad Tommy didn't take me to see no mummies," declares Danny in a tone that makes me wonder whether he wishes I had. "Dead gorillas is bad enough."

When we reach the other side of the park, Samuel proposes we walk up Fifth Avenue. Danny, however, insists we go by way of Third. After having been overruled on the cab, he isn't about to be overruled on the choice of route home. Danny prefers Third Avenue because, unlike Fifth, it has more action: shops, stores, restaurants, people.

Outside Woolworth's on 86th Street, an old wino wishes us a merry Christmas and sticks out his cap. "Hey there young fellows, how about some change for a thirsty old man at Christmastime? Just a little change for some Christmas cheer."

"We're not young fellows," replies Danny. "We're the Three Kings of Orient Are!"

"What's a little change to a king?" shoots back the wino.

"All I have is myrrh," says Danny. "You don't want no myrrh. Trust me. Ask him," he says, pointing to me. "He's the one with the gold."

"Sorry," I say and keep on walking.

Danny, however, reaches into his pocket, pulls out a dollar, and places it in the old man's cap. "Merry Christmas, my good sir!" he declares with a big grin and a deep King Balthazar bow.

"Thank you, your royal harness," slurs the surprised wino.

"He'll only use it to buy booze," I whisper when we are down the block.

"So what if he does?" Danny shrugs. "It's Christmas."

Sometime after New Year's, I accompany Dad on a speaking engagement at Mount Hermon, a prep school in Northfield, Massachusetts. Dad says he lectures at schools, colleges, and large churches in order to raise people's awareness about places like East Harlem, to tell them about the work of the Parish, and to raise money. Not necessarily in that order.

We arrive at Mount Hermon on a bright, cold Sunday in the early afternoon. With its vine-covered buildings, tall trees, and snow-covered everything, the school looks like one of the New England colleges depicted on the walls of Prexy's, "The hamburger with the college education." The Headmaster brings us into a lecture hall packed with students and teachers. For almost forty minutes, twice as long as his sermons, Dad speaks about East Harlem. He says that the dirtiness of the streets and buildings and even the poverty and suffering of the people aren't what make Spanish Harlem a discouraging place in which to live and work. You get used to the noise, the litter, and the lack of green. What you don't get used to is the hopelessness in the eyes of the young men and women hanging out on the stoops and street corners. It is not acceptable in 1960, in the most prosperous country in the world, to have so many kids who don't believe their lives are important, who have given up hope in their futures, who are dead at an early age. He tells the audience about the Parish and its youth work, Narcotics Committee, and Mom's Reading Program, about the hope of the Good News itself. He ends by reading a quotation about how the tragedy of life doesn't lie in not reaching your goal; the tragedy lies in having no goal to reach.

The audience applauds and applauds, and many of the teachers and some of the older students swarm around Dad, like fans at a Yankees game begging Mickey Mantle for his autograph. Watching from the front row, I feel proud that this celebrity is my father.

A young faculty member approaches and sits in the seat next to me. I can tell immediately where his questions are headed. I'm used to them by now. Whenever I go on these speaking engagements with Dad, even the ones to a downtown church, someone always asks: What's East Harlem like? How is it to live there? Aren't you afraid? I can count on these questions almost as much as I can count on the old ladies on the bus above 96th Street asking me if I'm lost.

"Hi, you're Reverend Webber's son, aren't you?"

"Yup."

"My name's Jonathan Merrill." He sticks out his hand. I shake it.

"Tommy."

"Hi, Tommy. You look a little bored. I'll bet you've heard that speech before, huh?"

Mr. Merrill is marking time, feeling me out, warming up to his big question. In fact, I wasn't bored listening to my father. I had listened pretty closely.

"I was wondering what it's like living in East Harlem."

"It's all right."

"It must be tough. I mean, being a kid like you growing up in such a poor, rough neighborhood."

I look at Mr. Merrill. Although he seems genuinely interested, I don't feel like talking about East Harlem. Mr. Merrill and all the other Mr. Merrills who are so eager to talk with me never ask me regular kid questions, like what I want to be when I grow up or who my favorite ballplayer is: it's always East Harlem, East Harlem, East Harlem. And if he means a white kid like me, he should just say so. I don't want to be a spokesperson for white kids, or for the Parish, or for what it's like living in East Harlem.

"It's pretty much like any other neighborhood," I answer. "Nothing special."

"It seems like something pretty special to your father," suggests Mr. Merrill.

"I guess you'll have to ask him then." I turn my face away from my questioner to the stage, where Dad is still talking with a group of eager faces.

On our way home, I stretch out across the front seat and place my head on Dad's lap, the way I always have since I was two or three. Even though I'm twelve, it's the only way to sleep comfortably in the car. From Dad's back pocket comes the familiar tobacco smell of the handkerchief he uses to clean his pipes. His strong right arm lightly brushes the side of my face when he makes a turn. Unable to sleep, I think about my conversation with Mr. Merrill. Why had his questions made me angry? Why hadn't I told him how I really feel? East Harlem isn't like the other places I know. It's not like Claremont Avenue, or West 77th Street, or Park Avenue south of 96th Street, or Sorrento, Maine, or Northfield, Massachusetts. East Harlem is different, very different. Why hadn't I tried to explain that, despite what Dad said, East Harlem isn't just a concrete jungle filled with litter, drugs, gangs, and teenagers with no hope in their eyes? The guys I know all have great hopes, dreams, schemes for the future. Danny's going to be a star of stage, screen, and television. William's going to bring the Knicks their first championship in a million years. Samuel's going to work for *National Geographic.* Even Rabbit has serious plans. He dreams of going into the air force, of flying airplanes.

In the darkness of the front seat, feeling close to my father, I remember what Johnny said about living in East Harlem, what he said about Mom and Dad, and I ask Dad if it's true he and Mommy are happier now.

"I thought you were sleeping."

"No. Just thinking. Johnny says you're happier now, happier than before we moved."

"He does, does he?"

I can feel Dad smile to himself even though I can't see his face in the darkness above me. I hope he doesn't make a joke. My question's not a joke—I really want to know.

"Are you?"

"Yes, I'm happier. We should have moved a long time ago. East Harlem is where I belong. Mom's happier too. She loves her Reading Program. The Group Ministry has voted to allow her to use the entire second floor of the Parish office building, and she's expanding the program to help kids get into good schools and colleges. Mount Hermon says they'd be very interested in accepting a promising student or two from East Harlem."

"You mean a Negro student?" I ask.

"Or Puerto Rican," says Dad.

As we drive on in silence, I imagine what it would be like for one of my East Harlem friends to attend Mount Hermon, how it would feel to be the only colored boy in a sea of white people. I imagine that living at Mount Hermon would be more difficult for them than moving to East Harlem was for me. At least I live with my family. They would have to live in a dormitory with white roommates. They could never get away from teachers and students wanting to know what it's like to live in East Harlem, what it's like to be a Negro.

Dad interrupts my thoughts. "Mom is a little concerned about Johnny. She's worried that he's having trouble fitting in, that moving to East Harlem has been harder for him than for the rest of you kids because he's older."

"What about me? She worries about me too much," I say, wanting to impress Dad with how mature I'm becoming.

"Not that much." He chuckles. "You have the knack of getting along wherever you are. Mom says you're irrepressible."

"What's irrepressible?"

"Hard to keep down."

"Oh." For a moment I think about whether this is true and, if so, whether it's a good thing. "Do you think so too?"

"Yes," he says. "You're about as irrepressible as I am. Only when you get to be my age, people sometimes wish you were a little less irrepressible."

"Does Mom wish it?"

"Sometimes."

After a long pause I say, "Daddy, you can tell Mommy Johnny's okay too."

"He is?"

"Yes. He told me."

CHAPTER 9

MY DAYDREAM ABOUT playing guard for the Knicks is suddenly interrupted when Libby's sermon catches my full attention. Her text for the day is the famous passage about love from Paul's first letter to the Corinthians. Libby's not dwelling on love, however. Instead, she comes back again and again to verse eleven: "When I was a child I spoke as a child. I understood as a child. I thought as a child. But when I became a man, I put away childish things." Libby says that children are concerned solely with their own needs, whereas Christians are concerned with the needs of others. Children ask God to grant their wishes, Christians seek God's guidance so that they can learn, and then do, His will. Children are self-centered; Christians are God-centered.

Libby's words sting. Everything she says that children do, I do.

Despite feeling let down that God hadn't seen fit to change Dad's mind about the move, I still pray to Him for things I want, even little things, like a new baseball mitt. I still call on Him when I'm scared or feeling sad. I'm not as grown-up as I like to think. And even though I know better, I still think of God as a kindly, white-haired old man like the grandfather in *Heidi* or as a bearded, wise Abraham Lincoln looking down from his throne at his Washington, D.C., memorial. But if He's not at least something like a man, to whom or what am I praying?

Whatever God looks like, I sit in my pew and pray for Him to help me put away childish things and become a good Christian. It's not right to be self-centered when all around me are winos, junkies, men hanging out on the street without jobs, and friends with ugly welts on their backs. Since the move to East Harlem, my desire to follow in my father's footsteps and become a minister has grown. More than ever I want to join Dad and the other members of the Group Ministry in their fight against poverty. If, along the way, I need to figure out how and when God decides to answer prayers, and what He looks like, I still have time. I'm only twelve.

To prepare for my future ministry, I decide to read the entire Bible straight through, from the first page of Genesis to the last page of Revelation. It doesn't seem important to memorize chapter and verse numbers until I meet my first Jehovah's Witnesses, who knock on our apartment door in pairs searching for souls to save. They are willing to stand in the hall as long as I am willing to stand at the door and talk or, as is more often the case, listen. In their presence I feel like a halfhearted Christian. They can quote chapter, verse, and line to make your head spin. When I ask Danny how he handles Jehovah's Witnesses, he looks at me like I must be nuts and says that he's never home when he hears them knocking.

"How do you know it's them?" I ask.

"Aint nobody knocks like Jehovah's Witnesses," he replies.

Though I know it puts me at a disadvantage with the Witnesses, I'm glad Dad and the other Parish ministers don't push memorizing the Bible. Nor are they big on rules and regulations, like Catholics or the stricter Protestants. Yes, we are to fight the evils of the world. Yes, we are to imitate Jesus, to do unto others what we would have them do unto us. But the Gospel should also make us happy. The ministers of the Parish tell jokes, play games, hold parties, and even drink and dance along with their parishioners. At home we play poker for pennies, and Dad smokes a pipe, occasionally swears, and certainly has a drink from time to time. I once overheard him remark that he doesn't trust any man who refuses to have an occasional drink. I haven't a clue what drinking has to do with trusting somebody, but I like the fact that Dad is no goody-goody minister railing against drinking, smoking, dancing, and having fun. He's a regular guy, even if he does wear a collar and occasionally gets calls from God.

I also like the idea that the East Harlem Protestant Parish is nondenominational, that we're not Congregationalists or Baptists, Methodists or Presbyterians, but simply Protestants. Dad thinks that debates over this or that religious doctrine are about as silly as arguments over how many angels can stand on the head of a pin. According to Dad, we are Ecumenical; our only denomination is Jesus Christ.

Even though I plan to follow in my father's footsteps, I dread those Sundays once a month when it comes Dad's turn to preach. He keeps his sermons short, never more than twenty minutes—he encourages us to time him—and they aren't boring. But he has the distressing habit of what he calls "salting" his points with examples from our family life; you never know when you might pop up in one of his sermons. One Sunday, he gets a big laugh by informing the entire church that his second son spends hours each day in front of the mirror combing his hair. I don't catch the point he's trying to make because my ears are ringing too loudly. I want to crawl under the pew and disappear. Dad has no right to tell people about my personal business; it's worse than sneaking a look into someone's apartment through a pair of binoculars. Besides, it isn't even true. I never spend more than half an hour combing my hair.

When we get home from church, I tell him I don't appreciate being used as an example or anything else in his sermons. He looks at me sheepishly, the way he always does when he knows he's been caught dead to rights, and says everybody combs his hair.

"They don't do it in front of the whole church," I cry.

Although I think a lot about God and religion and becoming a minister, I mostly keep my thoughts and feelings to myself. The few times I've tried to talk about religion with Danny he hasn't seemed too interested. He acts like religion is easy for him, like you have to be a little off to worry about what God looks like or how He answers prayers.

Nor do we talk much about God on the courts. One day I do ask Junie why he crosses himself before every foul shot, and he says it's like a little piece of good luck, like a little prayer.

"You mean you're asking God to help make your shot?" I ask.

"Not God exactly. But yeah, sort of. It's just something we do. When I cross myself before I shoot, it gives me confidence. I feel like I'm not all alone at the line. Like I've got somebody backing me up. I know I still have to do the shooting."

As I walk around East Harlem, I see churches and other signs of religion everywhere. Nuns in their habits and priests in their collars and black robes stand on the steps outside Saint Cecilia's on 106th and Saint Lucy's on 104th. I see crucifixes, statues of saints, and bottles of holy water and oils in the windows of storefront *botánicas*. Pictures of Pope Pius XII, the Virgin Mary, Jesus, and saints of all sizes are everywhere. Each block, except for the Italian ones and the ones filled with projects, contains at least one

Negro Holy Roller church or one Spanish *Aleluya* church or both. When I walk by, their doors are often open, and I can hear the guitar-playing-tambourine-smacking jubilation of the congregation. Inside, people sing, wave their hands to the ceiling, praise Jesus, and shout *"Aleluya"* and *"Gloria a Dios."* On Saturday afternoons and Sundays after church, the neighborhood vibrates with the praying, preaching, and singing broadcast through loudspeakers set up on the sidewalks in front of the *Aleluya* churches. There is nothing in El Barrio more numerous than churches except possibly bars. Booze and beatitudes, East Harlem's two balms for the aching, sorrowing soul.

For a long time Dad has been talking about taking a visit to hear Father Divine, and one Sunday afternoon Danny and I finally accompany him and some of the Parish regulars to the great banquet prepared each week at Father Divine's Harlem temple. Dad has explained to us that Father Divine is a Negro who has declared himself God and founded something called the Peace Mission Movement. He encourages people to work hard, to live clean lives, and to believe in the equality of all human beings. Along with donations from its followers, the Peace Mission Movement raises money from its many businesses, including restaurants, gas stations, clothing stores, and hotels. Dad also says that Father Divine insists upon the absolute separation of the sexes among his followers—so absolute that, like the Shakers, they're not destined for a long history.

We are shown into a grand social hall, where two long tables are set up on either side of the room, one for the women, one for the men. The women wear white dresses down to their ankles and white gloves up past their elbows; the men are in dark wedding-funeral suits. The dinner is a never-ending feast of roast duck,

151

turkey, lamb stew, chicken fricassee, potatoes, noodle salad, string beans, all kinds of other vegetables, and a long procession of cakes and pies. The food just keeps coming and coming, and if you don't want any particular dish, no problem, just pass it on down.

After almost an hour of eating, a large man with broad shoulders and a big stomach rises at the head of the men's table and explains that, unfortunately, Father Divine himself cannot be with us today. Father is away addressing an important meeting of the Detroit brethren. But we should not despair, he has sent along a personal message for our spiritual upliftment. A hush descends over the room as the words of the divine father begin to issue forth from loudspeakers hanging high on the wall at the front of the hall. His voice is a light tenor, not at all the deep bass King James Version voice of God I heard all those Christmas Eves at the Seminary sitting in the darkness beside the Van Dusen Christmas tree.

As Father Divine warms to his message about the importance of frugality coupled with the avoidance of liquor, gambling, and sex, the room's quiet lifts from the congregation like the morning mist off Frenchman Bay. The stern looking brothers and the joyful sisters begin talking back to the loudspeakers, shouting, "So glad, so glad," "Yes, Lord," and "Thank you, Father." The believers throw both hands up into the air, wave their palms, close their eyes, and shake their heads in rapture. It is frightening, thrilling. One of the women becomes so glad she falls off her chair and rolls onto the floor, where she is tended to by the other sisters, a small, tight circle of fluttering, white-robed angels. Danny and I look at each other, stunned. I bite my lip and pray to Jesus that I won't start giggling and that the man at my right, shouting ever-louder "Speak it"s and "So glad"s, won't be the next believer to hit the floor.

At the height of the sermon, Danny gives me one of his watch-this grins. Slowly he closes his eyes, throws back his head, raises his long arms to the ceiling, and hollers out for all he's worth, "So glad. So glad!" His cries rise to the ceiling, where they mix and dance with those of the other shouters. Thankfully, the spirit filling Danny isn't strong enough to wrestle him off his chair and throw him onto the floor.

When I begin seventh grade, Mom and Dad allow me to stop attending Sunday school in order to sing in the Ascension adult choir. The choir is eager for teenagers who can sing, especially tenors. I persuade Danny to join with me, even though choir warm-up before church means he has to get out of bed an hour earlier than he's used to each Sunday.

Ascension's choir is directed by Reverend Ted Ward. His wife, Martha, plays the piano and sings a beautiful soprano. Ted is a short, thin Negro man with a neat mustache and a baritone voice big enough to sing the National Anthem at Yankee Stadium without a microphone. Each week he struggles to teach us two selections: a classical, four-part choir anthem sung before the sermon and a simple spiritual or gospel song for the Offering.

One Thursday evening while we are working on the spiritual "Sometimes I Feel Like a Motherless Child," a discussion breaks out over whether it's a completely sorrowful song or whether the lyrics allow a ray of hope. Half the choir, especially the women, argue that there's nothing sadder than a child without a mother. The other half, mostly the men, point out that it says sometimes, *sometimes* I feel like a motherless child. The *sometimes* suggests there are other times when the singer's feeling not so sad.

Then Danny speaks. He says that anything but sorrow would ruin the song. The singer's singing out his sadness, his deep down sadness. He's lost his pops. He's lost his moms. He's a long, long way from home, and he can't bear it. He's so far from home, he's so sad, his face is in the ground. It's only "sometimes" cause he tries not to think about his sadness all the time. If he did, he would lay down and die. Aint nothing but sadness in that song.

No one speaks. Not a soul. Not even the outspoken Mary Peters, who can never get enough of the Hallelujah Chorus.

Finally, Reverend Ted asks Danny to sing it for us. Martha begins to play and Danny sings with his whole self, his eyes closed, his voice filled with deep down sadness. In the middle of the song, Reverend Ted stops conducting and lets the tears roll down his face.

Along with singing in the choir, now that I'm thirteen I start attending weekly confirmation class with Libby Newton. The two other teenagers signed up to take the class with me are often absent, and on several evenings I talk alone with Libby in her small church office. One night we get onto the subject of the miracles, and I express my doubt that Jesus ever walked on the water or that Mary was a virgin when Jesus was born. When Libby asks why knowing for sure about such things is important to me, she surprises me. Of course it's important. If the miracles aren't true, if Mary wasn't really a virgin, that suggests other parts of the Bible might not be true as well; it might all be just one big set of fairy tales or a mythology book.

Libby says there are many kinds of truth, literal truth and symbolic truth, for example. How Jesus was conceived can be seen literally as a miracle or it can be seen as a symbolic expression of God's power and presence. Either way, Jesus lived and died on the cross and became an example for us all of how to live. I ask if she's saying that Jesus is Jesus no matter what we think about his conception or the miracles, and she replies, yes, that no matter how he was conceived Jesus was still the Son of God, just as all of us are the sons and daughters of God.

Rather than shoring up my religious convictions, Libby's confirmation class makes me begin to question them. Before our discussions, I more or less accepted what I heard around home and in church. In my own mind things were pretty simple; you lived life as best you could, and then, if you weren't too bad a person, God forgave you your sins and you went to heaven. Now, however, many things were being brought into question. Maybe Jesus was born like any other child, never raised the dead or healed the sick, and is no more the Son of God than we are all the sons and daughters of God. Even heaven and hell seem far-fetched. It's hard to believe in the physical resurrection of the body or that there's a Devil somewhere making sinners grit their teeth and beat their breasts into all eternity. I like Libby's idea that things can have symbolic importance, but if everything's symbolic, what's actually real?

One weekend, near the end of my confirmation classes, as I struggle with these questions, the Group Ministry and their families drive to Parish Acres for a two-day retreat. As part of the program, one night after supper in the old barn now converted to a social hall we watch a movie about Martin Luther as a young man, his religious doubts, the struggles with the sins of the flesh that caused him to lash himself across his bare back. I sit spellbound, identifying with Luther, having doubts but at the same time wishing to be called by God to some heroic task, like fighting the terrible injustices of the Catholic Church. After the film is over I wander out onto the deserted baseball field, alone like Jesus in the wilderness. I'm desperate to experience something like what happened to Saul on the road to Damascus, when God bounced him off his horse and he became Paul, like what happened to Dad on the bow of his destroyer escort when he was ordered by God to become a minister. Fevered with religious excitement, I recite the Twenty-third Psalm and sing "A Mighty Fortress Is Our God." I long for God to speak to me, long to hear His voice booming from the dark heavens, calling my name. *"Thomas. Thomas. Go forth into the world and make fishers of all men."* If God calls me, I'm ready. I will cast aside all questions and doubts and become His servant, do whatever He calls me to do. I just need to hear His voice.

But the heavens are silent. What is God waiting for?

Danny and I are hard at work constructing a large placard on which we have drawn the Parish symbol of two shaking hands, one white, one colored. Below the picture of the two hands we write the words

TWO FOUR SIX EIGHT
NOW IT'S TIME TO INTEGRATE

Tomorrow we are marching in a Parish-organized rally in front of Woolworth's on 106th Street. We want to show support for our southern brothers and sisters who are picketing at lunch counters all over the South. It's the fall of 1960, and the South is exploding in demonstrations and sit-ins as Negro college students protest not only segregated lunch counters but segregated hotels, buses, and theaters, and the indignity of drinking from fountains labeled "for coloreds only." Pictures of Negroes lying on the floor with blood streaming down their faces as they are kicked and beaten by hate-screaming whites fill the newspapers. Every night on the evening news, we see scenes of Negro demonstrators running from white sheriffs chasing them with snarling dogs, clubs, cattle prods, and fire hoses.

Watching these shocking scenes on TV, Dad mangles the poetry of Langston Hughes, saying that sometimes when a promise is too long delayed, it explodes like a raisin in the sun. Mom praises the demonstrators for their nonviolence, saying that it takes courage to stand up to hatred without striking back. She says that even a coward will strike back but that a true hero, her kind of hero, will withstand the impulse to fight.

I want to know how America has become so full of racism and hatred. I've read about slavery, lynchings, and the Ku Klux Klan, but it seems like things are getting worse, like there's now more hate than ever. Negroes are supposed to be full citizens protected by the laws and the Constitution just like every other citizen, so how can it be that almost a hundred years after the end of the Civil War they are still denied the vote, denied fair trials, denied a tuna fish sandwich at a Woolworth's lunch counter? As I read the newspapers and watch TV, it seems like the South is a lawless, scary place. I know New York has segregated housing and segregated schools, but we also have a Negro congressman, Adam Clayton Powell, Jr.; our hotels, museums, and theaters are opened to all regardless of race; and everybody drinks from the same public water fountains.

Peggy wants to know if a raisin left out in the sun really explodes.

The next morning at the demonstration, we march in a circle on the sidewalk in front of Woolworth's. Led by Reverend Ted, we shout chants and sing spirituals.

> *Go down, Moses, way down in Egypt land,*
> *Tell old, old Pharaoh, to let my people go.*

Danny and I play with the words, and soon we have everybody singing:

> *Go down, Moses, way down in Dixieland,*
> *Tell old, old Jim Crow, to let my people go.*

As we walk together carrying our sign, Danny and I try, as always, to outdo each other in the singing and the chanting. When we aren't chanting or singing, we discuss Dr. King's principles of nonviolence. Danny boasts that if some overgrown southern cracker pushed him off his lunch counter stool, he'd smack his fat face. My father says that if Danny really feels that way he wouldn't be allowed to participate. Dr. King trains all the demonstrators before each sit-in to resist striking back, and they have to take a pledge of nonviolence.

"Even if they kicking you and spitting you upside your face?" demands Danny.

"Especially if they're kicking and spitting," answers Dad. "In the South there's no choice. The judges, the sheriffs, everybody's against you. You start fighting back and you're dead. Dr. King says they must counter physical force with soul force."

"I'm sure glad I'm not down south," I say. "Up here everybody can sit wherever they want, eat wherever they want. We've even got some colored cops."

"Colored cops are the worst," says Danny. "Always out to prove on your head how tough they are."

"At least we've got some."

"They're the worst," repeats Danny.

During the demonstration, a camera crew from CBS arrives, and Danny gets it into his head that we might make the evening news. Each time we march near the reporters, he starts in singing, shouting, and mugging for the camera. You never know who might be watching, he whispers.

For me, demonstrating is both fun and serious. I enjoy the excitement of being part of a movement that's demanding justice and equality, a movement that's changing history. Yet I know that marching on 106th Street among well-wishers and supporters isn't dangerous. No one is shouting threats at us, kicking us on the floor, or siccing the police dogs and fire hoses on us. We are not getting arrested and being taken off to jail. Our protest is symbolic and safe. The protests going on in the South are for real.

As the rally breaks up, a young television reporter asks Danny and me if we'd like to say a few words on camera. Danny accepts immediately, and when I agree, the reporter seems relieved. He obviously wants an integrated interview. Danny speaks first and says that Negroes have a right to be treated like everybody else, no better, no worser. Just like everyone in America, Negroes are promised life, liberty, and the pursuit of happiness, and that's what they want. The reporter then turns to me and asks why I'm marching. I reply that I feel it's important to let the demonstrators down south know there are a lot of people everywhere willing to stand up for what's right, whites and Negroes.

"We're on the move now," Danny shouts at the camera as the reporter signs off. "Aint nobody gonna turn us round."

At lunch Dad engages us in a discussion of the history of Civil Rights, about *Brown v. Board of Education,* about Truman ending segregation in the armed forces, about a man named Marcus Garvey, who thought the solution to America's race problem was to send all our Negro citizens back to Africa.

"No way I aint going back to no Africa!" says Danny.

"That wasn't the important thing about Garvey," says my father. "The important thing about him was that he was proud to be a man of African descent."

"Pride cometh before a fall," intones Danny.

I wonder to myself if God really wants people to be proud of being African. If He does, am I supposed to be proud of being English, Irish, Dutch, Swedish, and German? Am I supposed to be proud of being white? Why would God want me to be proud of being white? Most of the time I feel just the opposite. Often it's embarrassing being white, assumed to be rich, stuck-up, and prejudiced. And why would I feel proud to be white? I didn't do anything to become white. I didn't earn being white. Being proud of your skin color is like being proud of having blond hair or blue eyes. To be proud of something you should have earned it, like William can be proud of his basketball skills, Danny proud of his ability to dance, Dad proud of the work of the Parish.

Not that you should be ashamed of things you acquired by birth either. Kids I know conk their hair straight at night with boiled lye and then wear do-rags onto the courts. And some of the girls put on skin lotion that supposedly lightens their skin. The Puerto Rican kids talk about who has "good" hair and who has "bad" hair, and they joke that they must "improve the race" by marrying and having children with a girl who is lighter skinned than they are. But why? Who says light skin or thin lips are better or prettier? Brown skin doesn't get sunburned as easily. Full lips are probably more fun to kiss. I do like straight hair over kinky hair; it looks softer, nicer to run your fingers through, especially if it's the hair of a girl you like and she lets you. But that isn't being prejudiced, is it, preferring straight hair to kinky hair because it feels softer?

I'm sitting at my bedroom desk memorizing Latin conjugations. Danny, sprawled out across the floor behind me, is struggling to write a report on one of the leaders of the American Revolution. He has chosen Benjamin Franklin, mostly, he says, because he digs the glasses. I tried to convince him to pick Crispus Attucks and the Boston Massacre, but he flatly refused to write about anybody whose name sounds like a breakfast cereal. This afternoon, after we finish our homework, Danny and I are going to the Kennedy for President rally on 86th Street. The campaign is in its final weeks, and Danny and I are caught up in the excitement. Most of the Parish ministers originally supported Hubert Humphrey because of his stand on Civil Rights. Once John Kennedy became the Democratic nominee, however, they had no choice but to support him, anybody other than Vice President Nixon, who Dad says represents everything that's wrong with American politics. Danny, who's usually not interested in politics, liked the looks of Kennedy right from the start, even before the convention. Personally, I don't think Kennedy looks one bit presidential. Presidents should look old, wise, and somewhat sad, like Abraham Lincoln.

Danny keeps getting up, pacing the room, and going down the hall to see Peggy and Andy. When he stands and stares out the window for the third time, I ask him what's wrong. He says that it's just no good, that he can't understand half the words in the damn encyclopedia. I advise him to write his paper like it's a life story, to start at Franklin's birth and go right on. Who his parents were. Where he was born. How he did in school. What he did for his first job. Skip anything not important and plow right ahead until he dies. Danny says that the words don't come out. I tell him to pretend he's talking it to somebody. Talking aint the same as writing, he says.

In the next breath Danny says his brother, James, is reenlisting in the army for another four years and that his moms is bummed out about it. They had a big fight this morning, with James shouting there aint nothing out here for him. He's hoping this time they'll send him overseas, like to Germany. He wants to see the world. Danny's mother thinks that four years is enough, that it's now somebody else's turn. She's worried he'll get sent to some war.

"James says the army is better than college. They teach you a trade, send you places. You meet different people from all over. He's probably doing right; there really aint nothing for him out here."

"Couldn't he come home and go to college?"

"College? James? I don't think so. He only stayed in high school so he could get into the army."

"What's he like?"

"He's all right. It's not like we hang out or anything. Sometimes he tells me things. To take care of Mom when he's away, stuff like that."

Danny lies back down on the floor and stares at his paper. For a few minutes I hear his pen scratching away, but soon it stops again. He sits up and asks what I'm going to do when I finish college. I say I'm not sure, that maybe I'll become a minister. It's the first time I've admitted my plans out loud to anyone. Danny can't believe I'm serious. He seems surprised that anyone would want to become a minister. I add that at other times I think maybe I won't become a minister, that I wouldn't want to tell people what to believe when I'm not so sure myself. For Danny it's show business, anything in show business—dancing, singing, acting, whatever.

"The problem," he says, "is that it's not so easy breaking in. If I looked like you, things would be a lot easier. Can you imagine, Troy Donahue singing and dancing? He'd be the biggest star ever."

It bothers me that Danny thinks things would be easier if he looked like me because I know what he means is that things would be easier if he were white. Danny has read in some magazine that the Hollywood studios allow only one Negro at a time to play lead roles in the movies, and for the present at least, that one person is Sidney Poitier. All the other Negro actors must play supporting roles, and Danny has no desire to play supporting roles. He wants to be front and center, lighting up the screen. He wants to be a star.

With some help from me on the closing paragraph, Danny eventually finishes his report and we walk down to 86th Street.

Mom and Dad don't come with us. Although they're voting for Kennedy, they're not nearly as enthusiastic about him as we are.

The stretch of street from Lexington to Third is closed off, and a platform has been constructed outside the Loew's movie theater in the middle of the block. Mayor Wagner and a crew of New York political figures mill around on the stage. The crowd is so thick I can tell at once we'll never get up close. Danny hoists himself onto a corner mailbox, then leans down and pulls me up with him. We now command a perfect view. A policeman on horseback gives us a stern once-over but says nothing. Danny whispers that both the cop and his horse must be Democrats.

When Kennedy and his wife finally emerge from the lead car in a long cavalcade, the crowd shouts and claps. After introductions from several of the politicians, Kennedy begins to speak. He urges us to become pioneers in a New Frontier, to work with him so that together we can solve the problems of war and peace, of poverty and plenty. On Election Day, by voting Democratic we will be doing our part to forge a brighter, better world for ourselves and for our children. The large crowd thunders its approval. Danny and I clap, stomp, and try to outshout each other with bravos.

As the applause draws to an end, Danny jumps down from the mailbox and pushes his way through the crowd toward Kennedy's car. For a moment I lose sight of him, then as the long line of cars moves off, he comes bouncing back into view, holding up his right hand for me to admire like it's an Oscar or something.

"I shook his hand. I shook his hand," shouts Danny. "I told him I was a pioneer and shook his hand! He said, 'Tell your parents to vote for me.' And Jackie smiled at me. Can you imagine if he becomes president? I can say I shook hands with the President of the United States."

"Not if, when. When he becomes president."

"Right!" agrees Danny. "When."

As we walk back uptown, Danny says that I should forget this minister stuff and start preparing myself to run for president. "President Webber," he announces dramatically, testing the sound of it. "President Thomas Lane Webber."

"Then you could brag you did a lot more with the president than just shake his hand," I say, without admitting how much I like the ring of it myself. "You'd be a big shot."

"No, serious. You'd win easy. You'd get all the votes—rich, poor, colored, white, Puerto Rican, everybody. All of East Harlem would vote for you, twice. You'd be our neighborhood boy made good. Even I'd vote for you. And I'll sing at the ceremony for when you become president."

"You can sing the National Anthem."

"No. Please! Not the National Anthem. Something with soul. I'll sing, 'I Believe.'" Strolling down Third Avenue, Danny breaks into song.

I believe for every drop of rain that falls, a flower grows.
I believe—

"Deal," I say, cutting him off well in advance of the ending high note. "If I become president you can sing 'I Believe.'"

"Not if, when," says Danny.

CHAPTER 10

MAYBE ONCE A MONTH I find Tito waiting for me after school at the bus stop on Lexington or on Third Avenue at the bottom of the hill. He walks me to my building but never accepts my invitation to come up. On most days we stand in front of my building and gab about our summer experiences. At first, I thought he just wanted to rehash old times at camp. Now I think he likes being seen with me because people notice us as we walk down the street. Tito likes being noticed. Either way, I don't mind. When I walk around with Tito, I feel like I belong, like I've been adopted by a kid who owns the neighborhood. Tito eases through the streets the way William glides down the basketball court. When I'm with him I relax and let him do the worrying.

Today, Tito is on his way to his girlfriend's house and urges me to come with him. He wants to introduce me to Gladys and her family. I'm not comfortable visiting people I don't know, and I try to persuade him that we can't just walk in unannounced. He says it's no problem, he's told them all about me. Then he grabs my book bag and starts walking uptown on Lexington, down the steep side of the 102nd Street hill.

At 105th Street we take a right, and three buildings down the street, Tito leads the way up the outside stairs to the landing, where he pushes an intercom button. A voice asks *"¿Quién es?"* and Tito responds, *"Soy Tito."* Inside, on the way up, he counsels me to say *"encantado"* when he introduces me to Gladys's mother. *"Encantado,"* I practice, wondering why Junie never taught me that one.

On the third floor we are greeted by a pretty girl dressed in tight jeans and a long-sleeved red blouse. She wears several gold bracelets, a gold necklace, and gold earrings. Tito kisses her, they smile, clasp hands, and he whispers something in her ear that makes her laugh and blush. Then he turns in my direction. "Gladys, this is my friend Tommy."

"Hi, Tommy, pleased to meet you." Gladys steps forward and with a warm smile and an outstretched hand welcomes me into the García house.

Tito marches me into the kitchen where he kisses the cheek of Mrs. García, who is stirring the contents of a huge simmering pot with one hand and turning the food frying in three round skillets with the other. Tito introduces us. I say *encantado* and reach out to shake her hand, amazed at how young she looks, more like Gladys's older sister than her mother.

"Welcome to our home, Tommy. I'd shake but too sticky." She laughs, holding up her flour-covered hands. "You hungry?"

"No, that's all right, Mrs. García, thank you. I just ate." Although this is a lie, I remember Junie's *bacalaíto* all too well. In general, I try to stay away from things I've never tried before. None of the smells in the kitchen are smells I'm familiar with.

"Don't be shy," entreats Mrs. García. "I never heard of a young man not hungry on Friday afternoon. Any friend of Tito's is more than welcome. And please call me Lydia. How about you, Tito? I fix you a plate?"

Tito says he'll eat when Fito gets home, and we walk back into the living room, where Gladys is sitting on the sofa with three children around her. She introduces them as Aida, little Fito, and Carmen. Both Aida, who looks about eleven or twelve, and Carmen, who can't be more than five, already have pierced ears, like their older sister and mother. Mom says Peggy can't get her ears pierced until she's fourteen at the earliest.

Aida is the most beautiful young girl I've ever seen. Her skin is the smooth color of cinnamon mixed with white sugar. Her long, black hair gleams in the sunlight coming in through the window.

"You wanna play jacks?" asks little Fito, maybe age seven, from his seat on the floor.

"Fito, leave Tommy alone," instructs Gladys, holding hands with Tito on the couch. "He didn't come here to play with you."

"What did he come here for?" demands little Fito.

Somewhere in the back of the apartment, a baby starts to cry. From the kitchen Mrs. García calls out, "Aida, go get *el niño*. He needs changing."

Aida reluctantly rises to her feet and disappears down the hall. Soon she returns carrying a fat little baby whom she introduces as Hector and asks if I want to hold him. I reach for the baby and cradle him gently on my chest, holding him carefully with two hands the way I used to carry Andy when he was a baby. I'm still holding baby Hector, who is all hands, grabbing my nose and drooling on my neck, when a set of loud, rhythmic kicks pound the front door and in bursts a short, stocky man, with white, thinning hair, carrying two overflowing bags of groceries. "*¡Es viernes social! Maví, cerveza fría,* Coca-Cola *y* Drakes Cakes," shouts Fito, entering the living room laughing. "Let's have a party!"

"Papi, Papi," squeal little Fito and Carmen, running toward him and grabbing him around the legs. In my arms, baby Hector starts chirping.

Gladys and Tito stand up from the couch. Aida rushes to her father and throws her arms around him. He hands one of his bags to Aida and one to Gladys, exchanging them for little Fito and Carmen. Mrs. García emerges from the kitchen, wiping her hands on her apron, and plants a big, happy, kiss smack on her husband's lips.

After Fito and Lydia have separated, Gladys introduces me to her father.

I see my girls have put you right to work, he says. I say that it's not work, that I like kids. He says so do I and squeezes little Fito and Carmen, who both shriek with happiness.

I'm struck by how old Fito is. He looks old enough to be Lydia's father.

Plopping himself into the living room's only armchair, Fito shouts in the direction of the kitchen. "I smell *plátanos. Al jíbaro nunca se le quita la mancha de plátanos.* You know what's a *jíbaro,* Tommy?" asks Fito, turning toward me.

"No, sir."

"A *jíbaro* is a Puerto Rican country boy. You know what means *Al jíbaro nunca se le quita la mancha de plátanos?*" he asks, gesturing for me to hand him Hector. "It means no matter where a *jíbaro* goes or how much he dresses himself up, he still smells like plantains."

"Sort of like you can take Tito out of the street but you can't take the street out of Tito."

"*¡Ay, bendito!* That's it! Lydia, you heard what Tommy said? *Exactamente. ¡Exactamente!*"

Fito makes me sit with them at the round kitchen table while he, Tito, and Gladys eat. Mrs. García is in the living room with baby Hector. Aida stands behind her father, watching and listening. Fito asks why I'm not eating and I explain that I ate already. He tells Aida to pour me a soda, and when he sees me watching Tito dogging his delicious-looking chicken and rice asks if I ever tried *plátanos*. Without waiting for a reply, he tells Aida to dish me out some *plátanos* so they can turn me into a *jíbaro*.

Aida rushes to the stove and quickly returns with a plate of *plátanos*.

"You know what's *plátanos*?" asks Fito.

"No, what?"

"Fried green bananas," answers Aida.

I take a bite. The *plátanos* are delicious, crispy and a little sweet, sort of like home-fried potatoes with a banana taste.

"You really never ate *plátanos* before?" asks Aida.

"No, never," I answer. Her dark eyes widen in disbelief.

After his last bite, Fito wipes his chin, pushes back his chair, and rubs his stomach in satisfaction. Aida serves him a beer without his asking. "How about some music?" he demands. "*Es viernes social*, and I feel like dancing."

Gladys rises from the table and switches on the radio positioned atop the refrigerator. Latin music blares from the station. Fito rises and starts dancing with Aida. Gladys grabs Tito. Carrying baby Hector, Lydia comes in from the living room, followed by little Fito and Carmen. She hands Hector over to Fito and starts dancing with little Fito. I take Carmen by the hand and move my feet, trying to duplicate how Tito is moving his. Carmen takes one look and starts laughing. Aida breaks free from her father and takes my hand. It's like this, she says, demonstrating while I watch. One, two, three, one, two, three. It's easy. It's salsa.

One, two, three, one, two, three.

When the music stops, everybody claps and laughs. Fito falls into his chair. "You make a good Puerto Rican," he says and slaps me on the shoulder.

"*Sí. Porque tengo un corazón puertorriqueño,*" I respond with one of Junie's useful phrases. Junie has explained that nothing is more important to Puerto Ricans that having heart, Puerto Rican heart, *corazón*.

"*¡Ay, bendito!* He eats Puerto Rican. He dances Puerto Rican. He speaks Puerto Rican, and now he has a Puerto Rican heart. Must be Puerto Rican!" declares Fito. The whole family laughs, even baby Hector. "So, Tommy," Fito continues. "You know fractions?"

"Excuse me?" My brain is still stuck on one, two, three, one, two, three.

"My number-two daughter's real smart, they place her in accelerated. But she's having problems with fractions. You know fractions?"

"You mean like adding them and multiplying them?"

"Yeah, like that. Can you teach her?"

"Now?"

"Not now. It's Friday night. Some other day. Whenever you want."

"Okay. Fractions are easy once you get the hang of them. Sort of like dancing salsa."

"*¡Fantástico!*" exults Fito like he has solved a major family crisis. "You come here and teach her good. Then I don't worry."

Before we leave, Tito takes me into Fito and Lydia's bedroom, where Lydia is preparing baby Hector for bed. In the room is an altar with candles, flowers, two bowls of water, and what look like pictures of several saints and the Virgin Mary. I tell Mrs. García how nice it was meeting her and the rest of her family, and thank her for the delicious food. She smiles, makes the sign of the cross, and says in Spanish for *Dios* to guard and bless us.

When we hit the street, Tito asks how I liked Gladys and the family. I tell him how great I think they are. How Fito and Lydia don't seem like parents but more like just part of the family, like they're kids themselves. Tito says that lots of Puerto Ricans are like that but that I should never forget Fito's still the father.

"What's with the altar in the bedroom?" I ask.

"Those are their favorite saints. Fito and Lydia pray to them to keep watch over their family."

"Why the bowls of water?"

"To draw away the evil spirits. They're Catholic but also *espiritistas*. They believe in spirits, cures, curses. Like that."

"You don't?"

"Not really. You?"

"No."

"Just the same, watch out. Watch out or they'll do you like they did me."

"Do what?"

"Put a spell on you."

"A spell for what?"

"To make you part of the family," replies Tito with a big grin.

A week later, I arrive at the García apartment right at 11:00 on Saturday morning. Before I have a chance to ring the buzzer at the top of the outside stairs, Aida calls down to me from the third-floor window and buzzes me in.

Upstairs, I find her alone in the living room, wearing blue jeans and a white blouse. In her ears are big golden hoop earrings; around her floats the fresh, sharp scent of a newly cut lemon. Aida tells me that her parents are in their bedroom watching TV with the little ones. I can hear the sounds of happy voices pouring from the back. Aida says no one else is dressed yet. Fito has instructed her to feed me and to call him after I've finished helping her so he can thank me.

She leads me to the kitchen, where her math book and some work sheets are spread out on the table. "What would you like to eat? A buttered roll? Coffee? Juice? I could make some eggs."

"No thanks," I say as I sit down at the table and slide the math book across the table to her. "I just had breakfast."

I ask her to show me where she's at. She says page 63 and slides the book back to me without looking at it. I look over pages 63 and 64. They are full of examples of multiplying and dividing simple fractions.

"What's the problem you're having?" I ask.

"No problems."

"No problems? I thought you didn't understand fractions?"

"That was Papi's idea. I know fractions. To multiply you go across. To divide you flip-flop the numbers, then multiply across."

"Show me." I begin to wonder what I'm doing here, if maybe I do have to worry about the spell Tito warned me about. Aida picks up a pencil and quickly completes several examples from her book, both multiplying and dividing. No mistakes. "So why's Fito worried?"

"He wants to make sure because he can't check my homework himself. He has his heart set on me becoming a nurse. Papi says I'm his old age insurance. I'd like to be a nurse and help people. And blood doesn't bother me. But . . ."

"You have other ideas?"

"Sometimes."

"Like what?" She looks at me. When our eyes meet she looks down at the sheet of numbers in front of her. "Like what?" I ask again.

She's silent. Then she says softly, "A writer."

"You want to be a writer?"

"Yes," she answers, blushing and still looking down. "I love to write things, to make up things, to tell stories, to write poems.

Papi says I'm the family storyteller. But he still wants me to be a nurse."

I ask her to show me one of her poems. Aida gets up from the table, leaves the kitchen, and when she returns, hands me a single sheet of plain white paper.

Sometimes I dream who I would be,
If I lived in Puerto Rico.
Would I eat guavas off the trees?
Would I hear coquís *singing at night?*
Would I swim naked in a mountain stream
The way Papi did when he was a boy?
Or would I be careful, like girls are supposed to?
Would I wear jeans or a red dress?
Would I wear shoes, or sandals, or go barefoot?
Would I still be waiting to be señorita?
Would I be me?

"It's beautiful," I say.

"You like it?"

"Yes. A lot. A whole lot. Does it have a title?"

"Does it need a title?"

"Not necessarily."

"Maybe 'If I Lived in Puerto Rico.'"

"How about 'Waiting to Be *Señorita*'?"

Aida blushes, this time not looking at me at all. When she still doesn't say anything I ask, "Isn't the poem about waiting to become a young woman?"

"You know what's becoming *señorita*?" she finally asks, so low I can hardly hear her. "It's having your period."

"Oh." Now I'm the one blushing. I stand up, go to the sink, and pour myself a glass of water.

"Maybe I'll call it 'Would I Be Me?'" she says.

"That's a perfect title," I agree.

Returning from school one afternoon shortly after Kennedy becomes president, I discover that I have forgotten my apartment keys. When I knock on the door, no one answers. Johnny is still at school, Mom is probably delayed at the Reading Program with Peggy and Andy, and who knows where Dad is. I could go and look for him over at the Parish Office, but he might not be there. Besides, it's cold outside and getting dark. I plop myself down on the floor in front of our apartment door. The Reading Program runs until five every afternoon, and it's almost five now. Mom should be home any minute. I take *The Yearling* out of my book bag and in the dim light of the hallway begin my English homework.

After about five minutes, I hear the elevator door creak open, and our next-door neighbor from 10B, whom I know only as Lee, walks toward me. She is pushing a large shopping cart with two bags of groceries sitting on top of a heap of laundry. Lee is a dark brown, nearly black woman about my mother's age with small, squinty eyes. She seldom smiles and barely mumbles hello when we pass her in the hall or stand next to her waiting for the elevator. Even in the elevator she doesn't say much, despite Mom's attempts to draw her into conversation. If she does say something, she speaks so low and garbled that it's hard to hear her or understand what she's saying except when she yells at her kids; then you can hear her for blocks.

Next to Lee, her two sons, Robert, about nine, and Sonny, maybe four or five, walk glumly. Robert is a sad-faced kid who smiles even less than his mother; I have never heard him say anything. Sonny is more energetic and curious, like any five-year-old, and I sometimes see him running and laughing with the other little kids downstairs. When he's near his mother, however, he's just as quiet as Robert. From time to time, Lee knocks on our door to borrow some milk, sugar, or flour; otherwise, she sticks to herself. On several occasions Mom has tried to intervene when we hear the boys screaming and crying through the walls. Mom says Lee has admitted to her that when she drinks she sometimes beats the boys with an extension cord, and I've overheard Mom and Dad talking about whether they should call the child welfare authorities. Dad feels they should stay out of Lee's business unless the kids are really getting hurt, which they don't seem to be; anything is better than sending children into foster care. Mom says she refuses to sit idly by and let children be hurt. Whenever she thinks Lee may be beating her children she bangs on the door shouting for her to stop.

Along with teaching every child in East Harlem how to read, Mom's biggest wish is that she could teach all the mothers and fathers how to be good parents. She says too many East Harlem parents don't talk to their children, encourage them to ask questions, treat them like regular little people with their own opinions and ideas. Mom has a theory that children like Robert and Sonny act out in school because they're not allowed to act like children at home. Children who are good in school, like us, are the ones who cause trouble at home. The way we fight with each other and talk back to our parents would probably make Lee think we're spoiled. Maybe we are compared to Robert and Sonny.

When Lee reaches the end of the hall, she asks me what's the matter. I explain that I forgot my keys and that no one's home to let me in, but I'm sure Mom will be home any minute. Lee tells me I can't just sit on the floor in the hallway and orders me into her apartment. I try to say that it's no problem, that I'm fine. She'll hear none of it: I'm to come inside with her and that's final. She speaks in a tone that makes clear she's not accustomed to children who don't do what she tells them to do.

Lee's apartment is hot and stuffy and smells of stale, rotting food, like no one has taken out the garbage. There are clothes, cans, and litter strewn everywhere, and the sink is piled high with unwashed, greasy dishes. In the little room between the kitchen and the living room, she seats me at a table covered with dirty lunch plates and glasses. She tells Robert to take Sonny and go watch TV, then she washes out a glass from the sink and serves me some Coke along with two cookies. Though Robert looks at my cookies hungrily, he doesn't ask for one as he takes his little brother by the hand and seats him in front of the huge television that dominates the living room. Their TV must be twice the size of ours and has better reception. From my seat at the dining room table, I can see the cartoons the kids are watching perfectly. Lee shouts at Robert to lower the volume, and he jumps up to do so.

Without first putting away the groceries, Lee sits down herself across the table from me and pours herself a large slurp of Scotch from the bottle standing in the middle of the table. She doesn't add any ice or water. I'm feeling uncomfortable, and it's not just the heat and odor of the apartment. If it's when she drinks that Lee starts screaming and beating her children, I certainly don't want to stay for long. I keep both ears tuned to any sound in the hallway that might signal the return of Mom, Dad, or Johnny.

I have no idea what to say to Lee and am about to suggest that I go and watch television with Robert and Sonny when she starts telling me about her trip to the supermarket. It's the first time I've heard a full sentence come out of her mouth. Because she talks so low and her words run together, I can't follow her too well. Lee doesn't seem to notice, however, and keeps right on talking without pause except to take another sip of Scotch. It's the most I've heard her say in the three-plus years we've been neighbors, and I slowly begin to make sense of her words. She's complaining about how much food costs in East Harlem and how even when you pay good money what you get is often stale. She tells me how the snooty Puerto Rican girl behind the counter in Molly's told her she couldn't buy beer with food stamps. Even though Lee had given the girl five dollars along with the right number of food stamps, the cashier still acted superior just because she has a job. Who was she to talk to Lee that way, her parents probably can't even speak English, and anyway, what does she know about life or troubles or the difficulties of raising two children all by yourself? Who does she think she is just because she's Puerto Rican and has some sorry-ass little job? Welfare is the pits. She hates having to use food stamps right out in public, where everyone can see. Nobody likes welfare. They ask you all kinds of prying, personal questions, and when your social worker visits she looks in your refrigerator and snoops around in the bedroom, making sure you don't have no man living in the house with you. During Lee's last "face-to-face," her worker suggested that, because Sonny will soon be going to first grade, it's time for Lee to go to work.

"What job she expects me to get?" demands Lee. "I got asthma, high blood pressure, and arthritis in every bone. No way I gonna stand at a counter all day long."

As Lee is talking, I watch a series of roaches beat a path across her kitchen floor. If Lee sees them, she pretends not to, or maybe she doesn't care. To Mom every roach is a personal affront, a mortal enemy to be immediately cornered and executed, even if it means pulling out the refrigerator or removing all the silverware from the kitchen drawers. Mom says one of the reasons we have roaches is that Lee's apartment is such a mess; the roaches assemble there and then migrate over to our apartment. I wonder why they would bother coming over to our house, where no crumb is ever to be left on any shelf or plate, when Lee's apartment is such a roach heaven. In order to combat the roaches, Mom has gotten Lee to agree to have the exterminator man from maintenance come with his great silver can to her house on the same day he does our apartment. If he comes on different days, all the roaches rush from the sprayed apartment over to the next one.

Mom and Dad believe that welfare is a good thing. They say that the government needs to take care of poor people, especially single mothers like Lee with young children. Yet what Lee says is true. Everyone I know on welfare is ashamed and tries to hide it. The guys even joke about how the first and fifteenth of the month, when the welfare checks arrive, are called "Mother's Day." Twice a month people hang around the mailboxes waiting for the mailman and form long lines at the check-cashing stores up and down Second and Third Avenues. I'm not sure how Lee would survive if there was no welfare. What kind of job could she possibly get with her scowl and her mumble and her arthritis in every bone? Mom says that education and job training should be a larger part of the welfare program. It's hard for me, however, to picture Lee studying.

Just as Lee drains a final gulp of Scotch and is about to pour herself some more, I hear sounds in the hallway and Mom's voice at the doorway telling Peggy she should go right in and start her homework before dinner. I rise from the table and lean over to pick up my book bag.

"I was thinking to ask a favor," says Lee without leaving her seat. She hasn't poured herself that second drink, and she doesn't look at me. She just stares at her empty glass.

"What?" I ask, hesitantly. Usually if an adult asks me to do a favor I just say sure, even before I know what I'm going to be asked to do.

"I wonder if you babysit for Robert and Sonny sometimes."

Lee's favor catches me by surprise. I thought she was going to ask me to run down and buy her some cigarettes or ask my mother for some milk or something. Not wanting to be impolite or get her angry, I say that maybe I could, once in a while. Most nights I have a lot of homework.

Lee says that it will be only once in a while, Friday or Saturday night, and her boys won't be no trouble, they'll do what she tells them.

I suggest that she bring Robert and Sonny over to our house and let Mom watch them. Lee says she would never do that. She doesn't want my mother's charity. She'd prefer to pay me whatever I charge. She adds that Robert likes me, as if the fact that he likes me means I have no choice.

I look at Robert sitting on the floor in the living room. When he sees me look at him, he turns away quickly.

I explain to Lee that I'm not really into babysitting, which is mostly true. I don't even like getting stuck with Peggy and Andy. Once in a while I do babysit for my cousins, Mom's brother's kids, but only when Uncle Rick calls desperate at the last moment. Plus, he pays me $2.00 an hour, way over the going rate of $1.25.

"Does that mean you won't?" asks Lee.

"Like I said, I'm not into babysitting." I thank her for the cookies and Coke and advance quickly to the door, not looking at Robert and Sonny on my way out.

If I ever again forget my keys, I promise myself I'll wait behind the stairwell door, where Lee can't see me when she comes out of the elevator.

The doorbell rings just as I'm finishing my turn for the dishes. Here comes Rabbit, shouts Peggy from the living room couch, where she is watching Walter Cronkite with Mom and Dad. Ever since I invited Rabbit home to lunch he has gotten into the habit of appearing at our door without warning. Sometimes on returning home, we find him standing alone in the lobby waiting for us. Mom always welcomes him and offers him something to eat, but it's gotten to be a family joke. When we aren't expecting visitors and the doorbell rings, one of us will shout out, "Here comes Rabbit." More often than not, he stays as long as Mom lets him.

Rabbit sits at the kitchen table, dogging our Friday evening leftovers. I can tell he's down. More down than usual. Wondering if this is one of those Friday nights he's going to sleep on the roof, I ask him what's the matter. Without lifting his eyes from his food, he replies, "Nothing." Once through eating, however, he doesn't want to play a board game or watch TV. Instead we go back to my bedroom where he chooses a book from my shelf—one about the explorers of the New World—sits down on the floor, and begins reading. Rabbit is a big reader. With a book on his lap, he can become lost for hours while I do my homework. He doesn't even look up when I leave to go the bathroom or sneak a snack. Mom, always on high alert for any of my friends who show an interest in reading, has talked to him many times about joining the Reading Program. Rabbit always seems interested, but he never shows.

Tonight I don't want to leave him alone, so I pick up *Kidnapped* and sprawl out on the floor next to him. Although I'm trying to be a good friend, it's hard feeling anything but sorry for Rabbit. On the courts, he tries too hard to fit in, and his efforts are so clumsy that they have the opposite affect. When he's not there, the other guys talk about him brutally. They repeat for each other's amusement the stupid, bragging things he says, joke about his big ears, and make cruel comments about his father. Rabbit and his family are always moving. Every time you turn around, he has a new address. The guys say that when Rabbit's family gets behind in the rent, which is often, they stuff all their belongings into a couple of large garbage bags and sneak out in the middle of the night.

"Where's Rabbit?" goes the opening line of the routine.

"You mean Rabbit of 100 Street?"

"No, Rabbit of 107."

"You mean Rabbit of 111?"

"No, Rabbit of 104."

"I thought that's who you were talking about."

I don't laugh at the jokes about Rabbit, and Samuel, knowing Rabbit is my friend, doesn't laugh either.

I remember one afternoon when Rabbit was having an especially bad day, missing all his shots, dropping passes, and constantly throwing the ball away. Each time he messed up, he made an excuse like the pass was too high or he'd been hacked. Charles, who was on Rabbit's team, finally had enough and told him to go play stickball with his Spanish brothers, to leave basketball to colored guys and to white boys like me who can play.

Rabbit retorted that he was just as white as I was, that lots of Spanish people are white. Charles would have none of it, declaring that there wasn't no way Rabbit was white. Before Rabbit popped, I jumped into the fray.

"What are you talking about, Charles? Even I'm not white. Nobody's white. Look. Look here. Here's white." I put the back of my hand down next to the white of his polished Converses. "If anything, I'm more like a pale shade of tan."

"Aint no such race as pale tan," declared Charles.

"If I was white like your sneakers," I insisted, "I'd be a freak."

"You are a freak," piped in a guy named Slim, the second of Rabbit's teammates. "Any white boy can dribble like you, that's a freak."

"How about Cousy?" I demanded. "Who dribbles better than Cousy?"

"Only William and half the niggers in Harlem," declared Charles. Everybody laughed, and we all went back to playing basketball.

Back in my bedroom, Rabbit looks up from his book and asks if I'm going to my mother's reading program tomorrow. I say that I probably am, and he asks if he can come with me. I tell him sure, that he'll like it there.

Thanks, Tommy, he says and goes back to reading about Ponce de León and the fountain of youth until Mom comes in and tells him it's time to leave.

The next morning, Rabbit arrives at our apartment half an hour late. Mom has already left so that she'll be on hand and ready when the kids begin arriving at ten o'clock. He looks tired and sad, as usual, even though he's dressed in his Parochial school white shirt and formal dark blue slacks. He apologizes for being late and explains that he's been out much of the night with his mother, searching the local bars for his father, who's still not home. His mother is certain something serious has happened to her husband, that he's in jail, hospitalized, lying dead in a vacant lot. Rabbit is certain something serious has happened to the weekly paycheck.

At the Reading Program, Rabbit fills out his enrollment card and Mom explains that the first order of business is to determine his reading level. On his test, Rabbit scores at level nine, more than a full year above his grade in school. When Mom announces the results, he glows with pride, looking over at me to make sure I've heard. Mom tells Rabbit to return next Saturday with his home-work assignments; by then they'll have found a tutor to work with him. When she suggests that he choose two books to take home, however, his customary frown resurfaces. Sensing his uncertainty, Mom points out the "East Harlem Reading Program" stamp inside each book cover. If his mother or father has any questions about the program, or about the books, they can call. Rabbit thinks for a moment, then hungrily starts scanning the books in Mom's library. After reading through several shelves of titles, he settles on *The Bombing of Pearl Harbor* and *The Wright Brothers of Kitty Hawk.*

Mom recommends that he make one of his choices fiction, and Rabbits asks what fiction is. She explains that it's made-up stories, literature filled with imagination, poetry, make-believe.

"No thanks," says Rabbit, clutching his two books tightly to his chest. "I like to read about real people."

Outside, Rabbit asks me to walk him home so that I can be there to back him up about the books. He currently lives on 104th between Park and Lexington, not exactly on my way, but I agree to go with him. It seems important.

Turning onto his block, we hear loud shouting and see a crowd of pushing, wildly waving people gathered in a circle halfway down the block. As we draw nearer, Rabbit's face turns ashen and he whispers to me that it's his mother and father. They're screaming at each other in Spanish as the group of onlookers add in their two cents. Rabbit's mother is doing most of the talking. His father tries to throw in a slurred word or two, but it's clear he's on the ropes. Most of the crowd is against him. His eyes are bloodshot, his clothes are wet and dirty, he has a large, ugly bruise, glowing yellow and purple, on his forehead. One look, one sniff, and you know what happened to him, what happened to the weekly paycheck.

Rabbit's mother is a large, beefy-armed lady with gray streaks in her black hair. Her eyes are red from crying. All at once she stops shouting and begins to tremble. Then she steps forward and slaps her husband hard across the face. The crowd gasps. Silence drops suddenly over the street, and everybody freezes—everybody except Rabbit's father, who falls across the front steps of the building behind him. He holds himself with both hands around his waist, leans his forehead onto the steps, and sobs.

"Get out of here, Tommy," Rabbit hisses between his teeth.

"What about the books?"

"Just get out of here."

I turn and walk fast down the street, not looking back even after I cross Third Avenue. It was the last time I ever saw Rabbit.

CHAPTER 11

In the spring of 1961, after almost four years in Washington Houses, my family moves to a new apartment on 105th between First Avenue and the East River so that we can have an extra bedroom, a real dining room, and a second bathroom. In Wilson Houses we also have a handful of white neighbors. In what my father calls a grand experiment in social engineering, the City Housing Authority has determined that Wilson Houses, consisting of three twenty-story-high low-income public housing buildings, will rent its apartments to Negroes, Puerto Ricans, and whites in equal proportions. Although the City never finds nearly enough white families to reach its one-third goal, the handful of white people who do move in give Wilson Houses a different feel from Washington Houses, where other than a single woman and her little son, we were the only white people in our entire building.

Our apartment is in the middle building, at 425 East 105th Street. We have been assigned the thirteenth floor because we're one of the few families okay with living on thirteen. Peggy now has her own bedroom, as does Johnny. Andy and I will share a bedroom until Johnny goes to college in less than two years; then, for the first time, I'll have my own room. The apartment faces directly south, and we have a perfect view of downtown New York over the rooftops of the six-story-high East River Projects directly in front of us. We can also look east and watch the boats coming up and down the East River. To the west we can see the buildings of Washington Houses and beyond them as far as Central Park.

In Wilson Houses we are a longer walk from the subway and from Lexington Avenue, where I still catch my bus to school each morning. Walking back and forth to the bus stop, I quickly learn to stay away from the candy store on the northwest corner of First and 105th. This candy store seems to be the favorite gathering place of all the junkies, winos, and out of work young men in East Harlem. Mom says she's sure it's both a numbers joint and a drug shop, and she calls the local precinct to report her suspicions. The cops do nothing about it, however, and the corner of First and 105th remains a location to avoid. Whenever I cross First Avenue, which is just about every time I leave the apartment, I either walk up to 106th Street or cross to the south side of 105th and hurry into the middle of the block. One Hundred and Fifth Street between First and Second is an Italian block, and I feel safe once I'm well past the candy store. It seems strange, and a little sad, that after four years of living in East Harlem—four years in which I've never gotten to know a single Italian boy, four years in which all my East Harlem friends have been either colored or Spanish—

when I move to a new block and am feeling nervous I take refuge among Italians simply because they're white and I'm white.

Except for the extra bathroom, the change in address does little to affect our daily routine. Dad still runs the Parish and works at the main office, at 2050 Second Avenue. Mom still runs the Reading Program on the second floor, right above Dad's office. I still attend Collegiate every day, go to Union Settlement on Saturdays, and sing in the adult choir at Ascension on Sundays. I still hang out with Danny on Sunday afternoons after church, at Thursday night choir practice, and on Saturdays as we continue our adventures around the city. We visit the Bronx Zoo, the George Washington Bridge, the bell tower of Riverside Church, the Wollman skating rink in Central Park, and several times, Coney Island. On our travels we continue to sing doo-wop songs on the subway, watching everything speed at us through the first car window.

However, this second move changes my life in other ways that become clear only slowly. The amount of time I spend with my East Harlem friends, other than Danny, declines. Rabbit no longer knocks on our door unannounced, though I know the reason for this is not our new address but the fact that I witnessed his mother slap his father. I no longer play basketball on the 109 courts or the 121 courts and rarely go down to the two new courts of Wilson Houses. Most of my basketball playing is now confined to the Collegiate gym and the games we play at other private schools around the city. I'm becoming spoiled by hoops with nets, gyms with wooden floors, and contests moderated by referees with whistles. On the occasional Saturday morning when I do think of going over to 109, I find myself choosing to stay home and play my guitar. I sit for hours at my bedroom window, looking down at the streets while strumming and singing one of Mr. Hobbs's sad, lonely cowboy songs.

With the move to Wilson Houses, I realize how deeply I'm

being pulled into the world of Collegiate. When not with Danny, I spend much of each weekend at the apartment of one of my classmates and more and more I'm invited for whole weekends to one of their country houses in Connecticut, Massachusetts, or Vermont. My Collegiate friends invite me to birthday parties, Bar Mitzvahs, holiday gatherings, Broadway shows, sports events, and fancy restaurants. With them I can discuss things that are becoming interesting to me, like books, theater, history. We avoid talking about politics, however. Most of my school friends are Republicans, anti-Kennedy, and lukewarm about the Civil Rights movement. I also do not talk with them much about my life in East Harlem. My Collegiate classmates and their parents show little interest in life above 96th Street. It's almost as if, for them, East Harlem isn't there, as if 96th Street is the northern border of Manhattan. Even when traveling to and from the city, they stick to the West Side Highway or the FDR Drive so as not to see and hear El Barrio through their car windows.

Nor do my East Harlem friends seem to have much curiosity about how my school friends live. Like Junie, most of them prefer not to travel south of the DMZ. And, except for going to places like museums with Samuel and all over with Danny, I don't do much to erase the barrier of 96th Street. I try to keep my two worlds separate. I have never even invited Danny to see me perform in a school play, watch one of my basketball games, or hang out with me and my classmates. I worry that my classmates wouldn't understand Danny and might say something embarrassing to him. I'm also reluctant to have Danny witness the privileges and the riches of a world he isn't a part of. There are so many things Danny has never experienced, so many things he knows nothing about. How could he? He lives in a home without books. I begin to understand that for Danny college may not be an option. If he doesn't make it in show business, I'm not sure what he'll do. The conclusion that college and all the careers college opens up are probably closed to Danny worries me, and I determine to protect him from reaching this same conclusion himself. I never invite him into my Collegiate world. Not once.

Although we live only a few short blocks away, I now rarely pass by my old block on 102nd. On my way to school I stick mainly to 106th, a big, two-way street filled with stores and people. I no longer see Samuel, William, Junie, or any of the guys from the 109 courts regularly. When I do run into one of them on the street, or at the subway station, we say hello and talk briefly but never get together.

Toward the end of eighth grade a girl from one of Collegiate's sister schools, Nightingale-Bamford, invites me to be her escort to the Gold and Silver Ball. I'm now almost fourteen, and I think about girls constantly. I imagine kissing them, touching them, seeing them naked. I long to go out on dates, to have a girlfriend. I met Rachel at the Bar Mitzvah of one of my Collegiate classmates. She's pretty and easy to talk to. I accept her invitation with nervous anticipation.

The Gold and Silver Ball turns out to be a big society event, bigger than I had any way of knowing. Some classmates who are also attending inform me that the men wear tuxedos. When I apprise Mom of this requirement, she says it's ridiculous for a thirteen-year-old to wear a tuxedo, that my dark suit, my one and only suit, will do just fine. My heart sinks. I have a feeling it won't do just fine, and it doesn't. I end up being the only male in attendance not wearing a tuxedo. In the middle of the ball I consider feigning sickness and escaping into the cover of night, but I can't desert Rachel. I'm her escort. She invited me and I accepted. Besides, she handles my embarrassment well, as do my friends, who pretend not to notice that I'm a naked seal alone in a sea of formally dressed penguins.

On the way home, Rachel tries to hand me a five-dollar bill to pay the taxi fare, but I refuse it. Does she think that because I didn't rent a tuxedo I'm too poor to pay for a measly cab ride? When we arrive at her doormanned building on Park Avenue and 89th Street, Rachel insists that I accompany her upstairs. In a living room twice the size of our entire apartment, she takes my coat, hangs it in the front closet, sits me down on her couch, and goes into the kitchen. All is quiet. I can't tell whether her parents are out, asleep, or hovering somewhere in the back rooms. The apartment is huge.

Rachel returns with two glasses of Coke, sits down next to me on the couch, and asks if I had a good time. Trying to hide how miserable and out of it I felt most of the night, I say that I had a great time, I'm only sorry I didn't know more of the dances.

You did fine, she says and inches so close to me I can smell her perfume and feel the heat of her body. Although I sense she's waiting for me to kiss her, I'm uncertain. I've never kissed a girl before. What if she's just being friendly? What if her parents walk in?

Suddenly she rises from the couch and asks if I like Yeats. Before I can confess that I'm not sure who she's talking about, Rachel rushes from the room. She returns seconds later with a book of poetry. This time she sits so close to me that our legs touch, so close I can feel her breath as she begins to read a poem about a great bird swooping down on a helpless female, holding her breast to breast, with her thighs loosening and his loins shuddering. As Rachel reads, it occurs to me she might be expecting more than just a kiss. Though I like Rachel, she's not the girl I'm looking for. She's too different from me, too much a part of her protected, rich world. In a funny way, she reminds me of some of the East Harlem girls I know: sexually experienced, eager to lead me somewhere I'm not yet ready to go. The only neighborhood girls I feel comfortable around are those to whom I'm not sexually attracted, extremely fat girls, for example, or much older girls not interested in me as a boyfriend. With attractive girls my own age, I'm immobilized.

When Rachel finishes reading, she sets down the book and promptly kisses me. I put my arms around her. Her hands encircle my neck and back, her whole body presses against mine, her tongue slips into my mouth. As our tongues dance, I move my lower body away from her in an attempt to hide my growing excitement. In response, she only presses herself against me harder. Suddenly her whole body starts shivering, and she breaks into a sweat like she has the flu or something. Abruptly I pull away and ask what's the matter.

"Nothing," she pants; her face flushed, her eyes glazed over like a junkie's.

"I'm sorry. I have to leave. I've got to be home by one at the latest." Jumping up from the couch, I retrieve my coat from the closet. "Thanks for inviting me," I shout from the hall.

She remains on the couch, watching me from among the cushions. "Call me."

"Sure." I let myself out the door.

A few weekends later, I find Danny waiting for me at the entrance to my building with the news that he's lost his virginity. I tell him I don't believe it. Danny assures me I heard right and in a matter-of-fact voice describes how a girl from around his way pulled up her skirt in the vacant lot and let all the boys do her for a dollar. I ask if he also paid a dollar, if she let him go all the way for a dollar, and Danny is silent. Finally I ask him how it was. Nasty, he says.

Despite my initial disbelief, I know that Danny is bold and tries things and is probably telling the truth. Instead of bragging, he seems dejected, like he's found out something about the world and about himself he doesn't really want to know. But I want to know. I'm horrified, impressed, curious. I want him to tell me what it's like, to give me some details about the girl and her "dark triangle," like that of van Gogh's mistress Le Pigeon in Irving Stone's book *Lust for Life*, what it looks like, what it feels like. The image of the girl, whom Danny doesn't describe, lifting her skirt in the back of the vacant lot haunts me. How old is she? Is she pretty? Had they really done it in a vacant lot, on top of the garbage, with other guys waiting their turns and people watching from their windows? It excites and troubles me at the same time. If only I could be free and bold like Danny. If only I could stop worrying about what people might say, what they might think.

A knock on the door breaks my efforts to study for my eighth-grade final exams. I shout out Who is it? and Dad opens the door. He pulls over the chair from Johnny's desk, sits down next to me, and startles me by asking if I'd like to join the Riverside youth group. For a moment, I don't say anything. Although the thought of going to Riverside and meeting a whole new set of girls excites me, I don't want Dad to know how much in case it doesn't happen. He repeats his question. I lie and pretend that I'm not sure, that I haven't thought about it. In actuality I've thought about it a lot. Riverside Church has a large youth group that meets every Friday night for recreation, discussion, and social events. Sometimes they organize work projects to raise money for charity or take weekend trips to interesting places like Indian reservations. Johnny's been a member for almost three years, since ninth grade; he even attends on Sundays. Mom and Dad weren't thrilled when he chose Riverside over Ascension, but they didn't make a big deal about it.

Confused by my lack of enthusiasm, Dad says that Johnny

seems to enjoy Riverside and he thought I might as well. He figures I can meet girls my own age there, something it might be a little hard to do at Collegiate. He laughs at his own joke. There are no girls at Collegiate. Although my guess is that Mom put him up to this little talk, I'm pleased to think Dad is concerned about me, watching out for me. I inform him that Riverside has a rule you can't join unless you attend church there on Sundays and that, as he knows, I'm a member of Ascension; I sing in the choir and everything. Dad replies that he will talk to the people at Riverside. He's sure they'll make an exception in my case. I can be a part of both churches. Then I remember you have to be in high school and that I'm still in eighth grade. Dad says that he was thinking we'd get everything arranged now, then next fall I can join up.

"What about it? Do we have a deal?" he asks.

"Yeah. Thanks. But what about Johnny?" I ask. "He might not like it, me tagging along and everything. Riverside's sort of like his thing."

"I wouldn't worry about Johnny," says Dad, halfway out the door. "He's the one who suggested it."

The García household is in a high pitch of Fourth of July excitement. Lydia's in the kitchen cooking on all burners with the help of Gladys and a young woman from downstairs named Lucy. The radio is booming salsa from atop the refrigerator. I'm in the living room with Aida watching Baby Hector and Lucy's little boy, Carlito. Fito, little Fito, and Tito have gone to pick up the pig. The feast isn't due to start until late this afternoon, but Fito wanted me over early so he can show me how everything's done.

The men broadcast their return by yelling up from the street below. Gladys and Aida race to the window. Fito shouts for them to send me down. On the street I find Tito and Fito discussing what to do with the dead pig lying on a sheet spread over the back-seat of the car borrowed from Fito's young brother, Tío Jaime. The eighty-pound porker has already been sliced open and gutted.

"He's been marinating since yesterday," Fito informs me. "Garlic, oregano, salt, and lemons. You can't use too many lemons. We must have squeezed out two dozen."

Fito tells Tito and me to cover *El Lechón* with the sheet he's lying on and hoist him out of the car onto our shoulders and up the three flights of stairs to the García apartment. Despite his great bulk, the pig is easy to carry. His weight is evenly distributed over the length of a long metal *barra* that sticks a foot or two out of his mouth at one end and out of his backside at the other.

Once we have Mr. Pig upstairs, Fito orders us to put him in the bathtub, so that the ice can keep him cool. When Lydia hears where we intend to store the main course, she pleads not the bathroom; she and the girls will be needing *la ducha*. Fito assures her that the guest of honor will be long gone before they need to shower. *Adelante*, he commands.

Tito and I march *El Lechón* into the bathroom and prop him snout end up against the wall under the shower, with his butt end wedged between several bags of ice. As we're leaving, Fito closes the shower curtain. "We don't want him peeping on any of the ladies doing their business," he says with a big grin.

While Fito goes up to start the fire in a large metal bin they've already carried to the roof, Tito, little Fito, and I walk to Councilman Ríos's clubhouse to borrow two long folding tables. Tío Jaime arrives around noon with three huge coolers full of beer, *maví*, and sodas. As the two brothers crack open their first Rheingolds of the day, they get into an argument about whether the fire's ready. Jaime says they should start cooking the pig while the flames are still jumping from the coals, that way, *El Lechón's* skin will char, trap in the juices and soak in the wonderful burnt taste of the fire. Fito maintains that the pig should cook evenly throughout its entire roasting. He says the trick is to keep the coals glowing at a slow, steady heat so that the meat is cooked just right, tender and tasty, moist not dry, moist but not too moist. Jaime shouts to put it on now before the flames die down any further. Fito wants to know whose pig it is anyway. Jaime throws up his hands in disgust and tells his brother to go ahead and fuck it up for all he cares. Fito orders his brother to watch his language in front of the kids.

When Fito determines the coals are ready, and not one second before, Tito and I are sent to retrieve the pig and tell the girls to come and witness the opening ceremony. We go downstairs and find Jaime's wife, Tía Mercedes, stretched out and moaning on the living room couch. Apparently, she went into the bathroom to wash her face, pulled opened the shower curtain, and found herself eyeball to eyeball with *El Lechón*. Now she's being restored to life by Gladys and Aida with the help of damp washcloths and sips of orange juice laced with rum.

"It's just one of Tía Mercedes's *ataques*," says Aida as Tito and I carry the offending party up the stairs to the roof. "She'll be fine once all the work is done."

The family, Lucy, and various neighbors from the building circle around as Fito and Jaime mount the pig onto the spit. Little Fito is accorded the honor of being the first to turn the crank that rotates the beast over the coals. As the pig begins to roast, Jaime recites a poem in Spanish and everybody laughs. The poem, Tito explains to me, praises both the tastiness and the magical sex-enhancing powers of roast pig.

About four o'clock, Lucy and Gladys reappear with table-cloths and decorations and begin setting the tables and directing Carmen and some of the other children from the building in blowing up and hanging balloons. They also place four or five miniature American flags around the roof, including one positioned by Lucy over the doorway leading downstairs. As she reaches up to fasten the flag in place, her dress lifts, and I can see the tops of her legs, almost to her panties. Lucy has removed her curlers, brushed out her dark red hair, and changed from an apron to a short, white-and-pink summer dress that shows her bare shoulders and the tops of her full, round breasts. As if by some magic, the frumpy-looking cook in the downstairs kitchen has been transformed into a sexy young woman, a very sexy young woman.

Tito and I help out, carrying up the paper plates, cups, eating utensils, and food. We bring tray after tray, dish after dish: *pasteles, plátanos, habichuelas, arroz con pollo, carne guisada,* several salads. It's enough food to feed an army. *El Lechón* is still several hours from perfection when the guests begin to arrive: first the cousins, then the friends, then the families from the rest of the building. Two of the men carry small guitars called *cuatros,* and three others bring tall single drums and *güeros,* ribbed percussion instruments made from dried gourds. One of the men with a *cuatro* turns out to be Nestor, Fito's son from a former marriage. I'm startled to learn that Fito had another whole family before Lydia. I knew he was older than Lydia, but I had assumed he simply married late in life the way some men do. Nestor is short and handsome, with gleaming dark hair slicked straight back. Fito must have looked like that twenty-five years ago.

Two transistor radios on opposite sides of the roof are tuned to the same Spanish music station: El Barrio's version of stereo-phonic sound. In no time at all, most of the guests over ten, except for the older men deep in conversation around the spit, are danc-ing. The little children run everywhere, and nobody pays any attention until two of them get into a fight or one falls down and starts to cry. Then a rush of women converge, scold, comfort, and send the kids off to play again.

It's getting dark by the time Fito calls for silence and announces the ceremonial first carving of *El Lechón*. We all gather around the roasting pig. Before Fito can make the first cut, Tío Jaime shouts out that we should sing the National Anthem. Everybody joins in as Fito and Jaime, both veterans of World War II, stand rigidly at attention and salute the American flag that Lucy had placed over the doorway. As the song ends, someone shouts out, "Play ball!" and everybody laughs. Fito announces, Let's eat, and the carving of *El Lechón* begins. People line up as Fito serves out huge slabs of *lechón* right off the spit. My two large slices are manna from heaven: if not prepared by God Himself, at least cooked the way He intended it to be cooked, the Puerto Rican way.

The musicians begin playing and singing old songs from the Island: *boleros.* Fito calls for *"Lamento Jíbaro"* and sings as Lydia stands next to him holding his hand. I can't understand the lyrics, but *"Lamento Jíbaro"* is clearly a song about a man's love and longing for his home country. After Fito finishes singing, everybody claps, and he and Lydia hug and kiss. Then Nestor and the other musicians roll into a love song, and under the spell of *El Lechón,* Fito and Lydia begin dancing, pressed close together like two young lovers.

As the sun sets behind Central Park, the night cools and a gentle breeze blows over the roof. Lucy invites me to dance. It's a slow song, and she follows my lead easily. As she nestles against me, her breasts burn into my chest. Her free hand touches the back of my neck. Her head is on my shoulder, her face turned to my face. She whispers into my ear that I dance well, relaxes even deeper into my arms, and moves her bare hand on my bare neck.

When the song ends, Lucy squeezes my hand, places her free hand on my chest, and tells me that I'm a strong young man who must have a lot of girlfriends.

I'm searching for something to say to this woman who must be at least twenty when Aida interrupts, pulling my arm; Fito needs help with the firecrackers. She's silent as she leads me to where Fito is unwrapping some mean-looking fireworks.

The sun has now set. It's a clear, still night with a bright quarter-moon in the sky over the Triboro Bridge. With Tito's and my assistance, Fito launches a spectacular succession of red, white, and blue firecrackers in honor of the Fourth of July into the darkness over 105th Street. Everybody claps and whistles and pronounces Fito's show the greatest ever. Then, within seconds, the dancing, eating, and drinking resumes.

As I help him pick up the wrappings and the remnants of the firecrackers, Fito whispers to me not to worry about Aida's not liking my dancing with Lucy, that it's okay. A man's gotta do what a man's gotta do, you know what I mean? He gives me a pat on the back and a big wink.

Eleven o'clock passes, and the party shows no signs of slowing down. In fact, people continue to arrive with six-packs of beer and rum bottles, everyone eager to partake of what remains of the magical powers of *El Lechón*. I find Tito and tell him that I have to leave, that it's getting late and Mom will be worried. He says he'll walk down with me.

Making my rounds, I say good-bye to Lucy, Gladys, Lydia, Tío Jaime, and Fito. Fito gives me a warm hug, slaps me repeatedly on the shoulder, and asks if I liked the *lechón*. I reply that I did, that I liked it about as much as a *jíbaro* likes his *plátanos*. Fito laughs, slaps me even more enthusiastically on the shoulder, and says he told me he'd turn me into a *jíbaro*.

When Aida sees that I'm leaving, she reaches into her pocket and hands me a picture of herself in her sixth-grade graduation cap and gown. Lucy's old, she says after I thank her for the picture. Very old, I agree.

Outside Tito says he's on his way to visit a friend named Jessica, who lives on 111th. He explains that he and Gladys don't mess around, not yet, not before they marry. Until then he'll go to see Jessica. Sensing my disapproval, Tito says, "A man's gotta do what a man's gotta do. I can't go around jerking off for the next four years until Gladys and I get married. A real man doesn't jerk off. What about Lucy? You should go for her."

"She's old."

"Old like Lucy is good. Old enough to take care of you but not hassle you. Young enough to still be fine. I'd go for her myself if she didn't live in the same building as Gladys." We arrive at Third Avenue and stop for a moment on the corner before parting.

"Tommy, listen. Fito knows I got a girl on the side. He understands. As long as I do right by Gladys, take care of her, respect her, never embarrass her in public. Like that."

"Does Gladys know?"

"Hell no. You think I'm crazy? But you, you're free. Lucy's perfect. Go for her. She likes you."

"I'd rather find a girl more my own age."

"Until you do, go see Lucy," says Tito.

That night in bed, I take out the picture of Aida. I study her beautiful, fresh face and her clear, happy smile. The picture smells of Aida, fresh and lemony. Under the covers with the light out, however, it's Lucy I can't stop thinking about. I picture her round, soft breasts, her dark red hair, her bare legs reaching out from under her dress as she reaches up to position the American flag, the sound and feel of her breath in my ear and the touch of her hand on the back of my neck. Thinking of Lucy, I do what a real man never does.

After Labor Day, I start going to the Riverside Church Youth Group on Friday nights. As I walk down blocks so familiar yet so strange, I feel like two different people. One me, from 105th Street, is only visiting. The other me, who grew up on Claremont Avenue, is on personal terms with every crack in the sidewalk. I wonder what my life would have been like if we had never moved, if I had never met Danny, Samuel, or Rabbit, if I had never been transplanted to East Harlem. I picture myself five or six years ago galloping through the Seminary halls pretending to be the Lone Ranger. I recall my old playmates, remember my favorite Seminary students and professors, and picture my old third-floor bedroom. Remembering makes me sad. I regret that in order to become me I had to give up the Seminary, a place I loved.

My very first night at Riverside I fall in love. Lisa has a happy, inviting smile, glowing light brown hair, and intense brown eyes. What most attracts me to her is the way she delivers a heated opinion in every discussion. She throws her whole self behind her ideas without caring how they might sound or whether they might scorch the opinion of some poor guy who's less intelligent than she is. On the following Friday nights I try to position myself near her, to sit next to her at group activities. I think up clever things to say should we pass in the hallway, things calculated to make her want to stop and talk. Each time I see her, however, all I can manage is a smile and a weak hello. The seven days between Friday nights seem endless. I ask around about her, cool, like I'm interested but not that interested. Johnny knows her older sister, Vicky, and tells me that Lisa is both a year older than me and a full two years ahead in school because she started first grade early. She's in eleventh grade; I'm in ninth! And worse, she's dating a Columbia freshman. My sinking hopes are kept only slightly afloat by two facts: first, no sign of Mr. Columbia appears on Friday nights; second, whenever I'm able to catch her eye or say hello, she breaks into a friendly smile.

A group of us are leaving Riverside on a cold night in early

December when we discover that heavy snow has fallen during our three hours inside. A winter melee breaks outs as snowballs whiz through the air and shouts, taunts, and yelps of delight echo off the stone church wall. As I stoop to arm myself, a loosely packed snowball thumps off my shoulder. I turn to find Lisa standing behind me. Gotcha, she shouts, then runs.

I pack my snowball and take off after her. Instead of hitting her in the back, I catch her arm, turn her toward me, and draw back my throwing arm. No fair so close, she says. Before I can react, she slaps the snowball out of my grasp, reaches down, and scoops a pile of snow up onto my chest and into my face. Hey! I shout, bending into a squatting position and furiously shoveling snow at her with both hands. Without warning, she gives me a hefty push, and I fall onto my back. For a moment, she stands over me like a conquering gladiator covered with white, fluffy snow instead of red blood. She's both flushed with victory and worried I might be hurt. Before she can speak, I stretch out on the sidewalk and begin moving my arms and legs. She lies on the ground next to me and starts work on her own angel. As our arms reach out, our hands fleetingly touch. When we stand up to survey our handiwork, the angels' wings overlap. The two angels look happy together, made for each other.

With bare fingers Lisa wipes snow off her eyelids and forehead. She is completely white. I brush snow off her shoulders. Then she turns, and I brush off her back. When I'm finished, she does the same for me.

As the snowball fight winds down, small groups and couples go their separate ways. I ask Lisa if I can walk her home, and she suggests that I accompany her to the bus stop; she lives on 99th Street and West End.

"You're Johnny's brother," she says as we head toward Broadway.

"And you're Vicky's sister."

"And you live in East Harlem; your father's a minister."

"Yeah. How'd you know?"

"I have my sources," she says and looks at me with an amused smile. "I think it's so wonderful you live in East Harlem, that your father spends his life helping people."

"Being a minister and helping people is his calling. But East Harlem's not like what you might think. Someday I'll take you there. Show you what it's really like."

"I'd like that," she says softly. The tone of her voice makes me want to tell her things, show her things, explain things to her. She's not one of those people who wants to hear only about the gangs, the drugs, and the violence.

"How about your dad? What does he do?"

"He's dead."

"Oh . . . I'm sorry."

"It's all right. He died a long time ago."

"Do you remember him?"

"Sometimes. I remember sitting on his lap, the cigarette smoke on his breath, the quietness of his voice. Sometimes I imagine he watches over me."

"Like now?"

"Yes."

We arrive at the bus stop, and I tell Lisa that in East Harlem folks believe that people don't die, they just pass over. As I say these words, I'm overwhelmed with the desire to kiss her, to hold her so tight she'll forget about how cold she is, about her father dying young, about Columbia freshmen.

Her bus approaches, and we say good-bye. Lisa pays her fare, turns around, waves and smiles a big, more than friendly smile.

On Tuesday night, Lisa calls to say she won't be at youth group that Friday. I'm devastated. But then she invites me to join her, her mother, and her sister at the Riverside candlelight Christmas service next Sunday afternoon. Greatly relieved, I accept. We talk for a long time about everything. I tell her she should read *How Green Was My Valley* and *Go Tell It on the Mountain*. She suggests *Green Mansions* and *The Little Prince*. We talk about our families and friends, about the things we've done in the past and the things we hope to do in the future. I tell her how I've been planning to become a minister since age nine or ten but that more and more I'm thinking of entering politics. She says she'd like to have both children and a career, especially if she marries a man who likes children and is willing to help out with them. I tell her how much I like children.

On Sunday afternoon we sit in the first balcony of the towering Riverside nave and listen to a well-rehearsed professional choir sing Christmas music. Toward the end of the service, the lights in the church are turned off and candles are lit all around. A solo viola plays Gounod's "Ave Maria" as I reach out in the darkness and cover Lisa's hand with my own. She squeezes it and doesn't let go.

When Danny discovers where I'm spending Friday nights, he mounts a full-scale campaign to come with me. At first I put him off, worried he'll be a burden. I want to have a fresh start away from the neighborhood where everyone knows I'm the minister's son. More important, I don't want to have to worry about Danny, watch out for him. Nor do I want to have to explain him to others, why he diddy-bops, talks slang, and is always cracking jokes, why he loves to dance. Although there are a lot of Negro kids at Riverside, they seem more like me than like Danny. Their parents are teachers and doctors, they speak proper English, most of them have plans for college. Danny is East Harlem; I worry he won't fit in.

After several weeks of Danny's constant pressure, however, I relent and ask our youth group leader, Reverend James, if he can make a second exception for someone who, like me, doesn't attend

Riverside on Sundays. When I tell him about Danny, he smiles and says to bring him along.

To my amazement, Danny fits in immediately. He's still his fun, energetic self, but suddenly he loses his diddy-bop, drops his slang, and discusses religion and other serious topics without joking.

Although Riverside Church stands squarely in the middle of the Columbia University community, it is also right on the border of Harlem. Of all the New York City churches I've visited, it's by far the most integrated, by race as well as by wealth. Even its youth minister, Howard James, is a Negro. For both me and Danny, Riverside is like a bridge between East Harlem and the other worlds we are maneuvering through. It's like a little oasis, not East Harlem, not Collegiate or the Upper East Side. It's a world between the worlds of poverty and wealth, black and white. It's a world in which I feel comfortable, a world in which I can relax and be myself.

Danny and Lisa take to each other immediately. They have the same bounding energy and an eagerness to do and try everything. Sometimes when I'm with them I feel pulled along in their wake like a dinghy tied to a briskly tacking sailboat. At Danny's and Lisa's insistence, the three of us join the youth group's drama productions and appear in everything from an original play about an atomic bomb holocaust to Gilbert and Sullivan's *Trial by Jury.* At Christmas, the Riverside youth prepare a play for the entire church called "The Journey of the Three Magi." Danny plays the Christmas Angel, stopping the show by sweeping onstage in a long, white robe, with a thin, gold-painted clothes hanger suspended as a halo over his head. Lisa is assigned the role of the long-suffering Virgin Mary. I play the part of the funny, fat third Magi, wearing a padded stomach under my kingly robes.

"I always knew you were Melchior," says Danny.

"I always knew you were a little angel," I reply.

"Your mama's little angel," retaliates Danny.

The Virgin Mary just looks at us, pondering our words of wisdom in her heart.

One Friday night in the spring, after I've been going to Riverside for seven or eight months, I have an intense discussion with a Seminary intern named Steve. It begins by my questioning how it can be that each Protestant denomination has such different beliefs about the nature of God. To some, He's stern and doesn't allow dancing or a glass of wine despite the fact that Jesus himself clearly had an occasional sip; to others He means people to enjoy life to the fullest, as long as they don't hurt others. To some, God gets actively involved in everyday life watching over every lily of the field, to still others, He practices a strictly hands-off policy, allowing people to get in and out of their own messes without assistance. I want to know which view of God is right. To my surprise Steve proposes that I'm not asking the right question, that it's more important to ask what my God is like. I ask what he means by *my* God, asserting that God doesn't change, He's God.

Steve says every individual has his own idea of God. I ask if he really thinks there are millions and millions of different gods. He says he's not suggesting there are many Gods. What he's saying is that there is one God who takes millions and millions of different shapes inside the hearts and minds of individual human beings.

Steve's concept of an ever-changing, never-changing God is hard to accept, yet it seems right. I've heard enough sermons from enough different ministers and been in enough Sunday school classes and Bible study discussions to know that each person does have a different idea of what God is like. I should stop trying to figure out who or what God is and ask, instead, who or what He is for me.

Danny, never one for uncertain opinions, asserts that Steve is right, absolutely right. I ask if he honestly believes that God changes Himself all up and becomes whatever anybody wants Him to become. Danny replies that he didn't say all that. God is Himself no matter what anybody thinks. He doesn't change. But each person comes up with his own idea of God.

"So is He one thing or many things?" I ask impatiently, peeved that Danny doesn't seem to be having any difficulty with Steve's mind-boggling concept.

"Both," says Danny after short consideration.

"He can't be both. They contradict each other."

"No they don't. It's like growing up. When you're little you think your moms is the whole world. She knows everything, takes care of everything. Then you grow up. You see she's got her own problems. She's afraid, lonely, everything else. She hasn't changed. She's still the same old moms she always was. But for you she's changed. You see her different. Just like God, forever changing, forever the same."

I look at Danny, amazed.

"But you know, it's not God I have a problem with, it's church people. They can be gossipy like you can't believe, talk what they don't know behind your back."

"Is that why I don't see you in church anymore?" I ask, trying to imagine what gossipy things are being said behind Danny's back and who might be saying them.

"That and I got better things to do Sundays," he says.

CHAPTER 12

The summer between ninth and tenth grade, the summer I turn fifteen, Lisa and I go to the Virgin Islands for six weeks on a volunteer summer work project with Reverend James and ten other kids from Riverside. Lisa and I are now a couple. The feared Columbia freshman has long since been told by Lisa that she's no longer interested.

Every morning we hold Bible study before setting off to fix up and paint one of the local churches damaged in a hurricane. My religious certainty is growing shakier and shakier. Sometimes I'm no longer sure if I believe anything at all. I'm more and more distressed with a God who lets so much suffering persist in the world. And I'm growing certain that the Bible was written by people making up stories to explain the world around them, that the New

Testament specifically is one long attempt by the followers of Jesus many years after his death to justify their belief in his divinity. In reality he was just an exceptional man, a great prophet, but not God. Finally, I'm put off by churches and church people, who as Danny saw before I did, are often narrow-minded first-stone throwers. If church people aren't going to dedicate themselves to becoming better Christians, why do they bother going to church? Deciding what not to believe, however, is easier than figuring out what to believe. Inside I still feel religious and close to Jesus. I'm not rejecting Jesus, rather I'm questioning God.

One evening before bedtime, I write a long letter overflowing with religious conflicts to my father. At the end of the letter, I ask Dad to write back and tell me what he, himself, believes about two things. First, does he think God cares whether or not people convert to Christianity? If He does care, I'd like to know why and what happens to all the good non-Christians in the world. I refuse to believe they will burn in hell for all eternity. Second, I want to know what he believes happens to people after they die, whether he thinks that heaven and hell are real places or symbolic ideas, and if they are just symbolic ideas, what does happen to people when they die; do they simply turn to dust and ashes and that's it, gone forever?

Each day at mail call I look for Dad's reply. After three weeks with no answer, I realize he's not going to write back. I reached out to him, asked for help, and he ignored my plea. He could have written whatever he wanted, something, anything.

Meanwhile, in Bible study with Reverend James and the other kids, I become more and more antichurch. I can feel myself hardening against church people, the Bible, Christianity, against God. Like Dad, God hasn't answered. Not only does He continue to let racism and suffering reign in the world but He has let me down. He hasn't returned my call.

At the end of the summer, Dad picks me up at the Bangor bus station, where I arrive to join the rest of the family for ten days in Maine. In the car driving back to Sorrento, he says something about having received my letter filled with interesting questions. I turn my head to look out the window, anxious about what he might say next. But that's it. Apparently, mentioning his receipt of my letter seems enough to him, and he begins telling me about the fine weather they've enjoyed during their first three weeks in Maine and about the clams he, Peggy, and Andy dug up this morning for us to enjoy before dinner. Riding in the car with Dad, I feel completely alone.

Maybe because of Dad's not answering my letter and God's not answering my call, or maybe just because I'm getting older and beginning to question a lot of things, I'm now certain I no longer want to become a minister. I can't preach the Gospel when I no longer believe in it and am not even sure I believe in God. I can't lead others in worship when I find it more and more difficult to pray on cue or to recite passages like the Nicene Creed filled with dubious assertions about Jesus descending into hell and on the third day rising from the dead. I have no patience for sermons, prayers, or hymns so filled with Jesus they seem to exclude from God's grace all Jews, Moslems, Hindus, and Buddhists, not to mention agnostics and atheists.

Inspired by the stirring words of John Kennedy, I begin to envision a larger field of battle for myself, much larger than a church or a parish. The ministry is a safe calling for those not determined to take center stage in the drama of human history. For sixteen years Dad and the other members of the Group Ministry have labored long and hard in East Harlem, with little to show for it. Even Dad admits there are more junkies, worse schools, more poverty now than there were back in 1948, when the Parish started. What poor people need are jobs, education, and housing, not praying, preaching, and proselytizing. Instead of becoming a minister, I will become a political leader. I'll help build a forceful grassroots movement that will end poverty, racism, and inequality, a democratic uprising that will summon forth the best in all people, no matter what the color of their skin.

I'm white, but I live in a Negro and Puerto Rican community. I've experienced something of what it's like to be poor; I live in a public housing project, pass winos and junkies every day on the street, understand what it is to be an object of hate because of the color of my skin. At the same time, I attend school with the sons of the rich and the powerful. I can talk their language, move comfortably in their circles, help them understand why it's in their own best interest to end poverty, defeat racism, and create educational and economic opportunity. I can be a bridge between white and black, rich and poor, the powerful and the powerless. I have found my calling in my own way, on my own time, without God's assistance.

In the fall, just as I'm about to begin tenth grade, Johnny leaves for Harvard. His absence both at home and at Collegiate makes me feel more on my own than ever. Before we moved to East Harlem, he had been my wise, protective older brother, and I thought he could do just about everything better than I could, which he probably could. Best of all, he took me places. We went to the Nemo on 110th Street for the double feature on Saturday mornings and rode the subway to Yankee Stadium for doubleheaders on Sunday afternoons. We played in Riverside Park, visited Grant's Tomb, and shopped at Grable's for candy and baseball cards. His presence gave me the courage to caddy at the Sorrento golf course, where the local Maine boys could be pretty wild, and comforted me during our first weeks away at camp even though we were in different cabins. When we moved to East Harlem, he was my protection, walking with me to the bus stop, watching out for me. His presence helped me feel that my whole life wasn't uprooted, that some things were still the same in this strange new land. Even after Danny became my East Harlem mentor, I still looked to Johnny for insights into the adult world. I still felt close to him. We know each other so well we can communicate with a smile, a glance, a raised eyebrow. Now, with two hundred miles between us, it's like a part of me has broken off and floated away.

At Collegiate, I am no longer "little Webber," Johnny's younger brother. Teachers no longer ask why I'm not getting the grades Johnny is getting. Johnny was elected to the Cum Laude Society, and last year he was voted Head Boy, an honor bestowed by the faculty on that senior who best embodies Collegiate's values of high academic standards, character, and school spirit. Although I'm envious of Johnny's school success, I'm not exactly jealous of him. I'm proud for him and of him, proud that he's my older brother. I do sometimes wish I had a brain like his or a voice like his, but most of all I wish I could summon his presence at night. I wish I could ask him about things the way I used to, lying on the bottom bunk watching the weight of his body shape the springs and mattress above me.

The same week that Johnny leaves for Harvard, James Meredith attempts to become the first Negro to enter the University of Mississippi. As all the reporters comment, if Ole Miss falls it wouldn't be long before the entire South is integrated. At first, Governor Ross Barnett blocks Meredith's entrance, just as Governor Faubus blocked the entrance of the nine Negro students to Central High School in Little Rock years before. This time, however, Attorney General Robert Kennedy, the president's younger brother, immediately sends in the federal troops to quell the campus riots and orders his own assistants to escort Meredith to class. It's been more than eight years since *Brown v. Board of Education* declared that segregated schools are unconstitutional, and still schools are segregated just about everywhere. Dad says Kennedy is hesitant to push integration too quickly for fear it might cause the Democrats to lose seats in Congress in the coming elections and place his own 1964 presidential election in jeopardy. If Kennedy's being cautious for this reason, I think it's a disgrace. A real leader, like the one I intend to become, would mold public opinion, not bow to it.

Then in October, with thousands of federal troops still on the Ole Miss campus, President Kennedy speaks to the nation on television and tells us that the Soviet Union has placed nuclear weapons with the capability of hitting anywhere in the Western Hemisphere on the island of Cuba. He announces a quarantine of all boats and planes going into Cuba and makes clear that any use of the missiles anywhere will be considered a direct attack upon the United States by the Soviet Union. During the President's speech, Mom and Dad are silent. When Kennedy finishes, Peggy, now in seventh grade, asks if this means there's going to be a war. Dad says no, that there will be no war; even Khrushchev isn't crazy enough to start a nuclear nightmare. But I'm not so sure. I remember the small, fat, bald Soviet leader at the United Nations a few years ago, how he yelled, threatened, and banged his shoe on the table just like a crazy man.

That night I talk with Lisa on the phone, and she says her mother is so worried she has them packing suitcases so they can split on a second's notice if it looks like war's about to start. Everyone says if the Soviets strike, New York will be one of the prime targets, right after Washington, D.C. Lisa's mother plans to escape to a small summer cottage they own in western Massachusetts. Dad and Mom make no such plans. Dad says that in a full-out nuclear war there will be no place safe from nuclear fallout, and besides, our Maine cabin has no heat and it's late October.

Despite Lisa's mother's growing concern, and occasional hysterical comments about the coming war and Kennedy's incompetence from some of the students at Collegiate, I am strangely unworried, and my life proceeds pretty much as usual. It all seems so unreal, like back in elementary school when we practiced crawling under our desks during fake air raids, more like a game than like real life.

Then, in barely a week, it's over. Khrushchev backs down, and the Russians start to dismantle their Cuban missile bases. The negative comments at Collegiate fade away, and even Lisa's mother's fears are soon forgotten.

After spending last summer together on St. Thomas, Lisa and I are closer than ever. Every night we talk on the phone, often about the future and what it will be like when we get married and have children. On Friday nights I see her at Riverside, and we spend all day Saturday together. In the morning I try to intercept her on the way to Hunter High School on 68th and Lexington, waiting for her at the bus stop on Lexington and 96th Street, where she changes buses after coming across town. Mom says we see each other so much we might as well be husband and wife, and she worries out loud that I'm too young to be talking of getting married and having children. I think what's really bothering her is how soon it will before I, too, leave for college.

When not with Lisa, I spend my time playing football and getting ready for basketball season. On the football team I play split end and defensive halfback. Though I'm quick and have good hands, because of my small size—five-ten, 137—I play only in a couple of games at the end, well after the outcome has been conclusively determined. Basketball is a different story. I'm the only sophomore to make the starting five, and within a few weeks I am clearly established as the team's floor leader. After watching me during one game late in the season, our football coach takes me aside and tells me that he has decided to make me next year's starting quarterback, that I have the leadership skills our football team needs. He has no trouble getting me to agree to participate in an isometric exercise and diet program over the summer in order to build up my muscles, increase my weight, and strengthen my throwing arm.

As for my academics, I'm doing just so-so. I get good grades in history and English, only fair ones in mathematics, science, and French. My teachers think that I don't study hard enough, which I probably don't. At the same time, I know my mind isn't a quick one, like Johnny's or Peggy's. It's not easy for me to memorize mathematical formulas, scientific definitions, or French vocabulary. There are certain English words I have to look up over and over again, tricky words like *truly* and *sense* that can't be figured out by how they sound. I know I'm smart; I'm just not school smart like some of my classmates. I think a little differently, have my own ideas about things. And I'm good with people. I'm able to read them, tell what they're like; this comes from living in East Harlem, where studying on people is a survival skill.

Occasionally I run into Samuel on the street. We stop and talk, saying we'll do something together soon, but we never do. Then one Saturday he calls and invites me to go with him and his grandmother to church the next day for Fellowship Sunday.

Samuel's church is like no other church I've ever been to. We arrive ten minutes early, and the church is already full even though it isn't Easter or Mother's Day, only Fellowship Sunday. While everybody has their eyes closed during the first prayer, I sneak a peek and see nothing but rows and rows of people with their heads and hats bowed low, praying to Jesus. Although I'm the sole white person in church, I feel welcome. When Samuel introduces me during the service, the entire congregation shouts greetings and the women wave their handkerchiefs. Apparently they know my father, or have heard of him, and I am welcomed doubly as his son. At the end of a moving rendition of "Precious Lord, Take My Hand" sung by the choir soloist, the church erupts into Thank you, Jesuses and loud applause, and I applaud right along with them. I've often felt moved to clap in church, but it was never allowed. Mom says it would disturb the proper mood of worship and contemplation. I find it thrilling how, right during the sermon, the choir songs, and even the prayers the congregation shouts back their encouragement, praise, agreement, thanks.

On our way home Samuel and I get into a discussion about the service, and it turns out I liked it better than he did. He says he's embarrassed by all the shouting and carrying on. I argue that it's great, that it makes you feel people are happy to be in church.

"They sure are happy," says Samuel.

Two or three months later, returning from school, I meet Junie coming out of Woolworth's on 106th. Junie seems older. He's dropped out of high school and is working as a delivery boy at a supermarket on 83rd Street, apparently no longer hesitant to venture south of 96th. With pride, he tells me how he used his first paycheck to buy his family a Thanksgiving turkey, stuffing, sweet potatoes, cranberry sauce, pumpkin pie, the whole traditional American dinner. He even made them all sit down together at the table and eat at the same time.

"No *bacalao*?" I ask.

"No way. I did let Mom make her holiday *pasteles*, but that was it."

"Not even rice and beans?" I ask.

"No. I wanted us all to eat sweet potatoes, Tommy, sweet potatoes."

Before we part, Junie asks if I've heard the news about Samuel. I tell him no, and he says that he doesn't know for sure but the word is that his grandmother died and he's gone somewhere down south to live with relatives.

As soon as I get home, I call Samuel. A recorded voice tells me the number I've dialed has been disconnected. And just like that, Samuel disappears from my life. I think of him often, dressed in his Sunday best studying the gorilla scene at the Natural History Museum, and I pray that wherever he's now living is more like Grandma's sunny down south than like his own vision of the South with the KKK and another lynching every day.

Every Easter Sunday morning as we've done since I can remember, even before we moved to East Harlem, my entire family attends the Parish's sunrise service, held on the banks of the East River. We rise early, before the sun is up, and walk together to the flagpole in the middle of East River Houses, where we meet up with the congregations and ministers of all four East Harlem Protestant Parish churches. What I like most about Easter Dawn Service is that all the old familiar faces are there, not just the members of the Group Ministry and their families, but my favorite parishioners: the elders of one church or the other, the folks who help Dad run the Parish, Mom run the Reading Program, Bruce run the Narcotics Committee, Libby lead the church services, and Ted organize the choir. They are the old heads, the laypeople who organize things, make sure things are done right; the guides and mentors who watch over and instruct the Parish children, including the sons and daughters of the Group Ministry. The ones I like are the opposite of those other, gossipy church people, the holier-than-thou ones, the ones who talk what they don't know behind your back.

This morning I look for Danny, even though I know he probably won't show. He hasn't been at a sunrise service in two or three years.

The first person to greet us is Ramón Díaz. Ramón has been a member of the Parish from day one, helping Dad and the other ministers turn a fighting gang on 100th Street into a social club called the Puritans. Now he has his own office on the third floor of the Parish Office building, above the Reading Program. From there he dispenses wisdom and counsel free of charge. Dad says Ramón knows more about family court, housing court, welfare regulations, detox programs, and job opportunities than any man alive. Whenever anyone comes by one of the churches or the Parish Office looking for emergency assistance, they just send him up to see Ramón. Ramón once told me that most poor people don't want to be given something for nothing. They'd rather be shown how to get what they need for themselves. Most come looking for information, not handouts. It was Ramón who insisted that rather than give away the cartons and cartons of children's clothing and toys donated to the Parish each year at Christmastime, we should ask folks to pay a dime or a quarter for each item; that way they could feel proud to have paid for their family's Christmas presents.

In the growing crowd I spot Chassie Ortiz. She smiles and waves to us even though she must be over eighty and can hardly stand without leaning on her cane. Chassie never misses a sunrise service. She can be stern and disapproving, but she also has a sly sense of humor and an intense concern for anyone who seeks her help. Young and old turn to her for advice, and she gives it without hesitation. A few months ago, I walked her home from a late afternoon church function and she talked my ear off the entire way about the growing antiwhite sentiment in parts of the Negro community. She was particularly incensed that anyone would suggest white people should get out of Harlem and East Harlem, and go back to their own communities and deal with the racism there. Although I hadn't heard any such talk, she seemed intent on laying my mind at rest just in case I had. What are they talking about, their own communities? asked Chassie indignantly. White folks have as much right as anyone else to live and work in East Harlem. No one owns East Harlem, Tommy, and don't let anyone ever tell you different. East Harlem is free and open to everyone, just like America.

After everyone has gathered, including the senior youth chosen to carry the four church banners and Blake Hobbs with three of his trumpet students, Bruce Thomas leads us in prayer. I find myself standing beside Rhonda Edwards, and after our amens she flashes me one of her youthful smiles. Rhonda sings in the choir with me and is Mom's assistant at the Reading Program. Of all the Ascension church leaders, Rhonda is the most hip, and I often talk with her during rest periods at choir practice. Once when I mentioned something to her about how St. Paul is pretty tough on women, she shared with me her opinion that St. Paul had a problem and that to her way of thinking two clean sheets can't smut. She said religion is meant to lift us up, not make life harder than it already is. God has given us life and He intends us to enjoy it. Drinking, dancing, sex are not sins unless they're used in ways that hurt people. Besides, how does St. Paul know anything about women? He never married.

"Neither did Jesus," I reminded her.

"That's true," said Rhonda. "But you don't find Jesus carrying on against sex. He kept out of what he didn't know."

After Bruce's prayer we process in silence like the two Marys, through the projects and then up and across the Wards Island footbridge. Once on Wards Island we gather in a circle around the tomb site at the water's edge, and I look at all the familiar faces. At Ted Ward, our choir director, who taught me how to raise a joyful noise unto the Lord. At Carlos Ríos, the Parish's first lay minister, now a city councilman, who told me that the first rule of life, and of politics, is always to repay a favor. At Leonard Answick, my old

Sunday school teacher, more bent over than ever, who believes with all his heart that those who believe on the Lord do not die but merely pass on over to the other side.

Libby's short sermon is about forgiveness and rebirth and how blessed are the people who can believe in Christ's resurrection without having to put their hands in his bloody side like Doubting Thomas. Libby leads us in more *Aleluya*s than Aleluya Santiago used to when he was on a mighty roll. But her *Aleluya*s are a little thin, nothing like the soul-wrenching *Aleluya*s of the master. I wonder what ever happened to Mr. Santiago and his family. I wonder what happened to beautiful Evelyn, if she still wears a red ribbon in her jet-black hair.

When the service at the gravesite is over, we march back over the footbridge singing. In the old days, Danny and I would bellow at the top of our lungs from the middle of the bridge, each of us striving mightily to out-*Aleluya* the other. Danny figured out that to score heavily you had to shout out the first or last syllable, *ah*. If you got stuck on the *lu* part, as do many of the Puerto Rican street preachers, you had little chance of trumpeting a mighty sound. *AAA-le-lu-YAAA!* Up in front, Mr. Hobbs and his trumpeters would be blowing away; between their trumpet blasts and Danny's and my *Aleluya*s, we raised more than Jesus each Easter morning.

Today, walking back up and across the bridge without Danny, I think about all the other people I have met in East Harlem: about my old neighbors Mrs. Johnson, Mrs. Nicholson, Lee, Robert, and Sonny. About my friends from the courts: William, who taught me to dribble; Junie who taught me to curse in Spanish and pour out a sip of soda for my dead ancestors; Mr. Levy, who told me about the old days back before drugs and gangs when everyone looked out for each other and for each other's children. About Fito, who introduced me to *plátanos;* and Aida, who taught me to dance salsa. About Samuel now down south. And, most of all, about Danny. What would my life be like without Danny?

I decide that Mr. Levy was wrong. East Harlem is not different now than it was back in the days when the Third Avenue El brought all passengers up to El Barrio. East Harlem might have more drugs and gangs than it used to, but it is still filled with wonderful people, old heads and young heads, living as best they can and taking it upon themselves, with no thought of reward, to watch over and instruct the young, even if he's a Doubting Thomas, the second son of one of their parish ministers.

CHAPTER 13

It is still dark on the morning of Saturday, August 28, 1963, as we gather on the sidewalk in front of Ascension. The Parish has chartered four buses to carry us to the March on Washington for Jobs and Freedom organized by Martin Luther King and a broad coalition of Civil Rights leaders. I've never seen El Barrio so full of people this early on a Saturday morning. Usually the streets are quiet and empty as all of East Harlem sleeps off the effects of Friday night partying. This morning the neighborhood is jumping.

Danny is already there, waiting for me. Rather than risk not waking on time, he never went to sleep at all. We greet each other full of excitement. My only regret is that Lisa isn't coming; her mother, fearing violence, won't let her.

On the way to Washington, we're too excited to sleep. Riding south, we sing a mixture of old spirituals and freedom songs: "Go Down, Moses," "Oh, Freedom," "This Little Light of Mine."

In the absence of Reverend Ted, who's on one of the other buses, Danny is quick to assume the role of choir director. He stands in the front and conducts each song, shouting out the words in advance. Soon we're all swaying and carrying on in our seats. As we enter the city, we pass through a succession of Negro neighborhoods. People of all ages, sizes, and descriptions line the sidewalks, smiling, shouting encouragement, and waving handkerchiefs. I feel like a member of the Allied forces entering Paris at the end of World War II.

The March begins around noon, and we process arm in arm down the famous streets of our nation's capital: Pennsylvania Avenue, 17th Street, Constitution Avenue. Mom and Dad walk with Peggy. I walk with Danny. Holding hands in unity, it feels almost like old times, as if our small band of demonstrators marching outside of Woolworth's has multiplied into an army of untold thousands, as if one and one and fifty do make a million.

> *Black and white together. Black and white together. Black and white together, now.*
> *Deep in my heart, I do believe, black and white together now.*

When we pass the White House, Mom remarks how wonderful it would be if President Kennedy came and spoke. Dad says he won't be here, that the president is scheduled to meet with the March organizers later at the White House. I think to myself that once again President Kennedy is missing an opportunity to use his power and influence to speak boldly and dramatically in favor of Civil Rights. Though I'm drawn to President Kennedy, to his eloquence and sense of humor, I feel let down by his failure to become a great advocate for the poor and the oppressed. It seems that only Negro leaders speak boldly, put themselves on the line. Where are the white leaders willing to stand up and be counted?

At the Lincoln Memorial, Danny and I separate from the Parish group and squeeze our way down as close as possible to the speakers' platform. People are crammed in right up to the steps of the Memorial. Behind us, the crowd extends down and around the Reflecting Pool all the way to the Washington Monument. So many people are pressed so close together, there's no room to sit down.

Standing together, we listen to speech after speech from the leaders of the Civil Rights movement: A. Philip Randolph, James Farmer, Roy Wilkins. Between the speeches, Marian Anderson sings "He's Got the Whole World in His Hands," and Mahalia Jackson moves the crowd with "I've Been 'Buked and I've Been Scorned."

The last speech of the day is delivered by Martin Luther King, Jr., and as Danny declares triumphantly, it's a smoker.

> I have a dream that one day, down in Alabama with its vicious racists, with its governor having his lips dripping with the words of interposition and nullification, that one day, right there in Alabama, little black boys and black girls will be able to join hands with little white boys and white girls as sisters and brothers. I have a dream today!

Upon hearing these lines, a tight circle of four or five young men standing next to us whoop and holler and slap each other five. They then turn and include us in their celebration, slapping five all around. We are proud of Dr. King, proud he's our leader, proud he speaks with such power and moral authority, proud he doesn't talk down to us. Whether any of the others know what interposition and nullification are, I'm not sure. I know I don't.

On the way home, as Danny falls asleep on the seat next to me, I think about the day, about Danny and the other people on the bus, about how close I feel to them. I wonder if their anger at slavery, lynchings, and segregation ever slips over into hate toward white people. How could it not? Yet on this day, we are black and white together. We are united in the hope that, as Dr. King said, it is not too late for America to make good on its promise that all men, yes, black men as well as white men, would be guaranted the inalienable rights of life, liberty, and the pursuit of happiness. To create a country where justice will roll down like waters and righteousness like a mighty stream.

The next week during choir practice I happen to be sitting beside one of the church elders named Joe Gray, and I ask him how he liked the March. Joe is a short, solidly built, serious man who sings bass and rarely smiles. Trying to get him to show some enthusiasm, I rave about how great the March was with all the people, half a million plus. Though Joe agrees that the March was impressive, he says that marching is the easy part, finding people jobs is the hard part.

"Did you ever wonder," he asks, "why the government is so happy to let us march? Why they even encourage us?"

"Why?"

"Marching lets the steam out easy without any noise or disruption. It makes people feel like something's happened, that things have changed when, in reality, they haven't. But it only works so long. After a while people get tired of marching."

"What happens then?"

"Sooner or later if there are no jobs coming, people explode."

"Like a raisin in the sun?" I ask.

"Raisins in the sun don't explode," says Joe, "they dry up. Whoever gave you that idea?"

* * *

A few weeks after the March, Lisa leaves for Smith College and I face life without her for the first time in nearly two years. One Saturday morning, knowing that I'm down, Danny suggests that we go see *Seven Brides for Seven Brothers* playing at Loew's. He's heard it contains some outa-sight dancing and he's dying to see it. Insisting that a movie aint hardly a movie without popcorn, Danny buys us both popcorn and Cokes even though I've just eaten lunch and he's barely an hour from finishing breakfast. Loaded with food and drink, we settle into our seats down front. We've gotten into the habit of sitting close up to the screen so we can shut everything else out, feel like we're inside the movie.

As the lights dim and the movie is about to start, Danny reaches out and puts his hand on my thigh. He doesn't move his hand; he just keeps it there, still, waiting, on my thigh. For a moment I don't move either. I'm too stunned to do anything. Then I pick up his hand and return it to his side of our shared armrest.

During the movie I take in nothing. All I can think about is what Danny has done.

Walking home, we don't talk. Now that he's spoken, Danny's waiting for me to speak. But I don't. I don't know what to say. When we arrive at my building, he mumbles something about visiting his sister in the Bronx and we part.

For the rest of the afternoon and into the evening, half of me wants to call Danny and tell him everything's all right, to pretend that nothing has changed, that we can go on the same as before. The other half of me never wants to see him again. I can't believe he wants to be friends in that way. My shame and confusion is Danny's fault. He's to blame. He's the one who's gone and changed everything.

As I think about Danny, I realize that everyone else probably knows. Only I have been denying it, ignoring all the "signs"—his tight pants, his love of dance and show business, his lack of interest in sports and girls—in the hope that if I don't acknowledge them, they'll disappear. Reverend James, my parents, the church people, have known all along. It's taken Danny, Danny himself, to shake me awake and make me deal with the truth.

At Collegiate, my friends and I think we're very sophisticated about homos. We know all about them. They come in three types. Most conspicuous are the men who dress up as women and cruise 42nd Street looking for sailors or other lonely men horny enough to go along with their game. These homosexuals are repulsive, fascinating creatures, but if you're careful not to show any interest they let you alone. Then there are the older men who live alone, never marry, and often teach at all-boys' schools like Collegiate. Generally effeminate and a little fussy, these men are basically harmless and too worried about losing their jobs ever to make a play for one of us. Finally, there are the degenerate, lurking homos called pedophiles, perverts in long coats who try to rub up against you in the subway or who offer you a ride home while you're waiting alone at the bus stop. These are the dangerous homosexuals, who lure young boys into their cars or up to their apartments.

Danny doesn't fit any of these types. He's never shown any desire to dress like a girl, look like a girl, be a girl. He's strong. He lets everybody know they'd better not mess with him, or me, and the last thing he wants to do is teach at an all-boys' school. He does walk a little funny when he's not diddy-bopping, sort of gliding on his long legs and swinging his long arms, but a lot of people walk funny. I know he likes dancing, and he has a good friend, Miguel, who makes no effort to hide his homosexuality. But liking to dance and having a homosexual friend don't necessarily mean *you're* a homosexual. After all, look who my best friend is.

On Friday night I'm relieved when Danny doesn't show at Riverside. I'm not ready to see him. I don't know yet what I'd say to him. Nor does he appear the following Friday or the Friday after that, and I begin to worry about what he might be going through himself. When Reverend James asks me what's happened to Danny, I tell him that Danny's busy Friday nights for a while but he'll be back.

With Lisa away at college and Danny suddenly absent from my life, loneliness envelops me like a cold, steady drizzle. On weekends I wander aimlessly around downtown New York amidst the crowds and skyscrapers. I stroll for hours on Fifth Avenue, across 59th Street, up and down Broadway. I find comfort in the milling people of all races and ethnicities, in the anonymity of being just one unknown face in a bustling crowd, everyone going his own way on his own business. No one notices me or questions what I am doing here. No one hassles me, worries about me, reports on me back to my parents. Sometimes I watch the skaters in Rockefeller Center, then enter St. Patrick's Cathedral and sit quietly in the back. I feel out of place not being Catholic, not crossing myself in front of the altar as do many of the other visitors. At the same time I derive a strange comfort from the soaring spaciousness of the nave, the tinted light cascading through the stained-glass windows, and the general feeling that God is present, that if He listens to prayers anywhere, He listens to them here. Oh, God, I pray, let Danny be all right. Let our friendship be all right.

At school, I throw myself into my studies and extracurricular activities. Football practice and games take up every afternoon and Saturday mornings. I sing in the Glee Club and take voice lessons with our Glee Club Director. In the evenings I study hard and try not to think of Lisa and Danny. Occasionally I talk with Lisa on the phone, but it does little to fill up my emptiness and I don't tell her about Danny. I'd feel funny talking to other people about him before I talk to him myself. Besides, if he wants other people to know, it's up to him to tell them.

In October, on a weekend I don't have a football game, I visit Lisa at Smith and we double-date with her roommate and her roommate's boyfriend, who attends Amherst. The four of us go to an Amherst football game and then to a dance with a live band. Although everyone is nice to me, I feel like an impostor. Who am I kidding? I'm a junior in high school while the Amherst boyfriend is a junior in college. Lisa's living in a world that I'm not part of. She's dealing with different issues and pressures. She explains how hard weekends are for her, how the entire dorm empties on Fridays and Saturdays as all of Smith travels to Williams, Amherst, or Yale. When I agree that she should feel free to date other guys, my heart grows numb.

A month or so later, I receive a long letter from Lisa telling me about a blind date at Dartmouth. She writes of sitting in the back-seat of a car while her date kissed her. Although she didn't kiss him back, she did nothing to stop his kissing. As I read the letter, my stomach tightens. I don't want Lisa sitting all alone in her dorm room every Friday and Saturday night, but I don't want her sitting in the backseat of a car being kissed by a strange boy either. As I reread her letter, I feel myself harden against Lisa. It's frightening that love can drain out of me just as quickly as it filled me up. I'm angry at her for needing to go on dates without me, for getting into the car in the first place, for letting that boy kiss her. I write back explaining that I can't handle seeing her only every other month, that I'm uncomfortable dating other girls while she dates other boys. I suggest we break up for a while, see how we feel after two or three months. I say nothing about being haunted by the picture of her being kissed by Mr. Dartmouth.

Lisa calls the day she receives my letter. She doesn't try to talk me out of breaking up. She simply says she believes things can work out if we love each other. Then she asks if I still love her. In the background, I can hear the shouts, whoops, and laughter of life in her college dorm. I answer that I don't know, that I'm not sure.

"I'm sure," she says. "If we could only see each other, talk."

I say, "I'm sorry," and then say good-bye before she can do any more talking.

After I break up with Lisa, the void left by Danny's absence grows larger. No matter what I'm doing, I can't stop thinking about him. I want to ask him if he falls in love with a boy the same way I fall in love with a girl, or if it's different. I want to know what he thinks about having children, if being a homosexual means he will never get married, never have a family. I can't imagine never having children, never showing them how to sink a foul shot or strum a guitar. I want to ask him. I want to understand. But I'm also scared I'll discover that Danny is not the Danny I know but some strange person who dreams of having sex with other boys: a homo, a pervert. Maybe he doesn't even like me. Maybe he just wants to have sex with me. Maybe he has no interest in being friends if it's just friends.

In my quest for answers, I read *Giovanni's Room*. Until Danny put his hand on my thigh, I had avoided reading James Baldwin's novel about two male lovers in Paris, and I'm amazed to learn that in this book Baldwin writes from the perspective of a white man. The story, however, depresses me. Although the hero sleeps with girls, it's clearly other boys like Giovanni who most excite him. If Danny's like James Baldwin, or at least like his main character, he's deeply, fundamentally homosexual.

Despite my continuing questions about Danny, I don't talk about him with anybody. I'd feel uncomfortable going to either Mom or Dad. We don't discuss private personal matters at home; it's just not what we do. I've never talked with either of them

229

about sex of any kind, how can I talk with them about homosexuality? I might try talking to Mom if I knew she wouldn't worry about me, as she always does, and try to make me feel better. I don't want to feel better, I want to understand. I wish Johnny was still home, still sleeping in the bunk above me, sharing with me his older brother wisdom. But even he might not be able to help me with this one.

"Kennedy's been shot! Kennedy's been shot!" A seventh-grader runs down the hall outside my French class shouting the news.

At first, none of us believes it, we're all in shock. Then, moments later, our Upper School Director comes in and solemnly tells us it's true: not only has President Kennedy been shot in Dallas, Texas, but he's been pronounced dead. All classes and after-school activities are canceled. We're to go directly home. On my way out of school, I overhear one lower-school boy say to another, "I'm glad. I'm a Republican."

I head up to Riverside as I now do every Friday after school. I want to be with kids who will be upset and wounded the way I am, not with white, rich Republicans. I call home and tell Mom my plans. She understands.

Our usual Friday night program is replaced with a memorial service for our dead president, including prayers for Jackie, Caroline, and little John-John. In the small tenth floor chapel, Reverend James leads us in silent prayers interspersed with hymns, poems, and Scripture readings on the meaning of death. In the moments of quiet I vow to myself, to God, and to the spirit of John Kennedy to redouble my commitment to enter politics. I vow to work to achieve President Kennedy's goal of solving the problems of war and peace, poverty and plenty.

Reverend James is midway through the service when I hear a

noise in the back. I turn in my pew and see Danny enter the chapel and take a seat by himself near the door. Not wanting to catch his eye, I quickly look forward. I can concentrate neither on the passages being read nor on my thoughts about President Kennedy and my political future. After many long minutes I rise, walk to the back, and sit down in the empty seat next to Danny. I put my arms around him and we hug. Danny begins to sob. He cries quietly, without sound, his whole body shakes.

Following the service, Danny and I wait together on Riverside Drive to catch the Number 4 bus back to East Harlem. I tell him I'm glad he came. He says he had nowhere else to go. When I ask where he's been, he studies the sidewalk then says, Busy. Working up my courage to say what's really on my mind, I tell Danny that I broke up with Lisa. He asks what happened, if she got another boyfriend. I tell him that it was nothing like that, it was more like I couldn't handle her being in college. Danny chews on this piece of information, then says that people grow apart sometimes, that's how life is.

"Danny, I want you to know that—"

"Don't say it," he pleads. "Don't say anything."

"I have to. You're my very best friend in all the world, I just don't . . . I can't."

"I know."

"Do you understand?"

"Do *you* understand?"

Now we both study the sidewalk. I can hear the wind off the Hudson River blowing in the trees of Riverside Park.

"I understand you're you and I'm me," I say. "That's all I know. That and that you're my best friend."

"We're like brothers," says Danny.

"Yeah. Like brothers."

Again there's a silence between us before I say, "Today, as soon as I heard, as soon as it began to sink in, I wanted to talk with you, be with you."

"Me too," he says. "It's so terrible. I saw him last night on television, playing with Caroline. Then, bang, bang, he's dead."

"Remember when you shook his hand?"

"I was remembering that today. Who do you supposed killed him?"

"Some crazy."

"Probably some commie angry at how he stood up to Khrushchev."

"Crazy people don't always have reasons."

"No," says Danny. "Just a gun."

The bus ride home is crowded but strangely quiet. Danny and I have to separate in order to find seats. As we enter Harlem, the young black man in the seat next to me removes a knife tucked into his belt beneath his sweater and secures it, blade up, inside his sock, hidden under his right pants leg. At the sight of the weapon, I rise from my seat in order to put some distance between me and the knife.

Sensing my concern, the young man puts his hand on my arm and says, "Oh no, my man. The blade's not for you. It's just there to insure yours truly a safe walk home. There's gonna be some crazy shit out on the streets tonight."

In the weeks directly following President Kennedy's assassination, I decide not to play basketball this winter. Somehow after the March on Washington and Kennedy's death, dribbling a basketball up and down a court for hours on end has lost its appeal. I love basketball: the thrill of leading my team, of beating my man, of sinking a clutch shot with the game on the line. At the same time, when I think of all the hours I've spent over the years throwing a ball, it seems like such a big waste of time. And if I don't play basketball this winter, I can join the Drama Club, whose rehearsal time conflicts with basketball practice, and also have more time for my studies. It's our junior year and everyone in my class is thinking about college. Our college placement counselor has made it clear that only my grades stand between me and getting into my first choice. Getting into a good college seems a lot more important that shooting a ball at a round hoop.

When he learns of my plans to quit the basketball team, our Headmaster calls me down to his office for a private chat. Mr. Scott, a former coach himself, and very much into building up Collegiate's poor reputation in sports, is fit to be tied. Popping aspirins into his mouth and swallowing them without water, he berates me with a barrage of questions. How could I do this to my teammates, to my school, to him? Where is my loyalty? Just when we had a chance of becoming a winning basketball team for the first time in years, I have to quit on him. What am I thinking?

I explain how even if I kept at it I could never hope to play ball beyond college. How I want to concentrate on other things, especially my academics, so that I can get into my first-choice college. I remind him how often he himself cautions us to remember that academics come first. As I throw back his own words at him, I can see I have him on the ropes. Then he says something that surprises me. He asks what my father thinks of my decision. The truth is I haven't yet discussed my decision with Dad. In fact, I haven't told anybody other than my basketball coach, who must have spilled the news to Mr. Scott. I don't really know for sure what my father will think. My guess is that he'll regret my plans because of his own love of basketball but will staunchly support my right to make up my own mind. It hadn't occurred to me that Mr. Scott might stoop to calling my father and getting him to pressure me to change my mind. With this thought looming in the back of my head as a real possibility, I lie and tell Mr. Scott that Dad fully supports my position, that he believes at the age of sixteen I'm mature enough to make my own decisions.

Mr. Scott looks at me in silence for a moment, pops two additional aspirins into his mouth, and says, "Well, I guess that's that then. I'll be looking for that improvement in your grades next semester."

CHAPTER 14

Racing down the stairs on my way to buy some milk, I'm halfway between the fourth and third floors before I become aware of a teenager kneeling on the landing in front of me. He's so absorbed in what he's doing he hasn't heard me enter the stairwell. His pants belt is pulled tight around his upper left arm, and he holds a hypodermic needle in his right hand. A burnt bottle cap and a book of matches are discarded on the floor beside him. For a split second I flinch, hesitating in midair, then gravity and forward motion propel me down the stairs nearly on top of him. He jerks his head towards me, startled between fear and hunger, scared as shit. Before I know what I'm saying, I call out, "Good morning!" and catapult past, swerving by him just in time.

I'm almost to the ground floor when it hits me that the guy I've just seen is someone I know, maybe Rabbit, grown older, with a mustache. For a couple of years now I've been keeping an eye out for him, thinking I'd run into him on the street. After that ill-fated day, he never again showed up on the courts and never made it back to the Reading Program, where one afternoon Mom found his two books deposited in a paper bag on the stairs outside the door. Although I sometimes worry that he might have started using drugs, I try to convince myself that his love of books will somehow get him through. Now he could be overdosing right here on my own staircase. Slowly I turn and head back up the stairs.

I see immediately it's not Rabbit but a boy I know from Ascension named Victor, light skinned like Rabbit but with smaller ears. I see no sign of the needle, the matches, the bottle cap. "Hey, Victor." I sit on the stairs beside him. His eyes are closed. His head is propped against the wall. To myself I'm thinking that guys can overdose on drugs and maybe I should get him to the hospital or at least walk him around so he won't fall asleep and die on me.

"You okay?" I ask.

"Sure, fine," he says like I haven't just caught him aiming a long, ugly needle filled with heroin at his arm. "I come here to sit quiet, warm." His voice sounds far away, like the look in his eyes.

"You wanna come upstairs? Cool out in my bedroom for a while?"

He opens his eyes and looks at me. "Nah, I couldn't."

"You sure you're okay?"

"Yeah, I'm sure. I know what you're thinking, it's not like that. I aint a junkie. I only get high when I feel like it."

"You know Bruce Thomas? From the Parish? He runs a narcotics program. You know Reverend Thomas. He can help. We could go see him."

"For what? I'm in control, serious. I ride the horse, it don't ride me."

Not wanting to leave him here sleeping on the staircase, I ask if he'll walk me to the store. I know he's probably not telling me the truth about being in control. It's common knowledge that once a guy starts using a needle he's usually pretty much hooked.

"Okay, Tommy." Victor slowly rises to his feet, pushing me away as I reach out to help him up. "Can't stay inside all day."

We walk down the three flights of stairs and out onto the street. He doesn't weave, nod, stumble, or anything. Except for the glassy look in his eyes, I wouldn't notice anything different about him. He looks nothing like the most dangerous man on the streets. But then again, he isn't hungering for a fix. He's just had one.

On the street with Victor, I think again of Rabbit. I wonder if he's still sleeping on the roof, if he's graduated from high school, if he joined the air force and is off somewhere flying airplanes.

Outside the grocery store, Victor and I part. As I watch him walk down the street, I wonder where he hides the needle, how he keeps it from pricking him as he walks.

As my last year at Collegiate begins, I'm feeling pretty good about things, especially at school. I'm President of the Senior Class, President of the Drama and Glee Clubs, starting quarterback on the football team. My only ongoing worry is whether or not I'll get into Harvard. I visited Johnny there last spring, and after going to classes, walking around the famous yard, and writing a history paper in the Adams House library, I'm convinced it's the place for me. My major concern is that I'm not one of the top two or three academic students in my class, and this is the pool from which Harvard usually picks. Although my efforts to improve my grades last winter paid off, I still barely made it into the top third of my class. Now that my application is in, however, there's nothing I can do except wait until March 15th when all the acceptance and rejection letters go out.

When I'm not in school, life without a steady girlfriend is lonely. Since breaking up with Lisa I've gone out on a couple of dates with girls from Riverside, but the one or two girls I would most like to know better are already going steady. I keep hoping I'll find another girl to fall hard for, but she hasn't shown up yet. Sometimes I think of dropping by the García house and seeing how Aida is, maybe asking her out. I'm attracted to her, think she's gorgeous, yet something holds me back. For one thing, she's more than two years younger than I am and I'll be the one going off to college soon. For another thing, I worry that I'd be leading her on, that I'm attracted to her because of her beauty not because I enjoy doing things with her. I don't really know her all that well. What I do know is that if I ask her out, Fito and the whole family will think it's the first step toward our getting married.

One day I run into Gladys at the bus stop on 106th Street, and she tells me she's broken up with Tito. She explains that Tito has gotten too involved with the Dragons, hanging out with them all the time, fighting with the Viceroys and the other East Harlem gangs. She just couldn't take it anymore, being anxious about him, trying to get him to concentrate or their future together, not on fighting.

"Why do boys want to be in gangs?" she asks. "Why are they always fighting?"

"To feel safe on the streets," I reply, not really believing it myself. "To feel like they belong."

"Why did Tito need a gang to feel like he belonged?" she asks. "He had me."

I don't ask her, but I wonder if the real reason they split up is that she found out about Jessica from 111th Street.

Part of my duties as Senior Class President is to help organize the Upper School assemblies, held once a month on Wednesday mornings. Usually we invite a Collegiate parent or alumnus who is a famous performing artist or an expert on something like animal life in the Arctic or the architecture of Old New York. I have it in my head that at least once this year we should hear from someone black who will shake things up a little. My first choice is Adam Clayton Powell, Jr., the outspoken congressman who represents Harlem and East Harlem. I call his District Office, introduce myself as one of Congressman Powell's constituents, and ask to speak with him. The young woman who answers the phone informs me that the Congressman is out of the district, that I should write a letter outlining my kind request. Two weeks later, I receive a reply that Congressman Powell would be pleased to address the Collegiate Assembly scheduled for the third Wednesday in January and that his fee for speaking out of the District is one thousand dollars. When I show Congressman Powell's letter to our faculty advisor he says it's out of the question, the entire annual budget for assemblies is five hundred dollars and perhaps Congressman Powell is too controversial anyway. He suggests that in Powell's place we invite Congressman John Lindsay from the Upper East Side. One of the Collegiate mothers volunteers in his office and will surely be able to get him to speak, probably for free.

Striking out with Congressman Powell does not diminish my determination to find a black speaker for our Collegiate assembly. Dad suggests that I invite Dr. Kenneth Clark, the famous psychologist whose study of Negro children in the South was instrumental in convincing the Supreme Court that segregated schools can never be equal schools. This time, rather than calling, I pay an unannounced visit to Dr. Clark's office on 110th Street, where he helps run New Lincoln, an experimental interracial school. The

239

afternoon I visit, Dr. Clark takes me into his office filled with books and, while smoking cigarette after cigarette, talks to me from behind a huge desk scattered with papers. He seems amused at my unscheduled intrusion and agrees without hesitation to speak at Collegiate. Then he asks what he should talk about. I say it's really up to him, maybe something that will help us see what the world looks like from the perspective of black children in segregated public schools. He smiles and says he'll do his best.

The morning Dr. Clark speaks, I introduce him from the stage and then listen as he tells the Upper School students and faculty how his research with Negro children, how their play with black and white dolls convinced him that segregation had a negative impact upon their self-image. He adds that his work at New Lincoln has taught him the value of integration for white children as well; going to school with Negro classmates helps them to become more tolerant, better able to get along with people of all shades and ethnicities. The speech is fine as far as it goes. It is not, however, the smoker I was hoping for. I wanted Dr. Clark to make us feel uncomfortable, to provoke us to do something about segregation in America, in New York, right here in our own school. I was hoping to hear a call to arms, not a psychology lesson.

During my nine years at Collegiate, there has never been a Negro teacher at the school, and until this last year there have been only two Negro students, Richard and Godfrey Jacobs, the sons of a well-known Episcopalian minister. This year, with the Jacobs brothers now both graduated, there is one son of an African UN diplomat in our grade and several colored students from Harlem in the lower grades who were enrolled as part of a citywide private school program to admit black students of promise. Last year when an eighth grader from East Harlem visited the school Mr. Scott asked me to show him around. Billy wore a jacket whose sleeves were too short for his long arms, carried a book entitled *Black Like*

Me, and seemed nervous and out of place. I gave him a tour of the school and told him what a great opportunity it would be for him to go to Collegiate. I also told him how good it would be for the school, that Collegiate needed more black students like him, and that I hoped someday soon they'd hire some black faculty. I thought also to tell him not to hassle the money, clothes, huge apartments, and family vacations; to be himself and he'd do fine. Why I didn't, I'm not sure. Maybe because I didn't want to prejudice him. Perhaps his experiences at Collegiate would be different from mine, and, even if they weren't, there are some things you've got to experience and figure out for yourself.

In American history class, I search in vain for a white hero of historical significance about whom to write my senior research paper. I want to find a white person I can be proud of, a person who fought for the underdog, who stood up and had the courage to speak truth to power. Jefferson is out; he owned slaves. Lincoln is better; he spoke strongly against the evil of slavery. At the same time, he waffled on the race issue, saying he wouldn't want his sister to marry a black man. John Brown comes closest to being the white hero I'm searching for, but I shy away from a man who committed terrible acts of violence in the name of justice. And besides, something behind his eyes in those portraits scares me. Maybe he was as crazy as many historians portray him. Black heroes, by contrast, are plentiful: Frederick Douglass, Sojourner Truth, W. E. B. DuBois, Mary McLeod Bethune, Paul Robeson, Martin Luther King, Jr. I consider writing about Frederick Douglass, whose father was a white slave owner, but I know that's a cop-out. In America being half white doesn't count. I finally write a paper comparing and contrasting the leadership styles and historic importance of Abraham Lincoln and John Kennedy: two Presidents who, despite being tainted heroes when it came to race, had their inspired moments.

Confusion about race is still a part of my life, as it has been since my early childhood at the Seminary. As a five-year-old, I had no idea why adults would always laugh when, dressed in my baseball uniform, I told them proudly I was Jackie Robinson. Now seventeen, I know why they laughed but I still wish I could be black—black, that is, at will: black in East Harlem, white south of 96th Street. I'm even confused about what it is that makes a person black. Is it the blackness of his skin, his hair, his voice? Is it the blackness of his parents or grandparents or great-grandparents? How is it you're black when you're only one-half black? Or one-fourth? Or even one-sixteenth? How can you be black if fifteen-sixteenths of you is white? Are you black only if you look black? Are you black only if you espouse black causes? Are you black only if you talk, walk, and act black? And what does it mean to act black? Can't black people choose to act any way they wish? And are you equally black if you're from Panama, Haiti, or Senegal? Or is it different if you're Hispanic, West Indian, or African?

One thing I've learned for sure growing up in East Harlem is the wisdom of letting each person define for himself what he is. Some of the older folks at church object to the term *black*, currently favored by most Negro leaders, and you can still get in trouble on the street for saying anything other than *colored*. When meeting someone for the first time, I simply stick with his name, as Johnny advised me years ago. I wait until my new acquaintance calls himself colored, Negro, or black. If when asked a guy says he's black, or Puerto Rican, or Italian, or Jewish, then that's what he is. This policy applies even when a person who by all outward signs, of skin color and other physical characteristics, appears to be white proclaims himself colored or when a light-skinned Puerto Rican demands to be called white. Let a colored kid or Spanish kid dispute with him, not me. I only wish it wasn't so damn important. Who cares if someone is black or white, Puerto

Rican or Italian? What does that tell you about him other than the color of his skin, maybe, and that some of his ancestors came from Africa, Europe, or who knows where? But in America, it is important, and in East Harlem doubly so. It's your racial-ethnic group that identifies you, lets you know who's on your side, helps you understand to whom you belong. Unless, of course, you're white and there are no other whites around. Then you're on your own.

Many times in the past nine years, I've experienced being the only white person on the courts, at a party, in a store, at Sunday school, or in drama class. In these circumstances I feel the burden of proving that white guys can be cool, can dribble, dance, be regular guys, be unprejudiced. At the same time, I hate the pressure of being an ambassador for my race. I don't want to represent other whites any more than I want other whites to represent me. I'm just myself, me, Tommy Webber. Let every man speak and act for himself. When a colored person says something meant to be encouraging, such as "You're one blue-eyed soul brother," I have mixed emotions. It feels good to imagine that I'm accepted, that I've overcome the barrier of my whiteness. At the same time, I understand something of how it must feel to be the only Negro in the room and to be told, in effect, "You're not like other Negroes. You act differently. Why, you're almost white."

Last summer a riot broke out in Harlem after a white policeman shot and killed a black teenager. For two days and nights there were demonstrations, looting, and craziness in the streets, and I began to wonder if the raisin in the sun had decided to explode after all. The more moderate Negro leaders called for restraint and a cooling off period, while some of the more radical leaders, like Malcolm X, declared that it was time to get rid of all that "turn the other cheek" stuff and start handing out an eye for an eye and a tooth for a tooth. Malcolm X is one of the leaders of a new group called the Black Muslims, who I've seen walking around East Harlem selling copies of their newspaper, *Muhammad Speaks*. I've heard Malcolm X speak on the radio and know he likes to refer to "Martin Loser King," but I haven't paid much attention to what he or the Nation of Islam believe. All I know for sure is that they have no affection for white people. Once outside the subway stop on 103rd I approached one of their suited-up, bow-tied young men selling newspapers and tried to buy a copy. I told him I wanted to become more educated on the teachings of the Honorable Elijah Muhammad. The man turned his back on me, saying he was under no obligation to educate the white devil.

Whatever my confusion about race, East Harlem is more a part of me than ever. It has moved inside me and become a part of the way I feel, the way I think about the world. When I read history or engage in a political discussion, when I'm in a new situation trying to figure out how to act, I find myself looking at the world through an East Harlem lens. I'm on the side of black people and Latino people in their fight for justice and equality. I'm impatient when politicians counsel the leaders of the Civil Rights movement to move more slowly, when they say that change takes time. I find myself rooting for the college football team with the most black players or the black quarterback. I instinctively side with poor folks and suspect the rich. I listen to soul music, dance the East Harlem grind, and read black authors: Langston Hughes, Richard Wright, Ralph Ellison. Most of all I dream of returning to East Harlem after college, of starting a political movement that will transform the neighborhood into a model community of excellent schools, safe housing, plentiful jobs, and racial harmony. East Harlem is where I want to work, live, and raise my children. It's the place that formed me, just like Des Moines, Iowa, formed Dad, and Cleveland Heights, Ohio, formed Mom. I carry East Harlem within me wherever I go just as surely as I carry my likes and dislikes, my beliefs and values. Yes, I'm an American. Yes, I'm

English and a little Irish and who knows what else. But I'm more than just plain old white. I'm Tom of 105th Street, Tom of the Wilson Houses, Tom of El Barrio. I can diddy-bop, give skin, hold my own in a sounding match, eat *bacalao* with relish, and speak some pointed Spanish. I've been changed and molded by the neighborhood, taken El Barrio, like the air I breathe, into my blood. At my core, in my hearts of hearts, in my *corazón,* I'm an East Harlem White Boy.

Since this past summer, when he was admitted to an intensive dance program for promising young professionals, Danny has been totally absorbed in dancing. Every weekday afternoon and Saturday morning he takes class, and on Saturday evenings he and his new friends go dancing, cabbing around the city from one fancy club to another. In exchange for getting the crowd going, they are given their own table and free drinks. After several months of hearing Danny's stories about these clubs, I persuade him to take me along with him one Saturday night, and we make plans to go to Alhambra, just off Park Avenue on 60th Street.

When Danny appears at our apartment door, I immediately sense there's something different about him. At first, I think it's his fitted purple shirt, ruffled at the sleeves, and the fact that he's let his hair grow longer and applied some kind of cream or Vaseline so that it bristles wet even in the dim light of the hallway.

"You look different," I say as we wait for the elevator. Danny no longer races down stairs. He's a dancer now and has to be careful of his legs.

"Yeah?" he asks with barely a smile.

"No more dry look, huh?"

"Nobody wears their hair dry anymore. Dry's played out. Wet's where it's at. You like it?"

245

"I guess. It makes you look different."

"Good different, I hope," says Danny.

On the subway, we pay our fares and sit in a middle car. We're older, no need to stand at the front window to see what's coming at us, no need to sing doo-wop songs to impress the other passengers and ourselves. Instead, Danny instructs me on how to act when we get to the club; to stay close and copy what he does, to show the fake ID he got for me only if asked, to order a rum and Coke and drink it slowly. As Danny's talking, it suddenly dawns on me what's so different about him. It isn't his hair or his shirt, it's his teeth. He's gone and fixed his teeth. In place of the gap at the top of his mouth, there shines a set of perfect, pearly white teeth.

"You had your teeth fixed!"

He grins wide for the first time tonight. "They did a good job, huh?"

"They look just like real teeth," I exclaim in shock. Without a gap in his teeth, Danny's grin is different. In fact, his whole face is different, and I don't like it. He looks like a glossy picture in one of his fan magazines, more like Hollywood, less like himself.

"The only problem is I lost my whistle."

"Do they feel strange?"

"More than strange. At first it felt like my tongue was all cramped up inside my mouth. And my upper lip felt gigantic. Now I'm getting used to it. When I meet new people, it's great. They don't know anything about how I used to look."

"The new you."

"Yeah. Sorta like. What's the matter?"

"Nothing. It just takes getting used to. I liked the old you."

"Well, get used to it. You can't make it in show business with bad teeth."

"They weren't so bad. You didn't even notice after a while."

"But you noticed at first. That's the whole point. In show business it's the first impression that counts. If they think you look strange when they first look, they don't take a second look."

Danny strides into Alhambra the way he used to march into the Italian bakery on the corner of 106th, like he owns the place. At a table in the back sit four of his friends, two males and two females, all white. They're older than we are, probably near twenty. Wearing short skirts, heavy eye shadow, and dark lipstick, the girls are especially intriguing.

"This is my brother, Tommy," Danny says by way of introduction. "He's going to be President of the United States."

Danny and I order rum and Cokes and are served without question even though we're only seventeen. The club is dimly lit, with multicolored spotlights on the dance floor. Spectacular glass chandeliers hang from the ceiling. I feel big, bad, nervous, and glad I'm with Danny. The club is a new world, and I'm not sure how to act in it. I sit quiet, watching Danny and the others for clues.

During the evening, an older man comes over to our table, and Danny introduces him as the club manager. He sits down with us and after several opening pleasantries tells a joke about how when Rudolf Nureyev was a young dancer at the Kirov Ballet the other male dancers had to be careful not to drop the soap when taking a shower. I'm unsure of the exact meaning of the joke, but I join in with the group, including the two girls, who all laugh wildly. All except Danny. Danny is not amused. His jaw tightens as it always does when he's angry, as if he's chewing on something he doesn't want to swallow before spitting it out. For a moment I think he's going to slam the manager just as he slammed the mustached man who wouldn't return my softball years before. Instead, he jumps up from the table, pulls one of girls onto the floor, and dances like a maniac through five straight songs.

After that night, despite all my pleading, Danny never again takes me with him dancing.

*　*　*

Shortly before Christmas, I have an interview with the Harvard Dean of Admissions on his fall swing through New York City's private schools. We talk of my experiences growing up in East Harlem. He doesn't ask about my academic interests, my extracurricular activities, or my career goals. He's interested only in East Harlem. The day after the interview I learn from our college placement adviser that Dean Smith accepted me on the spot. Although I'm happy and relieved to be into Harvard, I wonder how Mr. Smith knows who he accepted. Even if being a white applicant from East Harlem does make me unique, don't I need to be more than that?

Playing my East Harlem trump card is something I'm slowly learning to do. The fact that I live in East Harlem seems to impress people. Each time I lay down my El Barrio card, however, I feel a little false, a little like I'm profiting from something that was given to me, from something for which I never had to work. I would rather have gotten into Harvard on my grades, on my ideas and opinions, even on my athletic skills, on something, anything, I had worked for and earned myself. And sometimes I feel that the admiration I receive for having grown up in East Harlem is based on false assumptions. After all, I'm white and middle class. I live with my family and both my parents and we vacation in Maine. I go to the oldest private school in America. I have never been beaten with a belt or anything else. I have never joined a gang or used drugs. I have never poured water over my Cheerios because my mother can't afford milk. Who am I trying to kid? Besides, it's Dad who gets the credit for moving to East Harlem. I was dead set against it.

The Sunday after I'm accepted to Harvard, I accompany the family to Ascension and Mom broadcasts the news to the entire church. I can see how proud she is of me; as she tells people her face glows with pleasure. Dad doesn't say much except that he hopes I can study with his old history professor David Owens. A couple weeks later, however, before a Group Ministry meeting in our living room, I overhear his reply to one of the other ministers who remarks how proud he must be now to have two sons going to Harvard. Dad says that he isn't proud, only grateful. Hearing these words, I realize that Dad will never be proud of me, that what I've been hoping for, working for, all my life will never happen. It just isn't in Dad to be proud of me. Pride's not a part of his vocabulary. Maybe deep inside somewhere he's proud, but he can't admit it, not even to himself. He isn't proud of my accomplishments at Collegiate. He's not proud of my getting into Harvard. No matter what I do, even if I become President of the United States, he'll never be proud of me, only grateful. Grateful for what, I wonder. That I didn't become a drug addict or a gang leader? And grateful to whom? To God? Does God get all the credit?

One of the reasons I'm upset is that I've always felt so proud of my father. He's been my hero since I first had heroes; he's still my hero. Of all the men I know, Dad is the man who lives closest to the ideals and principles he espouses. He doesn't just talk about the poor and the sick, he lives among them and works long, hard hours trying to help them. He doesn't just philosophize about the condition of the oppressed and imprisoned, he actively organizes to offer them hope and he fights against the powers and principalities that keep them oppressed. It's through his example that I've learned who I am and what's important in life. What greater gift can a father give his son? He may not know how to tell me he's proud of me, but he surely does speak truth to power. All the time I was looking at the television set and studying history searching for that one courageous, standing-up white person, he was already there right beside me.

CHAPTER 15

ONE WEEK IN THE spring as my high school days draw to a close, I begin to notice flyers posted on lampposts and in store windows around the neighborhood announcing plans to start a new community newspaper. A meeting is being held on Saturday at a clubhouse on 110th Street between Park and Madison. All are welcome. I decide to attend. I've been trying to figure out what to do this summer, and working for a newspaper might be just the thing. After all, John Kennedy was a reporter before he began his career as a politician.

By the time I arrive, around three-thirty, the storefront is filled with fifteen to twenty people, mostly guys a few years older than I am. The meeting hasn't started yet, and I find an empty chair in the back. In the front, three fellows are sitting at a table. Two of them look Spanish, college age; one wears a suit and a tie, the other a casual sweater and jeans. The third guy is much older. He's a dark-skinned black man with thick glasses, a beard, and a studious look. In the front row, sitting next to a slim pretty girl, I am surprised to see Junie, who never seemed like the type to be interested in working on a newspaper. When he sees me, he waves and smiles.

To begin the meeting, the guy in the suit rises and introduces himself as Manny. He's a senior at Hunter College, majoring in political science and journalism. He grew up right here on 110th Street. The young man next to him is Jorge, the next great Puerto Rican poet, and the older guy, Jeremiah, is a reporter for the *Amsterdam News*, Harlem's community newspaper. They have called this meeting because they believe it's time for East Harlem to have its own newspaper. Manny asks Jeremiah, who has agreed to advise them on how to get started, to say a few words.

Jeremiah explains that East Harlem contains about 200,000 residents, more than enough to make a good profit even if only ten percent of its families buy the paper. At the same time, we should know that New York City neighborhood papers like the *Amsterdam News* have a tough time selling enough copies to pay their expenses, especially at the beginning. People prefer the major dailies. What he recommends is to begin with volunteers and as much donated equipment and materials as possible and to publish only once a month. Most immediately we should answer three questions: Who is the target reading population? What is the name of the newspaper? And who will make up the editorial board?

Before anyone in the audience can answer Jeremiah's questions, Manny stands back up. What we are proposing, he says, is to start a monthly newspaper called *The East Harlem Times*, geared toward all the residents of East Harlem. It will contain news features, profiles of community programs and people, essays on issues important to the community, and one or two poems and literary pieces. Jorge and I will begin as the editorial board. Later it can expand as others of you become involved.

When Manny finishes talking, a young man dressed in dungarees and an army jacket stands up. "I think it should be named *The El Barrio Times,* or maybe better *La Voz del Barrio.* Yeah, dig it, *La Voz del Barrio, más suave,* no?"

"Let me remind you," says Manny, "that we want our paper to appeal to all the people of East Harlem, not just to the Spanish community."

"Is it gonna be in English or in Spanish?" asks the same guy. "Because if it's in English you could forget it."

Now Jorge rises to speak. Unlike Manny, he has an easy confidence. "It will be in both Spanish and English, *bilingüe.* On one side will be the story in English, on the other side *la misma historia en español.*"

"That's okay then," says La Voz del Barrio. "*Chévere.*"

"Half the people won't read it once they see the Spanish," shouts someone behind me.

"Half the people won't read it once they see the English," shouts someone else.

"How about *The Voice of East Harlem*?" suggests the slim, pretty woman in the front row next to Junie. "*The East Harlem Times* sounds too much like *The New York Times.* Who are we kidding?" Several folks in the audience laugh.

"We'll take it under advisement," says Manny.

"What about the board?" asks a round-faced Spanish fellow sitting off to the left. "If you're trying to appeal to the whole community, the board should be representative of the whole community. You need some colored people on the board. And perhaps a white person or two."

"No white people," shouts La Voz del Barrio.

"You mean no *blancos*," shouts someone else. Lots of people laugh.

"We'll take all your suggestions under advisement," says Manny, trying to regain control of the meeting. "For now, Jorge and I will be the sole board members. What we're looking for is volunteers. We need reporters, ad sellers, office help. Any of you young ladies know how to type?"

"You got an office?" somebody asks.

"You're sitting in it," replies Jorge.

"Before you ask for volunteers, I think the brother's suggestion merits a direct answer," says a dark-skinned man wearing a conservative black suit. He's clearly older than the rest of the people in the room, except maybe Jeremiah. "For too many years East Harlem has been controlled by white people, first the Irish, then the Jews, now the Italians. I would hope our newspaper, whatever name we choose for it, will be a newspaper of, by, and for the colored people of East Harlem, whether they be Negroes or Spanish or a bit of both, as many of us are. *Y yo hablo como un puertorriqueño orgulloso.*"

Many people clap. A chorus of "no white people, no *blancos*" sweeps the room. Several heads turn in my direction, and I begin to tense up. I've been the only white many times in many different situations, and for the most part, I've felt welcomed, especially when older people are present. This is the first time I've been in a group that clearly isn't that friendly to white people: openly hostile would be a better description. I know their anger isn't directed at me—they don't know me—but it sure feels like it is. I try to hide how uneasy I feel, how humiliated. Besides, I'd like to work on the newspaper. Manny and especially Jorge seem like interesting guys with a good idea.

"I vote no white people," calls out someone.

"*Y no blancos también,*" echoes someone else in Spanish.

"We'll take it under advisement," shouts Manny. "We'll take it under advisement."

"No advisement," proclaims a young man standing next to the proud Puerto Rican. "And before we vote, I suggest that our white guest in the back be asked to leave."

Now all the heads turn in my direction. Before I can say anything, Junie jumps to his feet and shouts. "Tommy aint white, Tommy aint white, he's from 102nd."

"He aint Puerto Rican," comments La Voz del Barrio. "He aint black."

I can feel the blood pulsing in the ends of my fingers. Silence reigns in the office of *The East Harlem Times.* All eyes focus on me, uniting into a single, hot spotlight. I rise from my seat and say I'm sorry, I would have liked to help. Then I turn and walk slowly out.

On my way home I try to convince myself that I don't care about what happened, that it's no big deal, that if the guys inside got to know me, the way Junie knows me, they would see me as something more than just a white face. In truth, I feel disappointed, hollow, like an unfair thing has happened and there's nothing I can do about it.

On the third Sunday in May, Riverside Church celebrates Youth Sunday. As president of our youth group, Danny is slated to say a few words at the regular eleven o'clock service. He's all excited about preaching in the giant nave, and he makes me promise to be there. To my surprise, he turns down my offer to help write his little sermon or at least listen in advance to what he's going to say. This time he's flying solo.

Standing straight and tall, high up in the preaching pulpit looking out over the nave in a long black robe like one of the ministers, Danny speaks for about five minutes. He doesn't seem a bit nervous. I'm the one who's nervous. He tells the congregation that youth who have parents and other adults to show them the way are lucky. What youth also need, however, are adults who listen, who take them seriously and try to understand what they're feeling. Too many adults preach at teenagers, tell them all the things they're doing wrong or should be doing instead of listening and trying to understand. When they have only such adults around, youth feel adrift, abandoned, homeless. To make his point, Danny quotes from a Bob Dylan song. He says that today's youth are no more rebellious than the youth of previous generations, that we're no different than youth have ever been, that we, too, hope to do our part to make the world a better place; it's just that "The Times They Are A-Changin'."

After the service, Danny and I ride home together, as usual, on the Number 4 bus, down Riverside Drive, across 110th Street, down Fifth to 106th.

I tease Danny about his becoming a minister. "Forget show business. You've found your true calling, Reverend Strayhorn."

"No way. That's your department."

"No more. You know that. I'm going in for politics."

"Politics, religion, what's the difference? Either way you've got to preach, tell people how to live. There's no way in hell I'm gonna tell other people how to live."

"You did pretty good this morning."

"I wasn't telling anybody how to live. I was helping them understand. You liked my Dylan?"

"It was great. Right to your point. Since when were you into Dylan?"

"Since always. I love Dylan. He speaks true. He's a poet. You ever study his words? It's not all 'Blowin' in the Wind.'"

"Yeah, but how about that voice? How do you get past that voice?"

255

"It fits the music. His voice makes you deal with his words." Danny launches into "The Times They Are A-Changin'." Walking side by side, I join in. We are well into the fourth verse, singing, "Your sons and your daughters are beyond your command," when I suddenly become aware of two guys directly in front of us. They command the corner of Park and 106th Street across from the El underpass. We'd been so absorbed in our duet that we hadn't noticed them. Now it's too late.

"Look at the *moreno pato* with his white girlfriend," says the older and taller of the two. They both wear Viceroy jackets; bandannas cover their heads.

"Ignore them," whispers Danny.

The leader steps squarely in front of Danny, blocking his path. "We don't allow no faggots in our neighborhood."

"This is our neighborhood, too," I say, trying to draw their attention away from Danny.

"Leave it alone, Tommy," says Danny. "Just keep on walking."

"Tommy. Hey, Tommy. *Tommycita!* Only way you gonna keep on walking is to walk over me."

"Let him by," says Danny.

"Let him by," squeals the leader. "Oh, please, please, let *Tommycita* by." The leader steps in my direction with a big, sneering grin and makes smacking sounds with his lips.

"Why don't you kiss my ass?" I blurt out, surprising myself even though it's definitely what I felt like saying. It just explodes out of me. For once in my life, I'm not going to say I'm sorry when I'm not sorry, or joke when nothing's funny, pretend that this guy's insulting threats are no big deal. If I get my ass beat, so be it.

The Viceroy leader, more surprised than I am, only says, "What?"

"I said kiss my ass, shithead!"

He swings at me. Instinctively I turn my head to the side, and his fist glances off my cheek. Lowering my head and shoulders like a middle linebacker, I dive at his knees. On impact, I wrap both hands around his legs and lift him up while still driving forward with my legs. He grabs me by the head, and we fall to the cement. I hear him grunt painfully as I land on top of him, and we roll over several times. With each roll, my face scrapes across the pebbly sidewalk. Finally, we come to a stop with me on top. He's hitting the back of my head. I'm punching his chest and stomach. Behind us, I can hear Danny screaming, "Motherfucker, motherfucker."

The next thing I know, Danny's tugging on my shoulders. "Come on, Tommy, let's make it. Quick."

Sitting on my attacker's chest with a choke hold around his neck, I've gone crazy. I press down on his windpipe with both hands and shout, "Apologize. Apologize, shithead! *Apologize.*"

"I apologize," Mr. Viceroy finally sputters, rolling over onto his stomach, coughing and gasping for air after I release my grip.

Danny pulls me to my feet, and we dart through the tunnel to the other side of Park Avenue and straight down 106th. We aren't exactly running, but we aren't walking slowly either. When we reach Third Avenue, Danny looks behind us. The street is full of Sunday strollers, with no sign of the two gang members and their boys. My head throbs, my cheeks burn, little drops of blood drip from my face.

"Here," Danny says, handing me his handkerchief. I press it to my bleeding cheek. We both look at each other for a moment. "You okay?" he asks.

"I guess." I dab at my face with the handkerchief. "We whipped 'em, didn't we?"

"Whupped 'em something terrible."

"What happened to the other guy?"

"When I went for him, he fled like a scared shit rat."

"You land any punches?"

"No. Just a couple of good slaps. That's all I needed. He was scared, not in shape. He aint no dancer. Jesus, Tommy, what got into you? You went crazy. You should have kept walking like I told you."

"And left you?"

"I was getting ready to run myself before you exploded."

"At least I didn't kiss him," I say.

Danny gives me a look. Then we both laugh. Walking down 106th Street, we laugh and laugh.

CHAPTER 16

I ARRIVE AT DANNY'S apartment to find him sitting on his bedroom floor surrounded by a disorderly array of clothes, suitcases, and half-filled boxes. Tomorrow morning he's flying to California. Months ago he bought a one-way ticket, which he keeps stored in the top drawer of his dresser like a prized possession, taking it out every so often to stare at it, hold it in his hands. He's proud that he's done what he promised his mother he'd do. He's graduated from high school. Now he wants out of East Harlem, and yesterday aint soon enough.

As Danny's farewell to New York, we've decided to go to the top of the Empire State Building. Despite the fact that we've both grown up in Manhattan, neither of us has yet made it up the Empire State. Danny has it in his head that he can't leave New

York without first climbing King Kong's mighty tower; he's worried he'll land in Los Angeles and someone will ask him about the Empire State. What then?

One look around the room, however, and I see we're not going to make it. Danny, still in the early stages of packing, seems at a loss what to pack next.

"You don't need to take everything," I assure him. "Just because your ticket is one way doesn't mean you can't leave some things behind. Your room's not going anywhere."

Danny's in no mood for my humor. It has dawned on him that he'll be leaving behind his entire collection of show business magazines and most of his beloved forty-fives.

"You won't need the magazines," I say in an attempt to make him feel better. "You'll see movie stars everywhere you look. I'll be the one buying magazines looking for pictures of you in them."

"I don't mind the mags so much, it's my records."

"Why don't you choose your top ten favorites? That'll be no room at all. When you play them you can get all misty-eyed thinking of home."

"Maybe my top thirty." He grins.

Knowing Danny, I grasp that the process of selecting his top thirty records will take all day. Instead of going to the Empire State, I suggest that he take a break from packing and we go up to his roof the way we used to. Danny likes my idea, anything to postpone the inevitable hard choices.

Up on the roof, the pigeons call and coo. We walk to the street side of the building, looking south, down and out over East Harlem to the majestic skyscrapers of midtown Manhattan.

"Maybe it's better we didn't go," I say, admiring the Empire State. "That way it will always be there, waiting for us, drawing us back."

We are silent for a moment, looking at our streets and our tenements, at our bridge with our river running under it.

"Remember when we first came up here?" asks Danny. "How you were blown away by the pigeons, how you couldn't believe there was some guy named Jesus?"

"And you had never heard of Riverside Church."

"And you had never seen a junkie on a nod."

"Remember monster cop?"

"That was a long time ago. When we were young."

"Now we're old and wise," I say.

"Hopefully a little," says Danny.

"When you come back to East Harlem, the TV cameras will follow you around the neighborhood like Burt Lancaster when he visited Union Settlement. You can show them the building where you grew up and the blocks you walked down and the stage where you first performed in public."

"And after you finish college, you'll run for politics and get elected President. All the newspaper headlines will read, 'From Washington Houses to the Washington White House.' Better than from a log cabin."

"And you'll sing at my inaugural."

"Yeah! Aint we bad!"

"So bad!"

"So glad!"

"*So, so glad.*"

We give each other skin, sliding our hands slowly across the palms, out across the fingers, and ending with a snap. Then Danny says, "Promise that when I visit you at Harvard you'll take me to class so I can listen and take in everything just like I'm in college myself."

"That won't be difficult. You can bop in with the other students and sit right down like you own the place. Nobody will notice."

"Make it a class I know something about."

"You mean like the sociology of the poverty cycle or more like Benjamin Franklin?"

"More like old Ben. I don't need some old professor lecturing me on rats and roaches."

He turns away, looking out over East Harlem.

"Danny, I have something for you. A going away present." From my pants pocket I pull out a small key and hand it to him.

"What's this?" he asks.

"I got it from Jesus."

"From Jesus downstairs?"

"Yeah, that Jesus." Danny is stumped, and I enjoy letting him hang. "You can't guess?"

"I don't see no Stutz Bearcat parked on the curb."

"It's not a cat. It's a bird. I bought you one of Jesus' birds. He says you can choose whichever one you want."

"What am I gonna do with a bird?" he asks.

"Anything you want," I answer. "Anything."

Slowly his mind takes in the possibilities, and his eyes pop in realization. He walks over to the pigeon coop and sizes up the birds inside. He closely observes each bird in turn but has trouble deciding.

"Help me pick one," he says finally. "I'm not doing this alone."

"It doesn't matter which one," I say, coming to stand next to him. "It'll probably just fly back home anyway. They're all homers."

"No way. After I set him free there's no way he's just gonna fly home to Jesus."

Danny turns the key in the lock, swings opened the door, reaches in, and carefully lifts out a small, quivering bird. Together we return to the edge of the roof, once again looking south over our East Harlem to the unvisited Empire State Building waiting for us, drawing us back.

"Ready?" he asks.

"Ready."

We count in unison, one, two, three. Slowly Danny lifts his arms forward and opens his hands as if in prayer.

Free at last, the bird soars up into the air.

In silence we watch as it flies over 96th Street.

EPILOGUE

Leaning on the ledge of my living room window, I look out over East Harlem, past the roofs of the surviving tenements, past the towers of Washington Houses, across 96th Street to the larger city, where the luminous Chrysler Building sparkles in the sunlight. On this September Saturday, most of East Harlem still sleeps. The omnipresent music and beat that is El Barrio does not yet sound from a community recuperating from *viernes social*. The shouts of two men arguing in front of the bodega across 106th Street break the early morning calm. Their voices echo up from the street in spirited Spanish. I catch the emphasis of their words but not their meaning.

It is 2003, and New York, at least my New York, remains a divided city. For forty-seven years I've lived in East Harlem, watching it, smelling it, ingesting it. Much has changed. Little has changed. Ascension Church, right below my window, is still there, only now it's called the Iglesia Pentecostal Macedonia and houses an overflowing Latino congregation whose double-parked cars block the street on Sunday mornings. The front of the church is secured behind a tall iron gate, and the voice of my father sounds in my head: "The doors of a church should never be locked."

Washington and Wilson Houses are still there, much as they were when we lived in them, except now they dominate the landscape as never before. In a neighborhood where an ever-growing number of vacant lots and boarded-over windows anticipate the coming of new buildings and large-scale renovations, and where welfare offices and schools are being converted into luxury apartments, they stand as a bulwark of protection against the gentrifying advancement of well-heeled Manhattanites inching their way northward across the DMZ. Only the blocks up and down Lexington still bustle with neighborhood businesses: *botánicas*, bars, bodegas, and beauty salons. But even here I see more boarded-up windows, more vacant lots, and fewer people. In 1948 East Harlem was estimated to house over 200,000 inhabitants. Today its population is barely 110,000. Where have all the people gone?

The faces of the people have also changed and not changed. In Jefferson Park, in the field adjacent to where the perennial teams of Puerto Ricans still play baseball, the square faces and short, sturdy bodies of Mexican, Guatemalan, and Ecuadorian soccer players are everywhere. Vanished are all but a stalwart few neighborhood Italians: Pat the shoemaker is gone; Sonny the pizza man, gone; Ralph and Joey of Puglisi's meat market, gone; Regina gone, her bakery on the corner of Second and 106th replaced first by a Korean fish market and most recently by an Iranian grocery store. The Italian faces that replaced the Irish faces that replaced the Jewish faces are themselves replaced with Mexican, Korean, and

Chinese faces, one immigrant group fading from the landscape as another begins to take root. In the recreation area of Franklin Plaza, I can see the solitary figure of an elderly Chinese man gliding through the slow, graceful movements of his tai chi exercises.

Dad and Mom still live in East Harlem, two stories up from the eighteenth-floor apartment on 106th Street and the corner of Second Avenue where I live with my wife, Andrea, a physician at Montefiore Hospital in the Bronx, two stories up from the apartment where we raised our two children. Dad, now eighty-three, runs a program for men locked within the New York State prison system. After the Parish faded to an end in the 1970s, he became President of New York Theological Seminary, turning it into New York City's leading institution for the training of black and Puerto Rican clergy. At about the same time, Mom passed on the leadership of her beloved Reading Program and became the first female General Secretary of the Health and Welfare Division of the Board of Homeland Ministries of the United Church of Christ. My brother Johnny is a public school teacher in Wisconsin. Peggy is an elementary school principal in Massachusetts. Blip is the president of a health consulting firm in Washington, D.C. My youngest sister, Katy, born when I was a sophomore at Harvard, is a social worker. After college I began my teaching career as a social studies teacher at a storefront school for high school dropouts on 110th Street, not unaware of its similarity to Dad's first storefront church on 100th Street. Since 1990 I have been the head of Edwin Gould Academy, a residential school for adolescent boys and girls caught up in the foster care and juvenile justice systems of New York City. Although there's not a minister among my brothers and sisters, we all sure can preach.

As for Danny, although he never reached his dream of becoming a star, he did have a successful career in show business, dancing for many years with the Alvin Ailey American Dance Theater and appearing in Broadway shows such as *Starlight Express* and *Grand Hotel.* In 1992 Danny died of AIDS. At his Riverside Church memorial service, I told how I always thought Danny would have become a big star if he hadn't gone and had his teeth fixed. What I didn't say was that when Danny died a piece of me died with him. Without Danny, my world is slower, sadder, less bright. I missed his presence when Aili got married and Matty got married and our first grandchild was born, and our second. I wish I could show him how Andrea and I have fixed up our little farmhouse in Pennsylvania. I long to sit with him on the back porch, watching the sun recede over the distant hill, talking about the old days and harmonizing doo-wop songs the way we used to in that long-ago world when we were young and all of life's possibilities lay spread out before us, ready for the tasting, like Father Divine's great banquet feast.

To my ears, "East Harlem" still has a special, almost mystical, ring like "Harlem," the African-American wellspring, but different, with a Latin flair: "El Barrio," a place so distinctive it has had books and songs written about it. I'm tied to East Harlem by memories that I relive on a daily basis as I walk past familiar places. I picture my father and mother as young parents, courageously sailing into uncharted waters, knocking on doors, calling on congregation members, building a life together. I see Rabbit sleeping against the 121 fence. I see Samuel every time a yellow cab stops, or does not stop, for an East Harlem passenger. I see Danny sweeping across Second Avenue with his smooth stride, late as usual. I think of him each time I hear our old songs, "There Goes My Baby," "Mama Said," "Stand by Me." And I picture myself, a nine-year-old towhead on my way to school, glad for a cold day when I could pull my hood tight over my face to hide its whiteness, determinedly diddy-bopping up the 102nd Street hill to the bus stop.

Fifty-five years ago, Dad helped found the East Harlem Protestant Parish. Some of my earliest memories are hearing him speak about the problems of drug addiction, poor schools, inadequate housing, gangs, hopelessness. His words would apply just as well today, except if anything, they would be more appropriate. Everything has changed. Nothing has changed. Despite all the time and effort of so many well-meaning individuals. Despite the Parish, the War on Poverty, the Black Power movement, the Puerto Rican Power movement. Despite community control and decentralization and the creation of local school boards and local planning boards and the election of many Puerto Rican and black political leaders. I recently asked my father if it dismayed him that, despite a lifetime of efforts, things seemed to be worse than they were when he first came to East Harlem. He replied that all a person is expected to do is the best he knows how. All the rest is in God's hands.

I remember looking out my bedroom window in the emotional days following the assassination of President Kennedy. As a sixteen-year-old surveying the streets of East Harlem, I pictured a great movement of the people, rising up, black and white together, to lead America home. East Harlem, my East Harlem, would become a city on a hill, a beacon in the night to light the way for America back to its fundamental values of freedom and equality. As I look out my window this morning, it is clear that no such movement ever came to East Harlem or to America. Perhaps it died with Martin Luther King or Bobby Kennedy. Perhaps it was stillborn in the jungles of Vietnam or in the despair of the crack epidemic or in the quagmire of our nation's growing political cynicism.

With the clarity that comes with time and age, I see now that no such movement was ever in the making; that history, like life, is always a struggle toward becoming, never a final victory. Yet it is the vision of what East Harlem, what America, could become that keeps me struggling. I prefer to believe that the great movement for social justice I dreamed of as a teenager in the early sixties is yet to be born. That it lies ripening within the hearts and minds of all of us who have not given up hope, who have kept the faith, who still dream of an America where justice rolls down like waters and righteousness like a mighty stream.

In a few hours the Mister Softee truck will sound its jingle, and children young and old will come running. Around noon, a street-corner evangelist from one of the still flourishing storefront churches will set up his soapbox and loudspeakers, and to the accompaniment of guitars and tambourines, all East Harlem will be called to Jesus. Children will emerge from every doorway, and the old-time games will sound in the street: hopscotch and double Dutch, b-ball in the school playgrounds. A little girl, her backpack overflowing with books, will enter 2050 Second Avenue, walk up to her tutor, and demand to share her latest poem. A fire engine will roar. A cop car will wail. An ambulance will race a dying stroke victim or a laboring young mother to Metropolitan Hospital. Death will arrive unexpectedly. Life will emerge hopefully, triumphantly, impossibly, rising up like that rose of song through the concrete sidewalks of Spanish Harlem.

And two young boys, one black, one white, or perhaps Chinese, will climb together to a tenement rooftop, look south out over East Harlem to the majestic downtown skyscrapers, and dream of flying over 96th Street.

ACKNOWLEDGMENTS

Flying over 96th Street was born as a somewhat sociological discussion of life in East Harlem, salted, as my father might say, with incidents from my El Barrio childhood. Through several rebirths, the sociology seeped out and the stories flooded in, until what finally emerged is the present memoir.

Along the route of this transformation, the opinions and critical reactions of many readers helped me to shape and sharpen my writing. Three women in particular stand out among the rest. First, my wife, Andrea, was there at the beginning, at the end, and at every step along the way, adding her encouragement, her ideas and her bons mots. It was Andrea who knew that "heads and hats bowed low" in prayer is more evocative than heads alone, particularly in a black church.

Second, my daughter-in-law, Katrina Fried Webber, encouraged me to accept that, at heart, the book is about my own coming of age and that I could not avoid the full implications of this fact.

Third, my first editor at Scribner, Rachel Sussman, saved the manuscript from a sure death on the slush pile and thereafter believed in it, fought for it, and worked hard to make it special. Rachel helped me understand what worked and why. Rachel, to you I am more than thankful.

Other folks also had an influential impact upon the book. During the last months of his life, my father-in-law, Angelo Bertocci, thoroughly red-inked an early draft with his personal and scholarly suggestions. My mother and father submitted to hours of interviews about their early days in East Harlem, and although much of what I learned from them about the formation of the East Harlem Protestant Parish never made it into the final cut, everything they told me helped me to see. My sister Peggy's enthusiasm bolstered my waning spirit at a time when I was doubting the book's worth. My dear friend Sasha Hourwich convinced me that sometimes it's okay to leave things unexplained, even unfinished, that that's how life is. Russell Weinburger believed in the value of the book when no one else outside my family and friends seemed to. Ted Solotaroff lent his light-filled Paris apartment and advised that when dealing with the multifold suggestions of editors I should pay most heed to those that got the writing arm moving again.

My second editor at Scribner, Rica Buxbaum Allannic, added her keen insights, polishing touches, and positive spirit. Nan Graham and Susan Moldow supported the project from the first thirty-page submittal through to the end. Julie Barer was and is more than an agent. She is supporter, critic, editor, guide.

The Board of Edwin Gould Academy and its President, Jo Ann Zucker, allowed me to take a five-month sabbatical near the end of the writing process, and my executive team, Bruce Bishop, Mary Ann Dowling, John Hutson, and Edgar Walker, along with Claudia Worsley, kept the Academy ship afloat during my absence.

I am forever indebted to the people of East Harlem, past and present: the ministers, staff, and lay members of the East Harlem Protestant Parish and their families; the residents of Washington and Wilson Houses; the staff and children of the Reading Program and of Union Settlement; the guys on the playground; the owners of the bakeries, *cuchifritos* stands, and *piraguas* carts; the old ladies on the bus and on the elevator; the musicians on the street corner. You were the extended family, the school, the village that raised this child.

Finally, every word, every page of this book was written in partnership with Dan Clifton Strayhorn. Throughout I was conscious of his mischievous eyes peering over my shoulder, making sure I was telling our story right. Oh, Danny boy, my Danny boy, your life was too short but your spirit lives.

ABOUT THE AUTHOR

THOMAS L. WEBBER helped found Edwin Gould Academy, a coeducational, residential school for adolescents in the foster care and juvenile justice systems, and has served as its Superintendent/Executive Director since its inception in 1990. He is the author of *Deep Like the Rivers,* the acclaimed book on how African-Americans preserved and nurtured their values under slavery, and is considered an expert on the needs of so-called troubled youth and on the problems of inner-city education. Dr. Webber graduated Harvard College in 1969 and received his Ph.D. in education from Columbia University. He served for seven years as an elected member of Community School Board 4 in East Harlem, the neighborhood in which he and his wife, Andrea, raised their family and continue to live.